SOCIAL JUSTICE EDUCATION IN CANADA

SOCIAL JUSTICE EDUCATION IN CANADA

Select Perspectives

Edited by Ali A. Abdi

Social Justice Education in Canada: Select Perspectives
Edited by Ali A. Abdi

First published in 2023 by
Canadian Scholars, an imprint of CSP Books Inc.
425 Adelaide Street West, Suite 200
Toronto, Ontario
M5V 3C1

www.canadianscholars.ca

Copyright © 2023 Ali A. Abdi, the contributing authors, and Canadian Scholars.

All rights reserved. No part of this publication may be reproduced, stored in a retrieval system, or transmitted, in any form or by any means, without the prior written permission of Canadian Scholars, under licence or terms from the appropriate reproduction rights organization, or as expressly permitted by law.

Every reasonable effort has been made to identify copyright holders. Canadian Scholars would be pleased to have any errors or omissions brought to its attention.

Library and Archives Canada Cataloguing in Publication

Title: Social justice education in Canada : select perspectives / edited by Ali A. Abdi.
Names: Abdi, Ali A., 1955- editor.
Description: Includes bibliographical references.
Identifiers: Canadiana (print) 20220276846 | Canadiana (ebook) 20220276854 |
    ISBN 9781773383071 (softcover) | ISBN 9781773383088 (PDF) |
    ISBN 9781773383095 (EPUB)
Subjects: LCSH: Social justice—Study and teaching—Canada. | LCSH: Social justice and
    education—Canada. | LCSH: Culturally relevant pedagogy—Canada. | LCSH: Critical
    pedagogy—Canada. | LCSH: Multicultural education—Canada.
Classification: LCC LC192.2 .S63 2023 | DDC 370.11/5—dc23

Page layout by S4Carlisle Publishing Services
Cover design by Rafael Chimicatti
Cover image by Adobe Stock/pavkis

23 24 25 26 27   5 4 3 2 1

Printed and bound in Ontario, Canada

Canadä

CONTENTS

Acknowledgements   *vii*

Chapter 1   Social Justice Education in Canada: An Introduction   1
Ali A. Abdi

Chapter 2   Critical Multicultural Education as a Platform for Social Justice Education in Canada   17
Ratna Ghosh

Chapter 3   Educating against Anti-Black/Anti-African Canadian Racism   31
George J. Sefa Dei and Claudette Howell Rutherford

Chapter 4   On Decolonial Thought and Writing Black Life   49
Marlon Simmons

Chapter 5   A Duoethnographic Perspective on Supporting Muslim Children, Youth, and Their Families in Canadian Schools   61
Antoinette Gagné and Dania Wattar

Chapter 6   The Islamic Call to Prayer as Public Pedagogy in Mississauga, Canada   83
Sameena Eidoo

Chapter 7   Social Justice through Indigenization and Anti-Oppressive Teaching   103
Anna-Leah King

Chapter 8   Postsecondary Education's Chronic Problem (or, It's About Time)   117
Alison Taylor and Robyn Taylor-Neu

Chapter 9   Critical Pedagogy in Teacher Education: Disrupting Teacher Candidates' Deficit Thinking of Immigrant Students with Origins in the Global South   131
Yan Guo

Chapter 10   Cultural Capital Re/constructions and the Education of Minoritized Youth   147
Dan Cui and Ali A. Abdi

Chapter 11   Challenging Normalized Ableism in/through Teacher Education   163
Bathseba Opini and Levonne Abshire

Chapter 12   For Goodness' Sake! Teaching Global Citizenship in Canada with a Critical Ethic of Care   177
Rae Ann S. Van Beers

Chapter 13   Education for Refugee Learners under the Framework of Social Justice and Racial Equity   189
Neda Asadi

Chapter 14   Interrogating Equity Issues on Inclusive Postsecondary Education for Refugees and New Immigrants in Canada   203
Michael Kariwo

Epilogue   **Edward Shizha**   217

Contributor Biographies   223

ACKNOWLEDGEMENTS

I am immensely grateful to the contributors to this edited volume for sharing their excellent, original perspectives on social justice education in Canada. Perhaps as much as anything, the contents of this book represent and are reflective of the important perspectives and related analyses and criticisms currently being debated and advanced in this expanding area of research. The perspectives shared in the volume shall minimally widen both the epistemic and pedagogical boundaries of social justice education. My thanks also to the Canadian Scholars team, Lindsey Malinowski, Colin Owen, and Cindy Angelini, and Katherine Kurowski (formerly of Canadian Scholars) for their excellent support and patience during the preparation and completion of the book. A note of thank you as well to the five anonymous reviewers whose observations and responses through the peer review process were helpful in the overall amelioration of the volume's focus and contents.

CHAPTER 1

Social Justice Education in Canada: An Introduction

Ali A. Abdi

INTRODUCTION

With the wide multiculturalization, in relative terms, of Canadian society in cultural, home language, and attached schooling realities, formally complemented by the country's presumptive categorization as a pluralistic Western democracy, systems of education have been struggling with the needed accommodation of multi-background, multi-economic means and differentiated social-background student populations. These students are either of first generation, "visible minority" status or are members of immigrant and refugee families from mostly so-termed developing countries. More than 400,000 new immigrants came to Canada in 2021 (Government of Canada, 2021), in addition to an average of tens of thousands of refugees for the past few years, all in the midst of an already highly multi-ethnic society. As such, the role of schooling and education in assuring the just and viable integration, as opposed to assimilation, of hundreds of thousands of learners—indeed millions in the coming decades—into Canadian schools and public life is as important as ever. While the general idea of inclusion, complemented by some policies and the Multiculturalism Act of 1988, has spawned select practices of multicultural education for over three decades, the overall message itself and most outcomes have not achieved the necessary critical learning and teaching interventions to enfranchise all students in the country's multi-level schooling milieus. Indeed, as Ghosh and Abdi (2013) point out, the critical and potentially equity-enhancing constructions and applications of multicultural education have been at best limited. Equity-enhancing in the sense of going beyond the surface counting of things, including educational resources, which primarily indicate the ideas and possible practices of equality (equalization). More often than otherwise, and especially initially, most multicultural education programs in Canada constituted themselves in ceremonial, power-critiquing–shy, shallow festivities that continue to elevate the exoticization of visible differences among diverse-background school populations. In the context of this reality and partially instigated by the still-limited school system response to the needs of non-mainstreamed learners, a critical and thematically inclusive focus on social justice education is important and timely.

In this introductory analysis, social justice education should focus on multi-dimensional readings and understandings of the historical, political, social, cultural, and linguistic constructions, deconstructions, and reconstructions of education and attached possibilities of societal well-being. In so doing, a deeper ascertainment of how we currently understand the concepts and possible practices of social justice itself—that is, before we speak about social justice education—is important. Without such understanding of social justice in societal contexts and related outcomes, social justice education runs the risk of ending up in the non-critical, non–power-interrogating, and non-transformative situation of conventionalized multicultural education. As such, the already dangerously proliferating deployment of social justice in different and potentially nominally stylistic institutional contexts, including corporate situations, needs to be challenged by creating more comprehensive platforms that can practically, and with tangible outcomes, inform the extension of a more tangibly liberating perspective to spaces of teaching, learning, and social development. The point on social development is important here in that education, by its very nature, can and should facilitate actionable livelihood contexts that ameliorate the lives of people (Abdi, 2008). As such, the importance of acquiring a deeper historical understanding of social justice works against the trivialization of social justice education, which should touch the learning lives of those who will benefit the most from enfranchising teaching and learning situations. With this in mind, and with the intended aggregate realities of social justice education as historically located, culturally liberating, and with current and future knowledge empowerment possibilities, this volume engages the topic from multiple descriptive and analytical angles. With that somewhat comprehensive intention and focus—if with less than mechanically sequential manner—the contributors present diverse, multi-topical perspectives and critiques on diverse and continually differentiating aspects and pragmatics of social justice education. Such perspectives shall provide important and contemporaneously linked readings of the situation with inherent and forward-looking suggestive intentions to advance social justice education in contextually interconnected ways that should benefit the actual learning and future lives of students.

HISTORICAL AND THEORETICAL CONSTRUCTIONS OF SOCIAL JUSTICE

While certainly other cultures elsewhere in the world have minimally spoken about the constructs and practices of social justice for centuries (even millennia), the first available record of the term *social justice* is attributed to the Jesuit scholar Luigi Taparelli. In the 19th century, Taparelli used the term while questioning the ability of the then-prevailing political systems to respond to the needs of society. Others who contributed to earlier formulations of social justice include the British philosopher John Stuart Mill, in his works on liberty and utilitarianism, and the French thinker Jean-Jacques Rousseau, via his essays on social contract. Indeed, a few early glimmers of social justice–connected terminology from Mill's work could be extracted from his usage of such terms as progressive man, happiness for all human kind, and his focus on the rights of women (Mill, 1859/2015). Some years later, he further developed his perspectives on women's rights, which, without patronizing anyone, could qualify him as (just) selectively ahead of his gender-biased political and economic exclusions of his time. Indeed, in his 1869 work *The Subjection of Women*, Mill advances a few gender-equality and rights issues that are still in contention today around the world. As should be noted, though, he was not a bona fide advancer of women's rights. As Jennifer Ball (2001) noted in her feminist critique of Mill's focus, he was not for a complete paradigm shift in these and related situations.

In terms of Rousseau's social justice contributions and perspectives, these preceded Mill's by about one hundred years. Yet neither philosopher was outside the sphere of the enlightenment tradition, and as such, their work represents a limited cluster of social justice principles and practices not fully connected to then–extra European situations and therefore not fully applicable to today's search for counter-minorities oppression intentions and realities. Still the temporalities of knowledge and scholarship are not to be discounted in these and related intersections of life, being, and learning. Indeed, when Rousseau's perhaps best-known works that might concern educators, *The Social Contract* and *Emile* (1769/2018), came out, he was exiled from France, and the books were banned. In the first book, Rousseau's observations were, for my reading at least, as radical or even more radical than Mill's about a century later in terms of political and attached rights perspectives. Possibly as much as anyone else in 18th century Europe, Rousseau spoke—in a textualized and, by extension, enduring format—about the rights of citizens and how governments should be aware of and act on their binding relationships with the populace. Indeed, that work should be read (in relative time-space understanding and accounting) as an important citizenship perspective and analysis that make deeper sense to me in these times that are characterized by expansively multifaceted foci on global citizenship and human rights education.

As one heretofore contributor myself to the citizenship education literature (Abdi, 2015), I should perhaps appreciate more the pioneering works of Rousseau in this and related domains of life, which are also both thematically and critically attached to the constructions and programmatic intentions of social justice education. Beyond that work's seminal nature in advancing the rights of citizens, which is also constitutive of the thick contemporary blocks of social justice and social justice education, Rousseau's *Emile* should perhaps be understood as one of the first systematic studies to analytically ascertain and appreciate the agentic presence as well as the social education needs of the learner. In addition, and uniquely for educators and educational scholars especially in so-termed multicultural pluralistic democracies such as Canada, *Emile* represents a very relevant historical learning project, with tangible and contemporaneous attachments to the critical observations and analysis we seek to create in subjectively inclusive and diversely enriching educational experiences. As such, *Emile* minimally heralded—in a different context with different sociopolitical structures, and certainly with divergent content and curricular emphasis and outcomes—what has been dubbed child-centred education. While child-centred education in Canada might be read as a precursor to the current focus on social justice education, one need not discount the possible connections, in fragmented but somewhat heavy terms, to its ideational and practical affinities with our intentions here.

While the above observations seemingly accord some important credit for social justice constructs, analysis, and textualizations to European thinkers and philosophers (i.e., Taparelli, Mill, Rousseau), let me briefly return to my point on the certainty that other cultures and peoples elsewhere in the world have also conceptualized, theorized, debated, and practised social justice and, by extension, social justice education projects. In so doing, I am making the claim, as one important example, that over millennia, African societies have actually constructed and practised what represents, for all pragmatic undertakings, a wide and critically inclusive way of life and education known as Ubuntu philosophy of life. As a humanist philosophy of life and education, Ubuntu, in its most basic tenets, advances the radical inter-subjective humanization of all members of society (Tutu, as cited in Battle, 2009). Extending from this humanization of all members of society, the social structure and operational platforms of Ubuntu function on the principally inviolable attitude and actionable intersection of seeing our humanity through the humanity of the other.

With this in mind, the late Archbishop Emeritus and Nobel Laureate Desmond Tutu spoke about the possible elimination of inter-personal/inter-group injustices through this inter-humanization perception and practice in which we must realize that, by denying another's rights, we are doing the same to ourselves (cited in Battle, 2009). Moreover, in learning and pedagogical terms, Ubuntu philosophies of education apply the same full inter-humanization principle and practice where, as I have written recently (Abdi, 2021), Ubuntu-based systems of learning and teaching aim for the continuous and accountable inclusion of all members of society in all platforms of life and education, with clear refusal to create differentiated and, in social contexts, differently privileging or de-privileging systems of schooling. In addition, Confucian philosophy of education (based on the philosopher Confucius's thoughts and writings), which heavily influences both historical and contemporary cultural contexts of China and some other Asian countries, advances the value of viable and virtuous-enriching right type of education that should be accorded to all (Li, 2017). Recalling Ubuntu's humanization through education, Confucian philosophy also constructs education as a basic platform for the collective well-being of society.

Given the above, and with more than a century or two since those original writings on the issue, one of the most important modernist writings on political justice (later with some social justice attachments) is John Rawls's oft-referenced *Theory of Justice* (1971/2005). In this work, Rawls initially advanced the liberal democratic notions of the case by implicating the centrality of equality in national and, via American-centric reach, global public spaces. With the measurable limitations of this approach, Rawls should be credited for the way he later modified his orientation. In a couple of works on the area, including his book *Justice as Fairness* (2002), Rawls's readings of the issue were not all straight-line liberalist orientation or from abstractionist renderings of justice on a quasi–non-practical, if still conceptually desirable, platform for idealized political and social entities. It is with these and later inter-temporal comprehensions of the context that we need to grasp—as much as possible—the very complex but worth-striving-for notions of social justice and social justice education. To be sure, Mill's, Rousseau's, and Rawls's writings were all based on their Eurocentric readings of their world, which in today's multicultural contexts will fall short of the needs to enfranchise all, including those whose original countries were colonized by European or Euro-American powers.

RE-THEORIZING FROM SOCIAL JUSTICE TO SOCIAL JUSTICE EDUCATION

Though Rawls deserves some credit for his analysis on justice as fairness, with post-Rawlsian intentions we can appreciate the more inclusive topical writings of social justice as constitutive of representation, redistribution, and recognition by, among others, Nancy Fraser (2008), Axel Honneth (1996), Fraser and

Honneth (2004), and Charles Taylor (1995). With these important interventions, we have slowly entered, while still within the European and Euro–North American descriptive and analytical lineage of the case, into emerging and, policy-wise, important reconstructions of the situation. The central component of this change, which is so crucial for contemporary analysis and potential programmatic outcomes of social justice education and comparable sociopolitical contexts, is the shift from the mainly equality driven, to the more historico-culturally tolerant [sic] possibilities of equity in being, learning, and advancing for self and community actualization. In her well-received book *Scales of Justice* (2008), Fraser moves the readings and possible practices of social justice beyond the Westphalian, boundaried, and politico-legal frameworks. In so doing, she suggests pluri-cultural and sociopolitical intersections of operationalizing her previous perspectives (Fraser & Honneth, 2004) on recognition and redistribution via justice representation. Such transnationally representative justice, which she also somewhat expands later, in *Transnationalizing the Public Sphere* (Fraser et al. 2014), should be fit for social justice education analysis as well. Irrespective of this later work, the centre of Fraser's analysis revolves within and around her now established three-dimensional social justice perspectives: economic redistribution, cultural recognition, and political representation.

Honneth (1996; Fraser & Honneth, 2004), on the other hand, started with the saliency of the struggles for recognition in human contexts, relations, and daily interactions. Later, in the 2004 work *Redistribution or Recognition*, which was framed as a debate between Honneth and Fraser, the former's position on the primacy of social and political recognition was reaffirmed. While no analytical mediation is intended here, for social justice education workers, the important interplays between recognition and distribution can serve complementarily for the required learning and teaching platforms. Those recognition-distribution connections shall be helpful in reconstructing conceptual, theoretical, and practical social justice possibilities. These possibilities could contemporarily lead to equitably inclusive schooling that can enfranchise the lives of people. In realigning the interrelated corners and centres of Fraser and Honneth's perspectives, it is important, and perhaps situationally more relevant for the Canadian situation, to relay the critical kernels that Charles Taylor (1995, 2003) advances, especially around the recognition category, as these are analytically attachable to prevailing/emerging communal contexts. For my understanding, Taylor's perspectives do not diverge drastically from Honneth's observations on the issue but are perhaps more strident in their concluding inclusivity intentions.

Taylor (1995) affirms not only our primordial needs for recognition, but also the damages done to our onto-epistemological locations through denials of recognition or the misrecognition of those who have been/are subordinated (Taylor, 1995). Indeed, the failure of many educational systems to respond to the learning and social well-being needs of especially minoritized students begins in large part due to the lack of recognition during these first encounters with the institutional components of the physical school structure, the leadership (principal, others), and teachers. Facing these multi-level implementers of educational policies and programs is the young child, especially one from the so-called visible minority in the Canadian context, who comes to school with so much hope and aspiration until institutionally labelled otherwise. Indeed, pragmatist philosophers such as John Dewey (1963/1997, 2008), Julius Nyerere (1968), and Paulo Freire (1970/2000) shared their critical and comprehensive understanding of these complex but either constructive or deconstructive contexts for the learning development of young and adult learners in North America and around the increasingly more interconnected world.

In essence, these celebrated thinkers' pre–21st century, post-conventional, selectively anti-colonial, and critical pedagogy perspectives, with thick practical applications, can contribute few things to social justice education possibilities in Canada. To be sure, in appreciating the multi-pronged complexity of the situation and what can be extracted from those works and later works in the area (Dei, 1996; Dei & Kempf, 2013), we can harness multiple value-added possibilities to advance the rightful education for marginalized students in Canada. This will especially be the case for those learners whose lives have been touched, in intergenerational terms and formats, by colonization, racism, and serfdom in North America, Africa, Asia, Latin America, and elsewhere. In expanding our readings of justice into the social justice and social justice education platforms, and beyond the problematic equality paradigm, we need to appreciate and multi-directionally embrace the complexity of the contexts upon which we intend to explain things and operate. Justice, social justice, and social justice education—from early written conceptualizations in the European tradition and certainly in different formats elsewhere to the current multi-centric renderings by latter-generation critical scholars—were/are not detached from select and interactive moral/ethical, religious/spiritual, philosophical, cultural, and political connections, debates, and even unsolved disagreements. As such, we have to perceive social justice and social justice education as contested analytical and operational terrains that can minimally disturb the liberalist, extreme individualization (and isolation) of persons, learners, and their communities.

That appreciation of the complex historical cross-cultural designs of social justice and social justice education should accord us some more tangible and au courant affirmations for viable cultural emancipation and social development. This statement itself is, of course, problematic unless we read life in North America as a precarious and cartographic factoid that is dangerous for minoritized populations. This is important in the sense that the designs of education for multi-background, multi-ethnic, multi-linguistic, and multi–economically afforded populations have a direct impact on the fortunes of all, for a long time. Indeed, the danger here for those who are not on the well-connected side of schooling becomes exacerbated when non-functional equality rhetoric is introduced and sustained, as that directly widens the socioeconomic and political divide between the have-lots and have-nots, as the case has been in Canada. When equitably conceptualized, theorized, and operationalized, on the other hand, educational programs can subjectively, culturally, and pedagogically uplift the just claims of the educationally delinked. The rescinding of the false rhetoric of equality education and the pragmatic elevation of equity as a foundational platform for social justice education should inform both the topical and critical intentions and achievements of this work. Equity in the way it is located here conforms to the multi-connected historical and cultural constructions of education where the whole context of the learner is appreciated and taken into account.

ORGANIZATION OF THE BOOK

Besides this introductory section, the book contains 13 chapters that cover diverse topics, all within the general areas of more inclusive, more empowering, more representative, and more critical analyses and recommendations of educational systems and relationships. Some of the contributions, if not all, also suggest ways of deconstructing and reconstructing the current unequitable situation and aim for more viable educational and livelihood possibilities in this economically advanced and politically evolving northern country. Where occasioned and topically useful, the authors embed in their work the critical, in select recognitive, redistributive, and just representation intentions of learning resources and related social well-being possibilities. The chapters are arranged in an eclectic, counter–structural rigidity format, with all responding in their unique ways to their generalist and/or specialized social justice education foci. This way of sequencing the chapters is itself selectively representative of the diversity as well as the complexity of social justice education platforms that touch almost every aspect of schooling and education in national and undoubtedly extra-national contexts. Moreover, the chapters in this edited volume, which focus on education and related social well-being issues in Canada, should shed new, multi-pronged (if quasi-circular) light on the situation. As such, they should provide ameliorative recommendations for issues that concern the learning and social well-being rights of learners with different conceptual, theoretical, and practical formations and implications.

While most of the topics covered are thematically connected to the established perspectives of social justice education, a relatively new addition to the discourse is disability studies/ableism and education (chapter 11). This addition elevates both the epistemic and pedagogical value of social justice education as disability—in its encounters with the societally embedded normativity of ableism—concerns social justice, equity, and human rights education. With six million Canadians aged 15 and over having some kind of disability (Government of Canada, 2019), the role of schooling in educating about the issue is exceedingly important. It was with this in mind that the Accessible Canada Act (to ensure a barrier-free Canada) received royal assent in the Parliament on July 11, 2019. There might not be a more relevant space to discuss this and assure the movement, learning, and achieving rights for all members of society than schools, and certainly teacher education contexts, so as to assure a wider understanding and appreciation in both institutional and wider community spaces. As stated in the Act,

> **Disability** means any impairment, including a physical, mental, intellectual, cognitive, learning, communication, or sensory impairment—or a functional limitation—whether permanent, temporary, or episodic in nature, or evident or not, that, in interaction with a barrier, hinders a person's full and equal participation in society. (Government of Canada, 2019)

To reiterate for clarity, the chapters are organized eclectically, which should be responsive to the conceptual, theoretical, and practical fluidity of social justice education that could represent an inter-strengthening characteristic within this and other critical learning and teaching studies. Critical in the sense that social justice education and its affiliated knowledge categories aim to establish and sustain learning and teaching situations that enhance the cultural emancipation and socioeconomic well-being and political/policy enfranchisement of all learners and their communities.

In chapter 2, "Critical Multicultural Education as a Platform for Social Justice Education in Canada," Ratna Ghosh returns to an area where she is perhaps the premier global scholar, and certainly the most prominent in Canada: multicultural education. Here, she notes how the aim of critical multicultural education (CME) is to highlight the inequality and injustice that has been invisible and normalized. To critically respond to this, Ghosh presents the possibilities of CME as a lifelong process in its worldview and argues that it should not just be a subject to study. She emphasizes the important discursive practice that must address inequitable power relations to achieve historical perspective and an intersectional lens by relating what is learned to the experiences of students. With inclusive descriptive notations, she points out how CME should pave the way for the learning success of students, with the objective of achieving equity and fairness for all.

In chapter 3, "Educating against Anti-Black/Anti–African Canadian Racism," George J. Sefa Dei and Claudette Howell Rutherford explore the connections and possibilities of decolonial pedagogies and critical anti-racist practice to respond to the specificity of anti-Black/African racism. In an era when Black and African bodies, especially Black and African men's bodies, have become easy "targets" of white racism and whiteness is protected at the expense of black lives, Dei and Rutherford call for the nuanced examination of anti-Black/African racism in order to develop more effective ways of addressing the problem of systemic oppression in society. They argue that anti-Black/African racism is not a new practice but is rooted in Black and African histories of colonialism and enslavement, which need to be examined through critical, decolonial, anti-racist, anti-Black racism education. Dei and Rutherford pay particular attention to struggles for Black and African Canadian learners in schooling and education, pointing to lessons for the pursuit of concrete transformative educational practice to address anti-Black/African racism. In addition, they address the "philosophy of practice" as well as the "practical strategies" that work to address anti-Black and anti-African racism to think through new futurities for the community.

In chapter 4, "On Decolonial Thought and Writing Black Life," Marlon Simmons focuses on historical systems of colonial epistemologies as being embedded in different educational settings of the Canadian society, including universalized ways of knowing present and past social realities. With this, he notes, epistemologies inherent to Black life have come to be positioned in ways that ushered in vehement debates on what knowledge is, what counts as knowledge, and where knowledge resides. While knowledge emerging from the perspectives of Black life draws from historical accounts of social theory, many theorists situate their thinking in ways that epistemologically diverge from those accounts. With that, Simmons notes how decolonial thought is needed as a perspective of Black life to be re-materialized and bestowed with the rightful epistemological credibility. To do so, one challenge of this decolonial project is to theoretically trace certain social formations of Black life and understand how different knowledge systems unfolded through the experiences of the African diaspora, which needs to be endowed with intellectual currency and epistemologically installed within educational institutions. This thinking, Simmons notes, needs to be achieved through a reading of Black life via decolonial sensibilities that are necessary for fecundating equity and social justice education.

In chapter 5, "A Duoethnographic Perspective on Supporting Muslim Children, Youth, and Their Families in Canadian Schools," Antoinette Gagné and Dania Wattar describe and reflect on their experiences working with Muslim students and families in different contexts. From that experiential platform, they explore their contrasting and sometimes overlapping experiences as parents, teachers, teacher educators, and researchers supporting Muslim families. In addition, they discuss more ways of establishing promising pathways leading to positive school experiences for Muslim children and youth and the preparation of teachers to work with diverse students in elementary and secondary schools in Ontario. In so doing, Gagné and Wattar deploy recognitive justice perspectives and intersectionality theory as central to their critical reflections.

In chapter 6, "The Islamic Call to Prayer as Public Pedagogy in Mississauga, Canada," Sameena Eidoo notes how Mississauga City Council passed a resolution that the enforcement of the noise control bylaw be suspended to allow for the broadcasting of the evening call to prayer from local mosques and non-residential buildings used for worship during the month of Ramadan. The resolution stipulated that the call could not invite Muslims to physically congregate in violation of COVID-19 pandemic emergency orders. The resolution, proposed by the Muslim Council of Peel, was recognized by some and protested by others, namely a registered non-profit, Keep Religion Out of Our Public Schools, operating under a private Facebook group, Mississauga Call to Prayer on LoudSpeaker Unconstitutional. Three years earlier, a Peel District School Board (PDSB) meeting was disrupted by attendees shouting Islamophobic slurs and tearing pages from a copy of the Holy Qur'an in protest of the PDSB's religious accommodation allowing Muslim students to use school space for Friday prayer. Set against these anti-Muslim sentiments, Eidoo's chapter explores the public pedagogy qualities and contributions of broadcasting the Muslim call to prayers, which can serve as a declaration of the spiritual and religious freedoms that are vital for Muslim youth and families to live and thrive in this pluri-religious society.

In chapter 7, "Social Justice through Indigenization and Anti-Oppressive Teaching," Anna-Leah King discusses the issue in relation to Indigenous education. She notes how social justice in education has presented challenges for Indigenous people, especially since the colonization by white settlers. With the devaluation and the discrediting of Indigenous knowledges and traditional education systems, complemented by problematic objectives of assimilation, she notes how "our" collective Indigenous dream for higher education has yet to be fully actualized but adds that the vision is still here and, as of now, the hope for revitalization is great. King focuses on and analyzes issues and possibilities of decolonization and Indigenization, and in so doing, borrows important perspectives from the Truth and Reconciliation Commission (TRC), especially on the Calls to Action sections that deal especially with education, Indigenization, and anti-oppressive teaching and learning. She concludes the chapter with a brief forward-working proposal, with seven important principles that guide the lives of the Anishnaabe people.

In chapter 8, "Postsecondary Education's Chronic Problem (or, It's About Time)," Alison Taylor and Robyn Taylor-Neu explore how the time logic of capitalism is infused within the world of university students' discourses in terms of the relation between what is termed schoolwork and paid work. Through this analysis, the authors show the extent to which higher education institutions are co-extensive with the political-economic logics of their milieu. While the neoliberal university has been analyzed and critiqued from different angles and perspectives, Taylor and Taylor-Neu's discussion adds to current literature by demonstrating how a commodity-valuation orientation to time has become thoroughly normalized, to the extent that it is not easy to imagine how it could be otherwise. By highlighting students' narratives on the topic (i.e., the links between school and work), the authors demonstrate "why attempts to reimagine a 'socially just' university have left the fundamental structures unchanged." One possible avenue for reimagination, in their view, concerns the gift economy as an alternative political-economic logic of time.

In chapter 9, "Critical Pedagogy in Teacher Education: Disrupting Teacher Candidates' Deficit Thinking of Immigrant Students with Origins in the Global South," Yan Guo discusses how English as an Additional Language (EAL) students bring their own languages, cultures, religions, and educational backgrounds to school, enriching their educational environments. However, she adds, many pre-service teachers use deficit-oriented discourses, highlighting EAL students' inability to speak English and their difficulties in communicating in school. Examining this situation and drawing from critical and postcolonial theoretical perspectives, she demonstrates how a teacher educator has implemented some experiential strategies in order to encourage pre-service teachers to challenge their largely unexamined deficit thinking regarding their EAL students. Teacher education programs in today's highly diverse immigration contexts, Guo says, must be reconceptualized to address what it means to teach in multilingual, multicultural, and multiracial schools. Here, the label of difference, which can also spawn perceptions and incidences of racism, needs to deconstructed and reconstructed.

In chapter 10, "Cultural Capital Re/constructions and the Education of Minoritized Youth," Dan Cui and Ali A. Abdi note how the concept of cultural capital has been widely employed in social justice research to explain class-based cultural and social reproduction across generations. The existing scholarship on cultural capital tends to be unwittingly affiliated with whiteness without being sensitive to ethno-racial differences. In this chapter, the authors aim to extend the explanatory power of this concept into social justice research by reconstructing the epistemic assumption of what should be considered "the valued cultural capital" in minoritized youth education in Canada. The authors first review the debate on cultural capital research from both a Bourdieusian approach and non-Bourdieusian approaches, followed by an empirical study of how Chinese Canadian youth negotiate cultural capital reconstruction at their schools in Canada. The study reveals that racialized minority youth, particularly those from immigrant family backgrounds, have been disadvantaged in the educational field, where their cultural capitals were racialized, devalued, or not recognized since the dominant cultural capital is affiliated with white middle-class norms. Consequently, they add, such class affiliation contributes to these youth developing a sense of inferior racialized and classed habitus, which affects their self-esteem, healthy ethnic identity construction, educational performance, and career aspirations.

In chapter 11, "Challenging Normalized Ableism in/through Teacher Education," Bathseba Opini and Levonne Abshire locate ableism as a real challenge across many Canadian educational institutions both in K–12 and postsecondary settings. The authors note that addressing ableism, be it through pushing for change in societal attitudes or through advocating for accommodations and environmental accessibility, is often seen as an additional cost, monetarily and emotionally. Drawing on the idea of dysconscious ableism and the theory of critical disability, complemented by current research literature and their own experiences as educators, they argue for a critical examination of disability as a social justice and human rights issue in and through teacher education.

In chapter 12, "For Goodness' Sake! Teaching Global Citizenship in Canada with a Critical Ethic of Care," Rae Ann S. Van Beers notes how, with increased attention to encouraging global citizenship characteristics in Canadian students, educators frequently partner with various NGOs with the expectation that the activities such organizations promote will help to develop desirable qualities in the youth that they teach. Even though educators want to teach youth to be "good" citizens, the conceptions of goodness that underlie these activities are not always commensurate with the notions of good global citizenship that appear in the literature. She discusses how such discrepancies can result in the promotion of activities that actually transmit a form of charitable foreign aid mentality to students, all under the guise of global citizenship. Van Beers engages a critical analysis of the Right to Play organization as an example of how something as simple as children's play can serve neoliberal colonial ends by exporting Western notions of play as integral for both individual and community development, further perpetuating the notion that difference must be "fixed" by the benevolent West. She challenges Canadian educators to cultivate a critical ethic of care in their students with the intent of moving citizenship education away from historical, developmental notions of goodness and toward critically "good" global citizenship.

In chapter 13, "Education for Refugee Learners under the Framework of Social Justice and Racial Equity," Neda Asadi points out how education can play an integral part in creating a thriving society through providing equitable spaces for all learners: spaces where learners can access knowledge, develop their sense of self, and understand the destructive power of "Othering." She adds that students who have been forcibly displaced from their homes and seek to make Canada their new home are among some of the most vulnerable learners in Canadian schools. Because educational policies drafted to deal with these issues are not adequate, Asadi says that it is imperative to develop educational frameworks that are unique to the context of Canadian diversity, thus allowing the construction of policies and practices in a way that would redress the injustices faced by refugee learners in Canada. Relying primarily on the existing literature, including works by Nancy Fraser and Frantz Fanon, Asadi outlines and develops a theoretical framework for racial equity and social justice analysis to design and achieve educational policies and practices that can meet the existing gaps and can create equitable spaces for all learners, with a particular emphasis on refugee students.

In chapter 14, "Interrogating Equity Issues on Inclusive Postsecondary Education for Refugees and New Immigrants in Canada," Michael Kariwo discusses the challenges faced by refugee and new immigrant children and youth in Canada. To analyze this, he focuses on university education, where he interrogates issues related to who controls knowledge and how racism and discrimination manifest themselves within the academy. He adds that refugee and new immigrant students face several barriers, including language, technology use, and finance. As a result, he notes, some develop mental health problems, and those from war zones experience an exacerbation of their post-traumatic disorders. The students in this situation—who bring their pre-migration challenges, which require accommodation in the new country—need to be understood and supported. To deal with these realities, Kariwo intends to engage the transformative possibilities using race and social justice theories as well as transnational analyses.

DISCUSSION QUESTIONS

1. What was your general understanding of social justice and social justice education before reading this chapter?

2. How would you differentiate social justice education from general (non-critical) multicultural education?

3. What social justice theorists encountered in this chapter provoke your topical understanding of the area?

4. How do you think you can expand your social justice education practices in the field and in the classroom?

REFERENCES

Abdi, A. A. (2008). Democratic development and prospects for citizenship education: Theoretical perspectives on sub-Saharan Africa. *Interchange: A Quarterly Review of Education, 39*(2), 151–166.

Abdi, A. A. (2015). Decolonizing global citizenship education: Critical reflections on location, knowledge, and learning. In A. A. Abdi, L. Shultz, & T. Pillay (Eds.), *Decolonizing global citizenship education*. Sense Publishers.

Abdi, A. A. (2021). Freireian and Ubuntu philosophies of education: Onto-epistemological characteristics and pedagogical intersections. *Educational Philosophy and Theory*. https://www.tandfonline.com/doi/full/10.1080/00131857.2021.1975110

Ball, J. (2001). J. S. Mill on wages and women: A feminist critique. *Review of Social Economy, 59*(4), 509–527.

Battle, M. J. (2009). *Reconciliation: The Ubuntu theology of Desmond Tutu*. The Pilgrim Press.

Dei, G. J. S. (1996). *Anti-racism education: Theory and practice*. Fernwood Publishing.

Dei, G. J. S., & Kempf, A. (2013). *New perspectives on African-centred education in Canada*. Canadian Scholars.

Dewey, J. (1997). *Experience and education*. Free Press. (Original work published 1963)

Dewey, J. (2008). *The child and the curriculum, including schooling and society*. Cosimo.

Fraser, N. (2008). *Scales of justice: Reimagining political space in a globalized world*. Columbia University Press.

Fraser, N., et al. (2014). *Transnationalizing the public sphere*. Wiley.

Fraser, N., & Honneth, A. (2004). *Redistribution or recognition? A political-philosophical exchange*. Verso Books.

Freire, P. (2000). *Pedagogy of the oppressed*. Continuum. (Original work published 1970)

Ghosh, R., & Abdi, A. A. (2013). *Education and the politics of difference: Select Canadian perspectives* (2nd ed.). Canadian Scholars.

Government of Canada. (2019). *Summary of the Accessible Canada Act*. https://www.canada.ca/en/employment-social-development/programs/accessible-people-disabilities/act-summary.html

Government of Canada. (2021). *Canada welcomes the most immigrants in a single year in its history*. https://www.canada.ca/en/immigration-refugees-citizenship/news/2021/12/canada-welcomes-the-most-immigrants-in-a-single-year-in-its-history.html

Honneth, A. (1996). *The struggle for recognition: The moral grammar of social conflicts*. The MIT Press.

Li, C. (2017). Education as a human right: A Confucian perspective. *Philosophy East and West, 67*(1), 37–46.

Mill, J. S. (1869). *The subjection of women*. Longmans, Green, Reader and Dyer.

Mill, J. S. (2015). *On liberty, utilitarianism and other essays*. Oxford University Press. (Original work published 1859)

Nyerere, J. (1968). *Freedom and socialism*. Oxford University Press.

Rawls, J. (2002). *Justice as fairness: A restatement.* Harvard University Press.
Rawls, J. (2005). *A Theory of justice.* Harvard University Press. (Original work published 1971)
Rousseau, J. J. (2018). *The social contract & Emile.* E-artnow. (Original work published 1769)
Taylor, C. (1995). *Philosophical arguments.* Harvard University Press.
Taylor, C. (2003). *Modern social imaginaries.* Duke University Press.

CHAPTER 2

Critical Multicultural Education as a Platform for Social Justice Education in Canada

Ratna Ghosh

INTRODUCTION

We are living through a watershed moment in the history of human civilization. The world is in crisis, not only because of the COVID-19 pandemic and the way rich and powerful countries—like the poor and less powerful countries—have been unable to prevent the human suffering and deaths in their populations, but also because of uneven wealth distribution, the inequality of living conditions among people, climate change and devastation, and the increase in corruption and violence globally. The COVID-19 pandemic has revealed the effects of inequality that exist today and exposed major cracks in societies' institutions all over the world.

The coronavirus has caused a dramatic shift in geopolitical power and alliances. The geopolitical consequences of COVID-19 have been examined (on eight measures of power) in the Asia Power Index (Lowy Institute, 2020), which indicates that China's overall score has been rising while the United States' score has been declining. China's rapid recovery from the pandemic is in stark contrast to the inability of the United States to get a handle on the spread of the virus. The eight measures of power considered are economic capability, military capability, resilience, future resources, economic relationships, defence networks, diplomatic influence, and cultural influence (Lowy Institute, 2020). The International Monetary Fund has projected that China will be the only major economy in the world to grow this year (1.9 percent in 2020) (Lowy Institute, 2020). The United States has been in a decline on every measure of power (except resilience) and is being challenged as the pre-eminent powerful economic and technological country in the world, although it is still powerful. The European Union and countries in the East such as China are emerging as strong economic rivals, and along with other Asian countries, they are showing great technological progress. The economic consequences of COVID-19 at global and national levels have changed how we live, communicate, and educate. Technologies have taken over our lives, and there is a growing digital gap among the haves and the have-nots.

We are embarking on a new era. We need to seize this opportunity to reimagine pedagogy in more ethical terms. While the coronavirus does not discriminate, some groups are at greater risk of getting infected. The COVID-19 pandemic is putting the spotlight on the structural issues that give rise to the inequities in society. The aim of critical multicultural education (CME) is to highlight the inequality and injustice that have been invisible and normalized, in the hope that future generations will be active agents in building an equitable and sustainable world. The diversity in our population, regardless of our ethnic, linguistic, or related backgrounds, will be with us for good. Hence the need to understand the situation in ways that collectively enhance people's lives in places like Canada, where groups and individuals from all corners of the world have to live together, study together, work together, and achieve together for the overall well-being of the national project.

This chapter asks: What is the role of education in a world that is confronted with diversity and difference in multiple ways? How can education help to create a more just society at a time when the gap in inequality is growing among nations and within societies? Grounded on the principle that "universal and lasting peace can be established only if it is based upon social justice" (Constitution of the International Labour Organisation, 1919, preamble), this chapter aims to argue that education has the potential and the responsibility to prepare future generations for responsible behaviour in working toward a more equitable and socially cohesive world that preserves the environment and maintains peace. Most importantly, it is vital to carefully consider the type of education because education can be used for different purposes. Critical multicultural education is key to instilling the values of critical thinking, social justice, diversity, inclusivity, and global citizenship in order to work toward a just society.

RECOGNIZING DIVERSITY

The concept of social justice is meaningful only when it is seen in the context of diversity. As Amartya Sen (1979) points out, the recognition of the fundamental diversity of human beings has very deep consequences, especially in relation to the concept of social justice issues. Human beings are different in multiple ways, but it is the meanings given to these differences that make the issues political and result in inequality, prejudice, and discrimination. These meanings are socially constructed based on physical or cultural markers, including sex, skin colour, religion, and sexual preference. Being socially constructed, the meanings are not fixed but volatile, depending on the time and place. Different groups become the object of discrimination at different times. The important point is that victims of discrimination (racism, sexism, homophobia, etc.) all suffer negative effects, not only economically and socially, but also psychologically.

Societies are now recognized to be diverse in multiple ways. Globalization and technological advancement have accelerated the pace of diversity due to the movement of people across borders, which has been driven largely by migration; refuge from war, persecution, or natural disasters; and long-term or short-term work. Diversity implies variety, but it means different things to different people: diversity of ideas, characteristics, values, and so on. But demographic diversity usually suggests differences in ethnicity and culture, socioeconomic status, gender, religion, language, sexual identity and preference, and dis/abilities. Vertovec (2007) uses the word *super-diversity* to denote the multidimensional complexity in diversity (and its intersections). This term implies more than a focus on ethnicity and culture, as these characteristics are not homogenous given that the intersection of social class, gender, religion, language, and other differences results in very different experiences for any one group. This poses a significant challenge to societies that desire to minimize instability among different groups and create social cohesion. Similarly, the challenge to schools and teachers is to provide fair and equitable learning experiences to diverse student populations to enable them to participate fully in society.

SOCIAL JUSTICE CONSTRUCTIONS AND POSSIBILITIES

Article 1 of the Universal Declaration of Human Rights (UDHR; United Nations, 1948) says, "All human beings are born free and equal in dignity and rights." The UDHR is a milestone document in which people from all regions of the world agreed that the dignity and rights of each individual had to be protected by virtue of the fact that they were human beings. After the "barbarous acts … that [had] outraged the conscience of mankind" (United Nations, 1948, preamble) in the Second World War, the member countries of the United Nations overwhelmingly agreed that recognition of human dignity and rights was the foundation of freedom, justice, and peace in the world: there was global consensus on the UDHR. But despite its moral strength, the UDHR cannot act as a legal document, and after more than 70 years since its adoption, almost all of its 30 articles are being violated in all countries. These violations by state and other actors pertain to political, legal, and economic rights.

If we as human beings are equal, then it follows that we are worthy of equal opportunity to achieve our potential and live in the way that makes us happy.

However, we are well aware that human beings are diversely different (Sen, 2006) in terms of their various and fluid localities (historical, global) and positionalities (race, gender, language, religion, class, sexual orientation). Significantly, each of these factors and their intersections lead to differential power relations and distinct experiences. They are comparative, relational, and complex (Ghosh, 2012). People do not get equal opportunities in life (e.g., education, employment, place of birth) due to structural, social, and individual discrimination based on differences in their physical, cultural, religious, linguistic, or intellectual abilities. Differences among people exist in all societies, but they are particularly enhanced in demographically diverse ones.

So, what is social justice? With the broadening of the meaning of social justice, new terms have come into vogue but the concept is not at all new. Firstly, the earliest formal organized discussions of social justice go back to the 19th century Jesuit tradition in Italy and were responsive to the growing inequality in newly emerging contexts in industrializing Europe. With that, the focus was on the fair participation of all persons in the actions and benefits of the economy. Social justice, therefore, started with a political and socioeconomic recognition and re-allocation of demands, which, if analyzed in today's situation, should be even more salient. As indicated in this chapter, and as certainly is the case for Canada in the early 21st century, the divisions in society are even starker. Especially on the political and the economic platforms and economic and social relationships, surface multiculturalism and its educational assumptions have not dealt with the issues as effectively as expected. The contemporary situation is accentuated by sociocultural, schooling, and selectively related power relation differentials that directly sustain the absence of equity in the country's public resource management and distribution, including education and employment.

As such, the re-emergence of much-needed social justice issues and social justice education categories should fit better with critical multicultural education (Ghosh & Abdi, 2013; Ghosh & Galczynski, 2014), which focuses less on cultural festivities in school and more on empowering all students to succeed in school and in later life. With that in mind, *social justice* can be viewed as a politically charged and contested term that means different things to different people. To reiterate, it implies equal access by all to the resources of society. With its assumed roots in industrializing Europe (although certainly formulated and practised elsewhere in the world) to reduce the increasing gap between the rich and the poor, the concept began with a focus on economic justice but is now generally and gradually broadened to discuss and problematize issues of race, gender, and other sources of injustice, such as environmental destruction, that obviously encompass universal and global dimensions. Lack of social justice leads to inequality, and perhaps because there is a realization of economic benefits to equality, efforts to reduce inequality in all spheres have been stepped up.

According to a McKinsey & Company report, "'inequality' is not only a pressing moral and social issue but also a critical economic challenge.... All types of inequality have economic consequences ... advancing women's equality can add $12 trillion to global growth" (McKinsey & Company, 2015). When marginalized people are prevented from educational access and achievements, unable to contribute to research and the economy, not only is considerable brainpower lost, but this unequal treatment is detrimental to all. In an interdependent and still fully globalizing world, there is urgent need for social cohesion, but there is unlikely to be cohesion where there are stark inequalities that deprive so many, not only in different parts of the world, but within one country, such as Canada, which identifies itself as an advanced multicultural democracy. As noted by Canada Without Poverty (n.d.), one in seven Canadians (about five million people) lives in poverty, with racialized groups, women, disabled people, and young people being the most affected. With one in five Canadian children living in poverty, one could critically ascertain the negative impact on their learning and overall development opportunities. Overall, the Human Development Index indicates that greater equality in a country leads to greater prosperity. Conversely, income inequality results in decreased human development (Sakir, 2014). "Equality ... [and equity are] integral to human development" (Melamed & Samman, 2013).

THEORETICAL PERSPECTIVES

Postcolonial theory, critical race theory, and anti-oppression theory explain different aspects of social justice. Equality is explained most directly by theories of justice. Philosophers since ancient times have been involved with the question of what a just society might look like. In one of the most influential works of the 20th century, John Rawls (1971, 2002) progressively saw justice as fairness and what characterized an ideal society. Arguing that a single set of "just" principles does not capture the various forms of injustices in our global system, Amartya Sen (2009) sees justice at two levels: what constitutes a just society (normative) and, at a more practical level, how to reduce injustice and advance justice. He suggests a comparative perspective on justice that allows for variability in the situations of different groups. For him, the measure of inequality is the outcome and the obstacles encountered in reaching that outcome. His focus is not so much on the skills developed but on what people can do and be. Other thinkers such as Young (1990) and Pavlich and Ratner (1996) point to pluralistic understandings of justice that are also contextual, so as not to silence the experiences of those who do not fit into a universal system (Ghosh, 2012).

Kabeer (n.d.) discusses the multifaceted nature of injustice and exclusion. The cultural dynamics of social injustice—the norms and beliefs that define some groups as inferior—not only promote discriminatory behaviour but also erode self-confidence and self-worth, resulting in increased conflict and criminal activity (gangs, terrorism, and use of drugs). The economic dynamics of social injustice result from unequal access to and distribution of resources (education, health, employment), either due to structural barriers or individual prejudices. The policy dynamics of social inequality reflect the availability of and ability to obtain basic services (health and educational services). Political dynamics of social injustice are evident in the denial of rights and voice to certain groups. The intersection of all these aspects of inequality results in social exclusion that needs to be tackled with inclusive frameworks that critically appraise each aspect from multiple viewpoints.

Equality Legislation

Equality, a liberal democracy term that does not mean equity, and anti-discrimination legislation indicate the commitment of states to social justice and equal opportunity, and provide a legal framework as well as a moral guide. Aspiring to have harmonious social contexts that can foster and sustain prosperity for all, countries have policies that manage diversity in their societies. Multiculturalism policies are an example of this, and Canada was the first country in the world to have a federal policy on multiculturalism, adopted in 1971. It was Prime Minister Pierre Elliott Trudeau's (Liberal Party) vision to build a just society (his campaign theme) that led to the policy, which was entrenched in the constitution in 1984. Multiculturalism was provided with a legislative framework in the Multiculturalism Act (Government of Canada, 1988) by Prime Minister Brian Mulroney (Conservative Party), with a focus on equality to "ensure that all individuals received equal treatment and equal protection under the law, while respecting and valuing their diversity" (Government of Canada, n.d.).

The *Human Development Report* emphasizes that "The extent to which social justice has been achieved in a society must be based on the outcomes" (United Nations Development Programme, 2011, p. 19). Legislated rights are undoubtedly important, but equality of condition is just as important. And this makes removing barriers to achievement of those outcomes a measure of equality. As Melamed and Samman (2013, p. 3) point out, "We are aiming for societies to be equitable but not necessarily equal." Even when opportunities and conditions are the same, outcomes are dependent on individual preferences and values and therefore cannot be equal.

Canada has not yet reached the stage of a "just, multicultural society" without discrimination, but acknowledgement of a history of exclusion and "darker times" and efforts to deal with structural racism and discrimination, which have been slow and often ineffective, nevertheless have a moral force in the legislations. The COVID-19 pandemic has drawn attention to the vulnerability of certain groups, and global social movements such as Black Lives Matter have provided the impetus to step up equity efforts in institutions, especially in higher education. As Prime Minister Justin Trudeau, quoting Martin Luther King Jr., said, "The arc of the moral universe is long, but it bends towards justice" (Trudeau, 2015).

Critical Multicultural Education

Education has a significant role to play in the world we create. With the spread of formal education as we know it today, the revolution of rising expectations demands that education provides equal opportunities to lead a good life. Yet normalizing inequality has become the status quo. While all societies want to avoid conflict, as they became more and more diverse, the rhetoric has been to offer equal opportunities in order to integrate the various groups. Interestingly, the focus on inequality (both nationally and globally) in education, while useful in measurable aspects, ignores the fact that some are more equipped to compete and succeed in such systems. It also does not sufficiently highlight the fact that education has important historical, social, cultural, linguistic, and class constructions that enable some to achieve well in schooling, while marginalizing or even failing those who do not fit such background categories. This is where the concept of equity is important. Equity refers to fairness, whereas equality implies equal treatment or access. It would be worthless to give people of marginalized backgrounds the same opportunities as those who have been privileged, because the cultural and social capital would not be the same. Rather, the idea is to remove barriers to achievement (as noted above), and not to expect people to be equal.

The critical readings of the situation here should therefore entice us to pose the question: What is the role of education in a volatile world of globalization, both in countries of the North and South? That depends on what kind of societies we want. In Canada, the policy of multiculturalism is a distinguishing factor. Along with the shift in the conception of multicultural education from a liberal perspective to critical multicultural pedagogy, the focus has shifted from folklore, cultural preservation, and prejudice reduction strategies to discussions about discrimination (such as racism) and such democratic values as equality, fairness, and inclusion. While most educators accept that human beings are equal in dignity and rights, they are fully aware people are not born equal in many ways. Not only are they unequal in economic terms, but there are vast differences in their places of birth, their histories of oppression, and the structural barriers they face in society and school, which stifle their identities due to the social constructions of race and gender, religion, and physical/intellectual challenges. These inequalities not only affect their life chances but are also intergenerational. CME aims to address the removal of these barriers; this should also highlight the necessary discussion of equity-oriented critical multicultural education, which critically ascertains people's current conditions as resulting from previous oppressions and related ongoing disenfranchisements.

Most contemporary education systems emanate from learning ideologies of colonialism and have been in the grip of a neoliberal ideology and the effects of globalization, which have focused on the commodification of education. Good education is equated to high-stakes testing and high scores, intense competition, and preparation for the job market in the global economy. This instrumentalist form of education has obscured the commitment to humanistic values of compassion, community care, justified collective rights, and individual dignity and worth. The focus is on skills and training, not on critical thinking and global citizenship values, or intercultural communication and cooperation. Economic and technological skills are essential in any society, but cognitive, social, and emotional skills can all be developed alongside those in schools because education cannot be a zero-sum game. Furthermore, the dramatic pace of technological, scientific, and social change requires that attention in education be paid to student and teacher well-being in addition to learning and its attachments of assessment and promotion.

The delivery modes of teaching and learning have been transformed due to COVID-19. Technology has taken on a sudden and unprecedented significance during the pandemic, particularly in education. With face-to-face learning suddenly halted in all levels of education and in all regions and countries in the world, education (learning and teaching) has moved online. Delia Neuman (1991) points out that technology and equity are not inevitable partners. While inequitable access to computers for marginalized groups—which include visible minorities, girls and women, people with disabilities, and those in inner city schools and rural areas—was evident and inevitable given the inequality in different areas of the world and within each country, the correlation between internet access and social equality has increased significantly during the pandemic. Notwithstanding the potential of emerging technologies, the digital gap is widening. Access to computers is taken for granted in online education. However, not only are computers not available to all who need them, but broad access to teleconferencing and interactive programs is out of reach in many countries of the South and in rural, remote, and Indigenous communities of countries of the North, including Canada. This will inevitably lead to further inequality in society, in educational opportunities, and in future life chances.

Soft skills such as social and emotional learning are difficult to cultivate through online teaching, although the development of technologies that attempt to do so are increasing exponentially. Social justice education emphasizes skill development for active participation as citizens in a democratic society that values justice, equality and equity, and life and liberty. This should not be treated as an additional subject; it should be embedded in the pedagogy. The purpose of education is to prepare students for meaningful work and citizenship that values and respects diversity in society and nature. This involves explicit and implicit learning experiences. Valuing and respecting others implies understanding the power relations that make people's experiences different. These different experiences are the result of history, geography, and inequality of access and opportunities to develop one's potential. As indicated above, critical multicultural education focuses on events in history that have led to privileging and un-privileging power imbalances globally.

Paulo Freire's work (1970) is particularly important because he connects justice to education by emphasizing the transformative possibility of education and conscious awareness of inequality and injustice (Ghosh, 2012). Freire's theory of *conscientização*, or conscientization (critical awareness of one's reality through reflection and action), influenced the development of critical pedagogy and of critical multicultural education. Critical multicultural education brings together a critical focus on a "just society" with social justice education and strives to empower students to develop their capabilities by means of a multicultural lens. The focus is on power relations in society, how privilege is perpetuated, and the impact on diverse students and their ability to learn and develop their capabilities to do and be (Sen, 1993), and ultimately societies' ability to achieve justice.

Critical multicultural education is a worldview, not just a subject to study. It is a student-centred pedagogical framework that goes beyond intercultural competencies and knowledge of other cultures and religions. CME involves the development of critical consciousness about oneself as well as of others, especially those who are seen as different, through taking multiple perspectives. CME uses a historical perspective and an intersectional lens to develop critical understanding of inequities in society so that they can been seen as the result of differential power relations. As such, CME implies an openness to other cultures as well as different and often difficult points of view. It focuses on social and emotional aspects of learning, as it also incorporates cognitive aspects of learning and being. Therefore, it brings students' voices and experiences to critique the practices that have been normalized on subjects of race, sex, class, religion, sexual orientation, and other tough issues. It challenges monocentric worldviews and examines knowledge brought from various cultures and histories to include European, Asian, African, and Latin American histories and experiences. The idea is not only to critique and challenge but to foster critical thinking practices and consider various cultural perspectives so students acquire individual abilities as well as developing a social consciousness of rights and responsibilities to society and the world we live in. CME aims at understanding processes that have resulted in colonialism, slavery, and globalization, but it also endeavours to understand the contributions of various cultures (including Indigenous cultures) and civilizations to the development of science and technology. Most importantly, CME recognizes that unequal treatment and opportunities for some is detrimental to all peoples in all societies. CME is not just for minority students, because the benefits of social justice and the appreciation of diversity benefit the interests of majority groups in society as well.

Teacher Education

Of crucial importance for the success of critical multicultural education is appropriate teacher education. There is an urgent need to reconceptualize teacher education so that students are taught what they will need in the world they will live in. COVID-19 has shown that inequality is not only a moral issue; it is an economic issue, an environmental issue, and, most importantly, an educational issue. The COVID-19 pandemic has highlighted the inequality of online learning for those who have no money, not only in countries of the South but also in remote areas of countries of the North, such as Canada, and for those who are physically challenged and marginalized. Sensitivity to these inequalities is required of teachers who may not be aware that differences must be recognized. Why do we need to change how we educate teachers? Teacher education programs in North America have neither been able to conceptualize difference in their highly diverse societies nor aimed at teaching for social justice except at the nominal, rhetorical level. There is growing evidence that in the United States, pre-service teachers in training are not prepared to educate students in this fast-paced and rapidly changing world (Demulder et al., 2016), and teacher education candidates in Canada are likely no different (Ghosh & Galcznyski, 2014).

To teach with a critical multicultural, anti-racist perspective for social justice implies a paradigm shift in teacher education programs. We need to seize this opportunity to reconceptualize the content and methods of teaching, but most of all, we need a dramatic change in worldview. Critical multicultural pedagogy and social justice issues are not subjects that should be taught but rather a new, inclusive worldview that should permeate all courses and activities in teacher education programs in Canada and elsewhere. It is also important to recognize that many active teachers have been schooled during times when racism and inequality (inequity) were not normally questioned. It is also unlikely, during those times, that dialogical and participatory methods of teaching were the prevailing experiences in school. As a result of this, and not entirely of their own shortcomings, these teachers have not challenged the dominant group's privileges or the many inequalities that have been normalized in their societies.

In order for current and future teachers to develop a critical consciousness in their students, bring in multiple perspectives, challenge the dominant norm, and disrupt the way knowledge is processed, they will need to develop their own critical thinking and consciousness in aspiring to have harmonious social contexts that can create and sustain prosperity for all.

The key to this kind of change is to understand the processes and structures of power and expose the mechanisms of inequality and resulting inequities. Teachers need to examine their own assumptions, ways of knowing, biases, and prejudices, which may be difficult to do. Moving from an assimilationist system of teaching and learning to an inclusive and critical multicultural perspective implies a total reversal of their worldview. They need to see global interdependence, the complexity as well as the importance of diversity, and the value of bringing in student experiences to make the lesson more relevant to students' lives in a student-centred philosophy of teaching. Most importantly, teacher education programs need teachers who will examine their own beliefs and prejudices before they try to deal with and understand the other.

CONCLUSION

This chapter looked at social justice education within the framework of critical multicultural education and pedagogy at a time when the COVID-19 pandemic has put a spotlight on the many cracks in our educational institutions as it has of other social, economic, and political institutions. In highly multicultural educational contexts such as Canada's, the need to design and activate learning possibilities that enfranchise all students is as important as ever. While multiculturalism has been a government policy since 1971, later established as a parliamentary act in 1988, its application to education has been at best symbolic because it neglects to question the important power relations and outcomes that interact with people's daily lives. Hence, there is a need for critical multicultural education and pedagogy that are likely to achieve more inclusive and enfranchising schooling contexts for all. With this, and by realigning the equity potentialities afforded by the pandemic, there are opportunities to transform educational systems the world over for ethical and active citizenship rather than just tinkering with a new normal.

DISCUSSION QUESTIONS

1. How is liberal multicultural education different from critical multicultural education?

2. What does social justice mean in education? How can critical multicultural education develop awareness of social justice in education?

3. How can we transform teacher education to bring about a generation of teachers who are world-minded and aware of their own biases (conscious or unconscious) so that they can have truly inclusive classrooms?

REFERENCES

Canada Without Poverty. (n.d.). *Just the facts*. https://cwp-csp.ca/poverty/just-the-facts/#:~:text=1%20in%207%20(or%204.9,over%20the%20past%20two%20decades

Constitution of the International Labour Organisation. (1919). Part XIII of the Treaty of Versailles. https://www.refworld.org/docid/3ddb5391a.html

Demulder, E., Stribling, S. M. & Dallman, L. (2016, January 12). Reviewers of Schwarzer & Bridglall Promoting Global Competence and Social Justice in Teacher Education. *Teachers College Record*. https://www.tcrecord.org ID Number: 19286, Date Accessed: 3/16/2018 3:36:45 PM

Freire, P. (1970). *Pedagogy of the oppressed*. Continuum.

Ghosh, R. (2012). Diversity and excellence in higher education: Is there a conflict? *Comparative Education Review*, 56(3), 349–365.

Ghosh, R., & Abdi, A. A. (2013). *Education and the politics of difference: Select Canadian perspectives* (2nd ed.). Canadian Scholars.

Ghosh, R., & Galcznyski, M. (2014). *Redefining multicultural education: Inclusion and the right to be different* (3rd ed.). Canadian Scholars.

Government of Canada. (n.d.). *Canadian multiculturalism: An inclusive citizenship*. https://web.archive.org/web/20140312210113/http:/www.cic.gc.ca/english/multiculturalism/citizenship.asp

Government of Canada. (1988). *Canadian Multiculturalism Act*. https://laws-lois.justice.gc.ca/eng/acts/c-18.7/page-1.html (accessed June 7, 2018)

Kabeer, N. (n.d.). *Can the MDGs provide a pathway to social justice? The challenge of intersecting inequalities*. Institute of Development Studies, University of Sussex. http://www.mdgfund.org/sites/default/files/MDGs_and_Inequalities_Final_Report.pdf

Lowy Institute. (2020). *Asia power index*. https://power.lowyinstitute.org/#:~:text=The%20Lowy%20Institute%20Asia%20Power%20Index%20is%20t

McKinsey & Company. (2015). *How advancing women's equality can add $12 trillion to global growth*. McKinsey Global Institute. https://www.mckinsey.com/featured-insights/employment-and-growth/how-advancing-womens-equality-can-add-12-trillion-to-global-growth#:~:text=A%20McKinsey%20Global%20Institute%20report%20finds%20that%20%2412,to%20close%20gender%20gaps%20in%20work%20and%20society

Melamed, C., & Samman, E. (2013). *Equity, inequality and human development in a post-2015 framework*. United Nations Development Program. https://hdr.undp.org/content/equity-inequality-and-human-development-post-2015-framework

Neuman, D. (1991). Technology and equity. *ERIC Digest*.

Pavlich, G., & Ratner, R. S. (1996). "Justice" and the postmodern. In M. Peters, J. Marshall, & S. Webster (Eds.), *Critical theory, poststructuralism and the social context* (pp. 143–159). Dunmore Press.

Rawls, J. (1971). *A theory of justice*. Harvard University Press.

Rawls, J. (2002). *Justice as fairness: A restatement*. Harvard University Press.

Sakir, S. (2014). The ninety-nine percent and the one percent. *Research in Applied Economics*, 6(3), 196. https://doi.org/10.5296/rae.v6i3.5996

Sen, A. (1979, May 22). *Equality of what?* Tanner lecture on Human Values at Stanford University. https://www.ophi.org.uk/wp-content/uploads/Sen-1979_Equality-of-What.pdf

Sen, A. (1993). Capability and well-being. In M. Nussbaum & A. Sen, *The quality of life* (pp. 30–53). Clarendon Press.

Sen, A. (2006). *Identity and violence: The Illusion of Destiny*. W. W. Norton.

Sen, A. (2009). *The idea of justice*. Allen Lane.

Trudeau, J. (2015, November 26). *Diversity is Canada's strength*. Address by the Right Honourable Justin Trudeau, Prime Minister of Canada. https://pm.gc.ca/eng/news/2015/11/26/diversity-canadas-strength

United Nations. (1948). *Universal Declaration of Human Rights*. https://www.un.org/en/about-us/universal-declaration-of-human-rights

United Nations Development Programme. (2011). *Sustainability and equity: A better future for all*. 2011 Human Development Report.

Vertovec, S. (2007). Super-diversity and its implications. *Ethnic and Racial Studies*, 30(6), 1024–1054.

Young, I. M. (1990). *Justice and the politics of difference*. Princeton University Press.

CHAPTER 3

Educating against Anti-Black/Anti-African Canadian Racism

George J. Sefa Dei and Claudette Howell Rutherford

INTRODUCTION

In this chapter, we conceptualize anti-Black/African racism (ABR/AAR) as systemic oppressive practices, as revealed in the institutionalized values in our social fabric, which function both consciously and unconsciously to deny, negate, and devalue Black life; Black body experience, Black history, identity, culture, and knowledge; and our existential humanity. As violent oppression meted on Black and African bodies, anti-Blackness has a long history rooted in colonialism and enslavement, always playing out on Black culture, values, knowledge systems, histories, identities, and social locations (Dei, 2020; Dumas, 2015; McKittrick, 2006; Sexton, 2011, 2015; Sharpe, 2016). While our observational analysis should be applicable to all Canadian public schools with a minority of African Canadian learners, most of our examples relate to Black students' experiences in the province of Ontario. As the most populous province in the country, Ontario has more people of African descent (collectively labelled as Black people) than the other provinces and territories combined.

Among the key tropes of anti-Blackness and anti-African racism are ideologies of racial hierarchy, white supremacy, and Black sub-humanity. It is critical that we differentiate between anti-African racism and anti-Black racism. The former is centred on the devaluation, othering, and exoticism of the rich ethnocultural elements of Africa's languages, folklore, spirituality, and geographies. Whereas anti-African racism sets that which is of the continent of Africa in juxtaposition to Eurocentric ideals of legitimacy, civility, worthiness, and morality (Adjei, 2018; Dei et al., 2004; Dumas, 2015; hooks, 1992; Woodson, 1933), anti-Black racism is centred in Black skin colour and the deleterious racialized notions ascribed to Black skin. Consequently, both anti-Blackness and anti-Africanness thrive in the climate of an interpellation of supremacist ideologies and the rational capitalist and modernist logics of reasonableness, normality, respectability, and acceptability.

The problem of anti-Black racism (ABR) and anti-African racism (AAR) extends beyond schools. We see a nearly universal adverse rendering of African people and culture, and this anti-Blackness lives deep within both Black and white people. Yet amidst the effort to obliterate Black stories and livelihoods, we see a relentless perversion with and desire for ownership of African resources and cultures. In sum, when we focus on anti-Black racism in schools, we are referring to culture, climate, environment, and the socio-organizational lives of schools within which Black education is delivered and impacted. ABR/AAR brings to the fore questions of power, knowledge, and representation as reflected in the processes of educational delivery—the teaching, learning, and administration of education for Black, African, Indigenous, and other racialized learners. Education and schooling have been deemed and constructed as sites and catalysts for perpetuating racism and must therefore be the vehicles through which we initiate change. With this, education leaders can best serve the system by taking responsibility for how racism is borne and replicated within the system and how that same system benefits from anti-Blackness.

The quest for a socially just education for Black learners has to be unwavering. Amidst the recent global uprising and newfound focus on anti-racism in the year 2020 and beyond, we must be resolute and provide sustainable remedies. Enid Lee, pioneering Canadian anti-racist educator, is quoted as saying, "If you are not taking anti-racist education seriously, then you are promoting a monocultural racist education. There is no neutral ground on this issue" (Lee, 1991, p. 10).

As we become more aware of the glaring disparity in outcomes and the deep intergenerational pain and trauma inflicted on Black children by the system of education, it is also critically important that we increase our efforts toward reflective, transformative, and revolutionary change. In doing so, we offer a perspective of anti-Blackness and Anti-Africanness and its relationship to white supremacy in the context of schooling.

White supremacy and its tropes laid the foundation of what became the colonial project in Africa and around the globe. It was the catalyst for the transatlantic slave trade and other such atrocities and transnational genocides. Racialization and the hierarchical designation of attributes based on skin colour were critical components of colonialism. In an effort to dominate and tyrannize, European colonizers murdered, raped, and stole land from Indigenous Peoples across multiple continents, including North America. Specifically, Africans were forcefully kidnapped and violently dislocated from their lands and enslaved (Cooper, 2016). Their captors forced them to replace their names, culture, spiritual teachings, family structures, and language with those of white, Eurocentric ways of life. Education was integral to that process of devaluation and unlearning of culture (Vowel, 2016). David Gillborn (2005, p. 192) refers to white supremacy in education as a "set of concerted actions" that operate "always to the benefit of the racist status quo."

Neocolonialism is broadly defined as economic and sociopolitical power and influence to dominate and control marginalized populations and entities. The use of the term here is meant to disrupt the concept of postcolonialism and affirms the permeating remnants of colonial ascendancy and dependency on the colonial state despite political emancipation (Nkrumah, 1965; Sartre, 2001). For the purposes of this chapter, we can translate this to the perception that public education appears to afford opportunities, yet it infringes upon the freedoms of those who are severely underserved by the system. Though the demoralizing and destructive processes of enslavement, erasure, and dislocation still perpetuate today, the politics of imperialist neocolonialism now enforces assimilation and other more insidious forms of brutality. Assimilation is one of a range of strategies of elimination; it can be more effective than conventional forms of killing since it does not involve going against the law that is ideologically central to the cohesion of settler society (Wolfe, 2006).

With those social norms established over hundreds of years, anti-Blackness and proximity to whiteness have also occasionally been rewarding for other racialized groups, selectively referred to as *honorary whites*, who use such socially constructed honorific whiteness as a currency to gain incremental power at the expense of Black bodies in a racialized hierarchy (Bonilla-Silva, 2004; Stovall, 2006). This continues to be the most advantageous method of propagating the colonial project. This divisive strategy of structural exploitation and categorization continues in contemporary educational systems (Dumas, 2015) and needs to be challenged.

To do so, we first approach the concept of decolonization from the perspective that colonization represents white settler hegemonic dominance (Lawrence & Dua, 2005). Anti-colonial education is the removal and undoing of colonial practices that challenge the appropriation of Black and Indigenous land, people, knowledges, and histories with an intent to deconstruct the institutionalization of white privilege in educational politics and edifices.

Decolonization of the education system is the way forward in repairing centuries of injustice suffered by Black and Indigenous people. The work of dismantling an institution so deeply entrenched in generational bondage can seem impossible. However, we must remember that these same systems began as personal imaginings based on greed and self-interest. Systems are not faceless; they are created and upheld by people and are built and maintained by those who stand to gain from the unearned power wielded within that ecosystem. Those who represent the dominant, patriarchal, cisgendered hegemony (those who identify as white, straight, and male), benefit from the existing power structures by which we are governed and require the education system to continue to erase histories and convince new generations about the falsehoods of racial inferiority in order to continue to harness that omnipotence.

Colonialism can be characterized by the usurpation of power, land, and resources; the indoctrination of its subjects is sustenance for the colonial project. The deep manipulation of the Black psyche is a prerequisite for the deceptive tropes of white supremacy and is at the root of colonization. It can be argued that the school became the site of state-sanctioned psychological manipulation in order to maintain the systemic oppression set by colonial powers. The application of a decolonial framework offers us a way forward in dismantling the existing structures so that education functions as a causeway toward racial justice. Educational leaders who are serious about creating anti-racist schools and classrooms can employ this thinking in order to decolonize their own minds, pedagogy, and praxis.

An anti-colonial disruption of existing structures calls for a redistribution of power to include stakeholders who ascribe to anti-racist principles and who have traditionally been silenced and excluded from leadership spaces. Those who safely uphold and thrive in whiteness and have a reserved seat at the boardroom table would be required to relinquish their seat to those who are intent (regardless of their skin pigmentation) on interrogating anti-Black policies and praxis. An anti-colonial education threatens to shatter the saliency of white supremacy (Gillborn, 2008). This presents the most stringent barrier to decolonization. A racist education system is simply too beneficial for those who impute white dominance and garner its benefits. These contenders lack the vested interests that would engender and inspire a system to reach forward and serve the invariably "underserved." Despite the countless contributions to anti-racist scholarship and generations of Black resistance and advancement projects, the elusive potency of racism has forced the underserved and marginalized to remain as such because, in reality, white people's continuing resistance to authentically surrender even some of their own personal gains at best limits any meaningful work that can be done to achieve anti-racist outcomes.

MANIFESTATIONS OF ANTI-BLACK RACISM

Anti-Black Racism/Anti-African Racism manifests itself in everyday institutional practices, curricula, classroom pedagogies, and texts that negate, denigrate, deny, exclude, and discredit Black presence, contributions, and lived experiences. It also plays out in everyday microaggressions beyond racist name-calling, language, and accents (Dei, 2021). The question is: What does it mean to wear a Black body or Black skin in schools? The selective hyper-visibility and invisibility of Black physical presence in schooling is perversely consequential. Black bodies are surveilled and scrutinized (Conroy, 2013; Maynard, 2017). Maynard (2017) acknowledges that Black children have been excluded from the concepts of innocence and protection and are believed to be "impervious" to suffering. This rhetoric has been conducive to the systemic evacuation or pushing out of Black children from mainstream education. There is also the Black/African hyper-vulnerability to violence. The polarity of the Black student experience is illustrated in the following examples of the current school context. In September 2016, a school administrator in the Peel District School Board called the police to help restrain a six-year-old Black girl after school staff members were unable to control her behaviour. In February 2020, an Ontario Human Rights Tribunal ruled that two Peel police officers racially discriminated against that six-year-old Black girl when they cuffed her wrists and feet and kept her restrained for 28 minutes (Cheung & Sieniewitz, 2017; Paradkar, 2020). For the adults in that scenario to view a six-year-old child as an imminent threat and, further, to defend the decision to brutally shackle her is a disturbing reminder of how Blackness is a perceived threat in the interdependent societal systems that govern Black lives (Bernard & Smith, 2018; Maynard, 2017; Zirkel & Johnson, 2016).

In 2019, the family of a young Black boy attending high school in Newmarket, Ontario, filed a $1 million lawsuit against the York Region District School Board, claiming that administrators failed to act on numerous reports of ongoing racial harassment and physical attacks against their son. The young ninth-grader was repeatedly targeted and viciously beaten several times. The family made numerous requests to have him transferred, all of which were denied. He finally incurred a concussion during a videotaped assault, which was featured on the local news, spurring public controversy about the incident (Boisvert, 2019). It seems that Black skin is, by the nature of its existence, threatening, even on the tiny body of a six-year-old who, at the same time, is not accorded rightful institutional protection, even when the danger to her being is clear and present. This substantiates how Black pain is imperceptible and inconceivable to those in institutional leadership. Black children suffer tougher discipline measures and repercussions at the hands of those with no regard for their safety or with ostensible regard for others' safety (Howard, 2014; Maynard, 2017).

African Canadian males in schools are suspended at a rate four times higher than that of their white classmates, from kindergarten to 12th grade (Daniel, 2017; James & Turner, 2017). This is also evidence of the interdependent relationship between the criminal justice system and the education system, characterized by the school-to-prison pipeline that disproportionately targets and punishes

Black children, specifically Black boys (Conroy, 2013; Salole & Abdulle, 2015). Education, like the criminal justice system, is a site of control within society, and the racist filtering of students into the prison pipeline begins as early as kindergarten (Swain & Noblit, 2011). Suspension data from the Toronto District School Board, for example, states that 48 percent of students suspended or expelled from school from 2011 to 2016 were Black students (James & Turner, 2017). That is when their school population percentage is about four times less than that. The education system, built on Eurocentric values and systematic hypervigilance as well as the criminalization of Black students' behaviour, funnels Black children out of academic success and into the penal system (Bernard & Smith, 2018). Policies are disproportionately used against racialized students in a way that obfuscates the responsibility of the individual applying the policy (Swain & Noblit, 2011). Although Black bodies are not valued and protected against violence institutionally, they are disproportionately targeted and censured as perpetrators of violence (Maynard, 2017; Salole & Abdulle, 2015).

Exclusionary efforts to filter Black bodies from educational spaces are varied beyond physical removal from school buildings. For years, we have had empirical evidence of the streaming of Black students out of academic pathways and into applied-level courses (Codjoe, 2001; Schroeter & James, 2015; James & Turner, 2017). The Ontario government's July 2020 announcement that destreaming would be implemented starting in grade 9 (DeClerq, 2020) does not address or remedy the inherent racial bias that causes streaming to become a racially motivated abuse of power in the first place. It also does not take into account the fact that streaming begins in kindergarten, when Black children are placed in colour-coded reading groups or strategically placed in alternative classroom spaces (e.g., the Kindergarten Intervention Program) due to poor behaviour or lack of engagement (Howard & James, 2019). Another less overt form of streaming is the exclusion of Black students from specialized programming such as French immersion, International Baccalaureate programs, Specialist High Skills Major programs, and advanced placement programs. Black families are not considered for or referred into these programs. Canadian demographic data on gifted programs indicate that Black students make up only 3 percent of the gifted student population in the Toronto District School Board (TDSB), though they make up 13 percent of the total student population (Brown & Parekh, 2010). This number is steadily declining. As of 2017, Black students made up 0.4 percent of the gifted population. Of the 5,679 Black high school students in TDSB in the 2006–2011 cohort, only 23 had been identified as gifted (James & Turner, 2017). Conversely, Black students make up a significant majority of those streamed into non-gifted special education programming (James & Turner, 2017), which raises concerns associated with Adjei's (2018) critical exploration of the pathologizing of Blackness as a perceived disability.

WHAT ARE THE IMPLICATIONS FOR DECOLONIZING THE EDUCATION SYSTEM?

Black learners and their families are sold the rhetoric of "liberal inclusion," which conflates the notion of sameness with that of equality. bell hooks (2006) characterizes this "mainstream imposition of sameness as a provocation that terrorizes" (p. 23). Inclusion forces those who are unwelcome to remain on the fringes—to be absorbed into a state that is intemperate and punishes those marginalized by the unilateral monolith. There is also hostility toward Black/African claims of Indigeneity (Dei, 2020), which aims to divest Black bodies of our sense of self and further propagates the vicious theft of land and identity suffered during enslavement. As a result, Black children are not sure where they belong.

In the introduction of bell hooks's *Black Looks*, Samia Nehrez (quoted in hooks, 2006) writes, "decolonization continues to be an act of confrontation against the hegemonic systems of thought, a historical and cultural liberation which involves an exorcism for both the colonizer and the oppressed" (p. 1). Therefore, to decolonize education requires a comprehensive multi-disciplinary, multi-system reform of how education is meant to be utilized by the state to establish standardized ways of knowing. The system of teaching and learning must be engendered in knowledge and related pedagogical multiplicities and multi-centricities (Dei, 1996).

In the establishment of a new educational system that is no longer rooted in oppression and politicized stratification, we might begin to imagine a restructuring of curriculum development and assessment practices in consultation with Black Indigenous Elders and Knowledge Keepers as well as the wider Black communities as part of the teaching and learning community. With that, we shall perceive the need for an intensive audit of the present ideologies of metacognition and start reimagining what constitutes knowledge, learning, and doing—a re-envisioning of the goals and intentions of *learning and well-being* as opposed to *schooling*.

Decolonizing also offers a critique of modernity and post-modernity and not just a preoccupation with the problematics of the enlightenment discourses that privilege events, thoughts, values, experiences, and the historical processes and practices situated at specific points in European society and its historical, cultural, and educational constructs. We must look at the system as a whole and the underlying subcultures of education. Decolonization would mean a review of the hegemonic governance and hierarchical structure within the system of education.

The application of decolonial praxis presents an opportunity for those with legislative powers to scrutinize and amend the Education Act to disembowel the corresponding elements that bind white supremacy to educational goals and achievement. Authentic decolonization calls on us to abolish what Robyn

Maynard (2017) calls "racially structured institutions" that monetize oppression and compensate those who gratuitously maintain the disenfranchisement of Black bodies. With this monetization, policies are disproportionately used against racialized students in a way that obfuscates the responsibility of the individual applying the policy (Dumas, 2015; Swain & Noblit, 2011). As we work to demolish the structural racist currency of learning and education, we can rebuild a system that radically delegitimizes white ideals and proffers racial justice, beginning with a stark revision and reconstruction of those policies.

The ministries of education, professional colleges, governing bodies, and labour councils must all align unanimously with a set of ethical standards and accountability measures that prioritize equitable outcomes for all students. Publicly denouncing anti-Black racism is one thing, but exacting measures that build this tenet into the currency and capital for educational advancement is a more tangible level of commitment to change.

Doing so will translate into requirements to build capacity in anti-oppression and anti-Black racism as part of the teacher appraisal process and principal appraisal process. In the case of Ontario, these review processes would need to be correlated with established core competencies within the Ontario Leadership Strategy (OLS), the Ontario Leadership Framework (OLF, 2013), and other assessment tools designed by the Ontario Institute for Educational Leadership. These amendments should be reflected in the hiring rubrics and guidelines for educators, developed by the Ontario Ministry of Education and adhered to by human resources departments in each school district.

Active campaigns to include Black parents, learners, and educators at the decision-making table is crucial in creating a shift in the power relations in school settings. Black community elders and parent engagement in the development of school policies and the decision-making process itself can be largely arbitrated by school parent councils and involve more collaboration with the larger school community. Not only does this guarantee Black parents and guardians a seat at the table so that their interests are heard, but it also ensures that those decisions carry weight so that these parents/guardians can maximize their potential to advocate and influence outcomes. Black parents, students, and educators should have the opportunity to provide input on the design, dissemination, and analysis of school climate and achievement surveys. Parents and community advocates can be involved in the interpretation of data and the development of the reports that come from the data in order to close existing gaps in the system that affect Black children. This model has worked in the Africentric Alternative School, where the conceptualization of "the village" is actualized to support the functioning of the school community. We will explore this model more deeply in the latter portion of this chapter.

Curriculum Reform

The process by which curriculum is devised, authored, and delivered is not inclusive of Black voices and narratives. In Ontario, racial minorities represent 26 percent of the population yet make up only 10 percent of the 70,520 secondary school teachers and 9 percent of the elementary school and kindergarten teachers (Turner, 2014). Curriculum revision and development are happening in predominantly white spaces with little input from Black educators and scholarship. This needs to be addressed in order to untangle what Gillborn (2008) refers to as "a web of actions by teachers, policymakers, right-wing commentators, uncritical academics, and the media all working in one direction" (p. 192). Ministries of education, faculty, and curriculum leaders need to engage in collective and interrelated curriculum reform—from the graduate studies level right down to kindergarten—to include the African Canadian experience.

The curriculum was designed to further galvanize a white supremacist "master script" (Dumas, 2015; Gillborn, 2008; Swartz, 1992). However, an anti-colonial system would embolden educators to both employ and inculcate a commitment to critical consciousness and inquiry so that learners examine and challenge dominant discourse, using teaching and learning as a form of activism. As lifelong learners, teachers would invoke what Ladson-Billings (1995) refers to as culturally relevant and responsive pedagogy (CRRP) to explore possibilities, using an expansive set of materials that honours multiple sets of knowledge and diasporic histories.

All children should be learning about the remarkable innovations from Kush, Maroe, and Kemet. The contributions from within the continent of Africa to the foundations of mathematical, scientific, technological, and military advancements are well documented despite the past and ongoing erasure campaigns from mainstream education. The folktales of Anansi the Spider should be told alongside Aesop's commonly recited fables, "The Hyena and the Hare" alongside "The Tortoise and the Hare." Africentric stories and Indigenous folklore can be carefully curated and applied to unit and lesson plans to deliver core curriculum expectations across disciplines (Dei & McDermott, 2019).

As we survey the current curriculum, where are the stories of Black rebellion and resilience to balance the emphasis on those of the European empires? How many teachers tell the stories of Queen Hangbe of Benin, a warrior and leader of the Dahomey Amazons, a powerful army of women? Queen Hangbe is among many African women warriors who led revolutions and epic battles across the continent. These stories will serve as the critical counter-narratives that challenge predominantly white patriarchal supremacist stories prevalent in current curriculum. There is a Zimbabwean proverb that avows that "Until the lion learns to write, the story of the hunt will always glorify the hunter." Despite vast amounts of documented evidence of Black enterprise and brilliance, our stories are diminished, censored, and suppressed. We will not wait for these stories to be told as a means of validation. Rather, telling these stories will serve as part of a collective healing process of learning and unlearning toward rediscovery and connection with our African ancestral endowments.

Focus on Anti-Racist Policy and Strategies

The Ontario Ministry of Education has taken steps in the past to draft policy documents focusing on equitable outcomes in Ontario. Each of the province's 72 school boards have developed practices that align with *Realizing the Promise of Diversity: Ontario's Equity and Inclusive Education Strategy* (2009), *Developing and Implementing Equity and Inclusive Education Policies* (2013), and *Ontario's Education Equity Action Plan* (2017). However, the implementation of these policies has not led to any robust or comprehensive changes in how Black students fare in the education system in Ontario (Howard & James, 2019). Even though there are recommendations with a specific focus on anti-racism, there is little to no focus on anti-Black racism. The equity, diversity, and inclusion departments and staff and those charged with the work of human rights are diverting and diluting the work of critical race discourse in education (Agpeyong, 2010; Walcott, 2018). Walcott (2018) offers a critique on how the politics of people of colour (POC) and diversity do not have specificity and as such cannot continue to perform the necessary task of destroying anti-Blackness. The invocation of training and policies that focus on *diversity* and *human rights* obscures and stifles any delineation of Blackness and forces the exclusion of anti-Black racism from very tidy "courageous" conversations on inclusion, bias, and prejudice.

The provincial team at the Ontario Association of Children's Aid Societies' One Vision One Voice project, led by Kike Ojo, has developed 11 race equity practices that provide a framework for how the Children's Aid Societies across the province will amend and enhance operations to improve outcomes for Black children and families (Turner, 2016). Could the integration of a set of race equity practices, aligned in conjunction with a stringent anti-Black racism strategy, help to address the evident alienation of Black learners from the school system in Ontario?

Toward a Future for Black Education

As we anticipate what lies ahead for Black learners in Ontario—also extendable to the rest of Canada—some questions come to mind. Is there a desire on the part of the present system leaders to remedy the alienation and disenfranchisement of Black students so that they have the same achievement outcomes as their counterparts? Is the success of the current system being measured by the sum of its parts?

Are we as educators bound up and invested in the liberation and success of Black children within and beyond the realms of education? It is important to understand how the answers to these questions inform the intentions and limitations of the present public education system. In his discussion of cultural education and the academy, Stuart Hall (1992, p. 8) speaks of a "symbolic divide" and the drawing of boundaries. He says that no politics is possible without a sense of "us" and "them." In education, there seems to be a particular scheme of divide, a boundary where the intrinsic desire to teach and inspire ends and the barbs of power and self-interest begin. Rinaldo Walcott (2018) interacts with Hall's interpretations of "us" as practitioners and "them" as "audiences" in his discussion on Black studies in the academy, where he posits Black studies or—as we can postulate here—Africentric studies as a means to challenge and overthrow the institution of learning itself (Walcott, 2018, p. 91). Walcott applies Hall's directives, which suggest that there is something at stake in intellectual political practice that calls upon us to "act" in order to "reveal potentialities for reshaping the world in more just ways." Here we conceive of a Black Africentric education as a means by which we can invest in and liberate Black children (Walcott, 2018, p. 91).

We have indeed been fighting laws of segregation for decades with an aim to ultimately integrate—but at what cost? Have we been fighting the wrong fight, aspiring to assimilate to a white ideal and coexist in a system that was designed to destroy us and manufacture racist ideologies? What if we design a system that intentionally serves to enlighten and uplift Black students? Let us imagine a schooling system that incorporates Afro-Indigenous knowledge systems and assessment practices, including community space where Black grassroots organizations, social service agencies, and stakeholders across the system could collectively provide support and resources for Black children and families. Let us imagine a self-governed system, funded in part with public funds acquired through official reparations paid to Black Canadians. This separate but equal solution can be a venture undertaken in the not so distant future, which can affirm and elevate the education and advancement for Black learners, their families, and their communities.

In looking at the question of new educational futures, we revisit the Africentric school to offer a blueprint for radical liberationist action. The school has been operating successfully since 2009. Toronto's Africentric Alternative School, a publicly funded school in Ontario, is the first of its kind. The schooling and daily practices are built on the fundamentals of Africentrism, culturally responsive pedagogy, and collaboration with parents. The Africentric paradigm provides a space for African people to interpret their experiences on their own terms rather than through a Eurocentric lens (Dei, 2008). In a research study conducted by Philip Howard and Carl James (2019), the authors attribute the success of the school to a deep commitment from the staff and the cohesive family setting. There is a vested interest in the success and high achievement of each student. This can easily be related to what Ladson-Billings (1994) calls the "Dreamkeepers" (p. 209): educators caught up in the liberation of their students, teachers who dream about making educational success a reality for Black students. The school boasts high parent engagement and makes certain to centre diverse Black culture and accomplishments using the Ontario curriculum. Parents are integral to the learning ecosystem and are revered as "carriers of knowledge."

The argument for an Africentric school is about more than acquiring our own brick and mortar school building; it is about establishing our own system of teaching and learning, not as an alternative to the present experience but as a responsive counteractive experience. In a sobering overview of the present system failures that target Black youth, Bernard and Smith (2018) discuss the tenets of an Africentric worldview that offers a healing and restorative approach to education. They position three central beliefs at the core of Africentrism: (1) human identity is a collective identity, and context is central to this identity; (2) spirituality is as important as material aspects of life; and (3) affective knowledge is valid and essential in understanding the lived experiences of all people (Schiele, 1996, as cited in Stewart, 2004). Learning centred on oneself and one's ancestry sets a foundation and openness toward the understanding of broader views and social contexts. Africentrism is not intended to combat or oppose other frameworks. A common critique of Africentrism is a concern that the *centring* of Black stories, spirituality, and cultures will leave children sheltered and unprepared to face the world. This viewpoint ignores the fact that, for decades, white Eurocentric ideas have been at the epicentre of the educational body politic without objection. There is a wealth of research that can attest that Black diasporic literacy and exposure to Black role models affirm and strengthen the Black identity of Black students and are associated with enhanced academic engagement and commitment, not to mention a healing from destructive messages typically learned in social environments about Black people (Dei, 2008; Dei & Kempf, 2013; hooks, 2006; King, 1992; Zirkel & Johnson, 2016).

In her paper "Black Learners in Canada," Rosalind Hampton (2010) speaks of the collective benefits associated with the Africentric school model:

> Black youth would benefit significantly from community-based educational programmes that contextualize and inform their lived experiences and provide them with new ways of understanding and responding to the world around them. Community based education involves all community members and creates spaces for intergenerational learning and the transmission of oral history. In this way, educational programming within Black Communities can be pursued as a system of community development as well as a philosophy of education that responds to the crisis in public school systems. (pp. 103–104)

The premise and vision that initiated the Africentric school are based in the realization that the present system is not designed to foster Black success and achievement. The critique of the Africentric school model is mired with discussion of segregation, separatism, and unequal opportunities. The higher graduation rates, higher provincial test scores, enhanced self-esteem, and greater sense of belonging and engagement for students enrolled in the Africentric school substantiate the fact that when Black lives and potential are nurtured and centred, Black students succeed at a higher rate (Chen, 2013; Howard & James, 2019; Johnson, 2013). The correlations and gainful implications are just as heartening as they are conclusive.

CONCLUSION

In order to decolonize the existing public education system in Canada (with a more sustained focus on Ontario's situation in this chapter), all of the interconnected facets in the schooling context need to become deeply involved in an intentional, ethical shift to uncover and remove the racially oppressive colonial logics and deficit thinking that attack Black lives and families and lead to poor educational outcomes.

We cannot deny the ways in which anti-African and anti-Black racism are infused within the North American schooling system. Nonetheless, the relentless and intergenerational pursuit of a fair and equitable education for Black learners, a decolonized system of schooling, offers up a chance to endeavour toward reformist and radical teaching and learning. It is with this objective that we have to aspire toward an emancipatory educational experience that will allow Black students to unapologetically reconcile with their identities, and from there, realize their fullest potential.

DISCUSSION QUESTIONS

1. The collective aspirations toward equitable access to education for Black learners is contingent upon the dismantling of Eurocentric, white supremacist logics embedded within social institutions. How do we design and implement a system of education while circumventing the need to be legitimized and co-signed by those same institutional standards?

2. Though we are actively deconstructing colonial practices that govern the present system of education, how do we move beyond the binary notion of an Africentric system as an *alternative* to or in opposition to the current system?

3. As educators, how might we revise and extend language, content, and contexts to ensure authentic inclusion of multi-centred, Indigenous, intergenerational, and anti-colonial knowledges within and beyond schools?

4. Based on a holistic conceptualization of educational success for all, identify ways in which educational leadership can promote the relevance and practicality for decolonized instruction for Black, Indigenous, racialized, and non-racialized learners.

5. In an effort to shift the imbalance of power that perpetuates anti-Black racism and anti-Blackness, how might we assign value and establish meanings to honour an anti-racist script while working to break down colonial structures?

REFERENCES

Adjei, P. B. (2018). The (em)bodiment of blackness in a visceral anti-black racism and ableism context. *Race Ethnicity and Education*, *21*(3), 275–287. https://doi.org/10.1080/13613324.2016.1248821

Agpeyong, R. (2010). *Black focused school in Toronto: What do African-Canadian parents say?* [Unpublished doctoral dissertation]. University of Toronto.

Bernard, W. T., & Smith, H. (2018). Injustice, justice, and Africentric practice in Canada. *Canadian Social Work Review/Revue canadienne de service social*, *35*(1), 149–157. https://doi.org/10.7202/1051108ar

Boisvert, N. (2019, May 14). *"They didn't help me at all": Family files $1M lawsuit against York school board over racist bullying*. CBC News. https://www.cbc.ca/news/canada/toronto/york-school-board-lawsuit-1.5134169

Bonilla-Silva, E. (2004). From bi-racial to tri-racial: Towards a new system of racial stratification in the USA. *Ethnic and Racial Studies*, *27*(6), 931–950. https://doi.org/10.1080/0141987042000268530

Brown, R. S., & Parekh, G. (2010). *Special education structural overview and student demographics*. Toronto District School Board.

Chen, S. (2013). Schooling, interrupted: What France's last sociologist might have said about Canada's first Black-focused school. *Counterpoints*, *445*, 69–80. https://www.jstor.org/stable/42982033

Cheung, A., & Sienkiewicz, A. (2017, February 2). *Mississauga mom launches complaint after police handcuff her 6-year-old daughter*. CBC News. https://www.cbc.ca/news/canada/toronto/mississauga-mom-launches-complaint-after-police-handcuff-her-6-year-old-daughter-1.3964827

Codjoe, H. M. (2001). Fighting a "public enemy" of Black academic achievement—the persistence of racism and the schooling experiences of Black students in Canada. *Race, Ethnicity and Education*, *4*(4), 343–375. https://doi.org/10.1080/13613320120096652

Conroy, K. (2013). Black males and exclusionary schooling practices: "Common-sense" racism and the need for a critical anti-racist approach. *Counterpoints*, *445*, 169–181. http://www.jstor.org/stable/42982038

Cooper, A. (2016). Black Canada and the law: Black parents and children in the legal battle for education in Canada West: 1851–1864. In A. A. Abdi & A. Ibrahim (Eds.), *The education of African Canadian children: Critical perspectives* (pp. 19–42). McGill-Queen's University Press.

Daniel, B. M. (2017). Troubling and disrupting the "cradle to prison pipeline": The experience of Black youth in Ontario. In B. M. Daniel (Ed.), *Diversity, justice, and community* (pp. 99–121). Canadian Scholars.

DeClerq, K. (2020, July 6). *Ontario plans to stop grade 9 students from streaming into applied or academic tracks*. CTV News Toronto. https://toronto.ctvnews.ca/ontario-plans-to-stop-grade-9-students-from-streaming-into-applied-or-academic-tracks-1.5012149

Dei, G. J. S. (1996). The role of Afrocentricity in the inclusive curriculum in Canadian schools. *Canadian Journal of Education, 21*(2), 170–186.

Dei, G. J. S. (2008). Schooling as community: Race, schooling, and the education of African youth. *Journal of Black Studies, 38*(3), 346–366. https://www.jstor.org/stable/40034384

Dei, G. J. S. (2020). Teaching race, anti-Blackness and [African] Indigeneity: Personal reflections of a Black scholar. In G. J. S. Dei, A. Vasquez, & E. Odozor (Eds.), *Cartographies of Blackness and Black Indigeneities* (pp. 1–22). Myers Education Press.

Dei, G. J. S. (2021). Foreword. *Curriculum Inquiry, 51*(1), 1–14. https://doi.org/10.1080/03626784.2021.1847533

Dei, G. J. S., Karumanchery, L. L., & Karumanchery-Luik, N. (2004). *Playing the race card: Exposing white power and privilege*. Peter Lang.

Dei, G., & Kempf, A. (2013). *New perspectives on African-centered education in Canada*. Canadian Scholars.

Dei, G. S., & McDermott, M. (2019). *Centering African proverbs, Indigenous folktales, and cultural stories in curriculum: Units and lesson plans for inclusive education*. Canadian Scholars.

Dumas, M. J. (2015). Against the dark: Antiblackness in education policy and discourse. *Theory into Practice, 55*(1), 11–19. https://doi.org/10.1080/00405841.2016.1116852

Gillborn, D. (2005). Education policy as an act of white supremacy: Whiteness, critical race theory and education reform. *Journal of Education Policy, 20*(4), 485–505. https://doi.org/10.1080/02680930500132346

Gillborn, D. (2008). Coincidence or conspiracy? Whiteness, policy and the persistence of the Black/white achievement gap. *Educational Review, 60*(3), 229–248. https://doi.org/10.1080/00131910802195745

Hall, S. (1992). Race, culture, and communications: Looking backward and forward at cultural studies. *Rethinking Marxism, 5*(1), 10–18, https://doi.org/10.1080/08935699208657998

Hampton, R. (2010). Black learners in Canada. *Race & Class, 52*(1), 103–110. https://doi.org/10.1177/0306396810371770

hooks, b. (1992). Representing whiteness in the Black imagination. In L. Grossberg, C. Nelson, & P. Treichler (Eds.), *Cultural studies* (pp. 338–346). Routledge.

hooks, b. (2006). *Black looks: Race and representation*. South End Press.

Howard, P. S. S. (2014). Taking the bull by the horns: The critical perspectives and pedagogy of two Black teachers in Anglophone Montreal schools. *Race Ethnicity and Education, 17*(4), 494–517. https://doi.org/10.1080/13613324.2012.759921

Howard, P. S. S., & James, C. E. (2019). When dreams take flight: How teachers imagine and implement an environment that nurtures Blackness at an Africentric school in Toronto, Ontario. *Curriculum Inquiry, 49*(3), 313–337. https://doi.org/10.1080/03626784.2019.1614879

The Institute for Education Leadership. (2013). *The Ontario leadership framework: A school and system leader's guide to putting Ontario's leadership framework into action*. https://www.education-leadership-ontario.ca/application/files/8814/9452/4183/Ontario_Leadership_Framework_OLF.pdf

James, C. E., & Turner, T. (2017). *Towards race equity in education: The schooling of Black students in the Greater Toronto Area*. York University.

Johnson, L. (2013). Segregation or "thinking Black"? Community activism and the development of Black-focused schools in Toronto and London, 1968–2008. *Teachers College Record. 115*(11), 1–25.

King, J. E. (1992). Diaspora literacy and consciousness in the struggle against miseducation in the Black community. *The Journal of Negro Education, 61*(3), 317–340. https://doi.org/10.2307/2295251

Ladson-Billings, G. (1994). *The dreamkeepers: Successful teachers of African American children*. Jossey-Bass.

Ladson-Billings, G. (1995). Toward a theory of culturally relevant pedagogy. *American Educational Research Journal, 32*(3), 465–491. https://doi.org/10.3102/00028312032003465

Lawrence, B., & Dua, E. (2005). Decolonizing antiracism. *Social Justice, 32*(4), 120–143. https://www.jstor.org/stable/29768340

Lee, E. (1991). Taking multicultural, anti-racist education seriously: An interview with educator Enid Lee. *Rethinking Schools, 6*(1), (October-November, 1991). https://rethinkingschools.org/articles/defining-multicultural-anti-racist-education/

Maynard, R. (2017). *Policing black lives: State violence in Canada from slavery to the present*. Fernwood Publishing.

McKittrick, K. (2006). *Demonic grounds: Black women and the cartographies of struggle*. University of Minnesota Press.

Nkrumah, K. (1965). *Neo-colonialism: The last stage of imperialism*. Thomas Nelson & Sons.

Ontario Ministry of Education. (2009). *Realizing the promise of diversity: Ontario's equity and inclusive education strategy*. https://files.ontario.ca/edu-equity-inclusive-education-strategy-2009-en-2022-01-13.pdf

Ontario Ministry of Education. (2013). *Developing and implementing equity and inclusive education policies in Ontario schools*. Policy/program memorandum 119.

https://www.ontario.ca/document/education-ontario-policy-and-program-direction/policyprogram-memorandum-119

Ontario Ministry of Education. (2017). *Ontario's education equity action plan*. https://files.ontario.ca/edu-1_0/edu-Ontario-Education-Equity-Action-Plan-en-2021-08-04.pdf

Paradkar, S. (2020, March 3). Tribunal ruling on handcuffing of 6-year-old Peel girl is yet another wake-up call. But watch how it will be dismissed as a one-off. *Toronto Star*. https://www.thestar.com/opinion/star-columnists/2020/03/03/tribunal-ruling-on-handcuffing-of-6-year-old-peel-girl-is-yet-another-wake-up-call-but-watch-how-it-will-be-dismissed-as-a-one-off.html

Salole, A. T., & Abdulle, Z. (2015). Quick to punish: An examination of the school to prison pipeline for marginalized youth. *Canadian Review of Social Policy/Revue canadienne de politique sociale, 72/73*, 124–168.

Sartre, J. P. (2001). *Colonialism and neocolonialism*. Routledge.

Schroeter, S., & James, C. E. (2015). "We're here because we're Black": The schooling experiences of French-speaking African-Canadian students with refugee backgrounds. *Race Ethnicity and Education, 18*(1), 20–39. https://doi.org/10.1080/13613324.2014.885419

Sexton, J. (2011). The social life of social death: On Afro-pessimism and Black optimism. In *Tensions, 5*, 1–47.

Sexton, J. (2015). Unbearable Blackness. *Cultural Critique, 90*(1), 159–178.

Sharpe, C. (2016). *In the wake: On Blackness and being*. Duke University Press.

Stewart, P. (2004). Afrocentric approaches to working with African American families. *Families in society: The Journal of Contemporary Social Services, 85*(2), 221–228.

Stovall, D. (2006). Forging community in race and class: Critical race theory and the quest for social justice in education. *Race Ethnicity and Education, 9*(3), 243–259. https://doi.org/10.1080/13613320600807550

Swain, A. E., & Noblit, G. W. (2011). Education in a punitive society: An introduction. *The Urban Review, 43*(4), 465–475. https://doi.org/10.1007/s11256-011-0186-x

Swartz, E. (1992). Emancipatory narratives: Rewriting the master script in the school curriculum. *The Journal of Negro Education, 61*(3), 341–355. https://doi.org/10.2307/2295252

Turner, T. (2014, October 30). *Teacher diversity gap*. Turner Consulting Group. https://www.turnerconsultinggroup.ca/blog/teacher-diversity-gap

Turner, T. (2016). *One Vision One Voice: Changing the Ontario child welfare system to better serve African Canadians. Practice Framework Part 2: Race Equity Practices*. Ontario Association of Children's Aid Societies. https://www.oacas.org/what-we-do/onevisiononevoice/

Vowel, C. (2016). Monster: The residential-school legacy. In *Indigenous writes: A guide to First Nations, Métis & Inuit issues in Canada* (pp. 171–180). HighWater Press.

Walcott, R. (2018). *Against social justice and the limits of diversity: Or Black people and freedom*. Routledge.

Wolfe, P. (2006). Settler colonialism and the elimination of the native. *Journal of Genocide Research, 8*(4), 387–409. https://doi.org/10.1080/14623520601056240

Woodson, C. G. (1933). *The mis-education of the Negro*. Africa World Press.

Zirkel, S., & Johnson, T. (2016). Mirror, mirror on the wall: A critical examination of the conceptualization of the study of Black racial identity in education. *Educational Researcher, 45*(5), 301–311. http://www.jstor.org/stable/43996934

CHAPTER 4

On Decolonial Thought and Writing Black Life

Marlon Simmons

INTRODUCTION

Over the last decade, though not limited to that moment, there has been an insurrection of calls for Canadian Black studies as a field of inquiry within educational institutions. What I believe we are experiencing, be it in the academy, in K–12 schools, or on social media, is an ongoing dialogue among different political actors, educators, activists, social workers, and stakeholders to tend to difference across multiple temporalities as embodied in Black life. I also think that ensuing from these different epistemologies in this ongoing dialogue is a particular educator who invokes a type of thinking, which, in a sublime way, forms discursive and material disjunctures to some of the colonial articulations and hegemonic representations of Black life in the context of the institutionalized text. Put another way, what I think we are experiencing with this ongoing dialogue is a pointed critique regarding current conditions of anti-Black racism, one which is neither trapped in a binary nor reducible to a polemic.

Challenges exist when writing and implementing Black Canadian studies in academe—questions of epistemological representations of Black life and Black geographies over time, place, and text. These challenges have been present since the colonization of the African people. My concern is less with understanding whether these representations are new or whether they exist and more so with understanding and mapping the changing cartographies over time, how these representations become tangible in the present, and how thinking through these varied moments of epistemological representations of Black life could offer and build sustained possibilities for decolonial thought. The question of agency and power is paramount here. To have Black life become situated through positions of power in respective societies, to be self-determining through counter-colonial readings and practices should mark the reconstruction of historical artifacts and related colonial disposability of Black life. Black people have always been and continue to be resistant to Black disposability, the displacement of Black histories, and epistemic erasures, which organize colonial codifications deployed to devalue and disenfranchise Black life.

One of the challenges of this decolonial writing project is to theoretically trace certain social formations of Black life to understand how different knowledge systems unfolding through the experiences of the African diaspora come to be endowed with intellectual currency and epistemologically installed within educational institutions. With decolonization in mind, the aim of this discussion is to bring a critical reading of Black life into decolonial sensibilities and, by extension, decolonial practices necessary for advancing equity and social justice. By way of centring Black life within the settler colonial nation-state of Canada, I broach writing as a method of social inquiry (Richardson, 2000). Such social inquiry considers tensions and negotiations regarding educational research, Black life, decolonial thought, and epistemological sense of place as circumscribed through historical and contemporaneous configurations of anti-Black racism.

BLACK LIVING, WAYS OF KNOWING, AND EDUCATIONAL RESEARCH

Black life is in a never-ending ethical relationship with history in which the endeavour of having to retrieve itself from colonial histories is constant. Living, for Black life, becomes part and parcel of recovering the self through its otherness of thought. Living involves resistance. It also involves an otherness constituted through a primacy of the aggregations of colonization. Educators have historically been confronted with the question: What is Black living? Given the context, the question has been responded to in many ways. Black living comes infused with colonial histories of grief, material loss, and intergenerational trauma. Despite these colonial encumbrances, Black living has been resolute to the commitment and responsibility of valuing the Black self and Black culture, even with the ongoing anti-Black racism that persists in assigning demeaning signifiers to Black life.

One of the historical questions with which decolonial thought and writing Black life are faced is making sense of what permeates and undergirds the arrays of socioeconomic determinants and miscellany of circumstances encountered within everyday Black life. This moves us into the historical terms and conditions of epistemological belonging within specific philosophical paradigms ensconced within educational institutions. Objective forms of knowledge have dominated the humanities, social science research, and educational institutions for a long time. Though one can learn from these methods, understanding the incommensurability of Black experiences includes pursuing ways of knowing in which qualitative approaches to understanding Black living can work to find pathways to better Black life. Qualitative approaches to Black life include the type of questioning and the type of thinking required to have a particular delineating capacity to make sense of ongoing colonial configurations present within Black life. We also need to be cognizant of the socialization process in which Black living achieves entry into its local and global worlds, the concomitant conceptualizing frameworks in which it exists, and how these conceptual frameworks open possibilities and simultaneously limit such possibilities. At the same time, it is only through these working conceptual frameworks that Black living is able to experience instances in which it can extend its social, political, and economic horizons.

The study of race, colonization, diaspora, and decolonial thought has acquired and maintained its location within the hallways of educational research. With historical systems of colonial ways of knowing being embedded in different educational settings of Canadian society, institutional challenges involved undoing universalized ways of knowing present and past social realities. Epistemologies immanent to Black life have come to be positioned in ways that ushered vehement debates concerning what is knowledge, what counts as knowledge, and where knowledge resides. While knowledge emerging from the perspectives of Black life draws from historical accounts of social theory, many of the theorists situate their thinking in ways that epistemologically diverge and converge from them. Offering such an account allows for compound ruptures of historical and, specifically, institutionalized theoretical claims. Such ruptures are immersed in ongoing tensions.

One thread informing my knowledge of Black living is the idea of tracing the underpinning colonial conditions within the contemporaneity of Black life. In so doing, I am also interested in tracing these colonial conditions onto educational research. What does it mean to say that educational research, in particular humanities and social science research, must think of its epistemological historicity? To demand such thinking from educational research lends to an acknowledgement of its hermeneutic journey being perpetually constituted through particular colonial variants. That is, humanities and social science research are deeply entrenched within colonial histories as they become arranged, curated, and recovered within institutions of education. The study of humanities and social sciences brought a distinguishable ontological shift in educational research. I say this with an understanding of Black life through relations of colonial histories, which becomes precipitated with racial signifiers, giving rise to a system of meaning essentialized as pure and stable, constitutive of power, knowledge, and difference. These interchangeably mutable and immutable signifiers have throughout history denoted meaning for the past, present, and future of Black living.

SOLIDARITY, DECOLONIAL THOUGHT, AND WRITING BLACK LIFE AS PRAXIS

The temporal aspect bound in the experiences of Black living is vital to understanding Black life. Temporality as distinct to Black life ought not to be reduced to the idea of the passing of time. I think of it more as speaking to the specific periodization of history constitutive of Black experiences. I think that given the relational ontologies ensconced within Black life, one of the challenges faced is being cognizant of the diverging and converging routes to solidarity. These routes to solidarity demand that Black life get to some form of understanding of the self as shaped through the complex intertwined histories of colonization and Diaspora (Walcott, 2014). In contemporary public spheres, we have seen how solidarity among different communities shapes public opinion and garners attention from social media in ways that encourage the broader public institution's understanding, and by extension, educational reconstructions of the experiences of Black life.

With solidarity in mind, we can address the different social contexts and their economies, both locally and globally, to promulgate myriad forms of resistance which can form pre-emptive modes toward anti-Black practices. Solidarities are inherent to these pre-emptive modes where myriad Black communities need to join and partake. Such pre-emptive modes can create inter-human relationships and possibly serve as a shared sentiment and practice throughout the historical and current contexts of people, one necessary for life to coexist and collectively survive with the self-determination rights for different communities. To me, this kind of solidarity comes into being through interactions of history and memory, complemented by our actualities with each having constitutive modes of knowing that temporally diverge and converge through generations of struggle. How, then, might we make sense of the embedded epistemological struggle and solidarity that invariably becomes articulated through relational approaches to Black life? These epistemological modes are integral to the meaning-making process of decolonization and resistance to anti-Black racism, becoming in the process raw resources for writing Black life. Often, experiences of struggle in the present become encumbered through ahistorical narratives. These experiences bring some pressing questions and concerns, which lend to public memory giving rise to complex historical, political, and social realities. Wrapped within these realities, though, are possibilities for change, possibilities that grew from Black life wanting to know the Black self and the ways in which the Black self came to its present lived socioeconomic situation. From here, the concern can move to what possibilities the future holds for Black life, which enable the refusal of current political and economic conditions as absolute and unchangeable. This needed change ought to emerge from different communities residing in Black life, as that could inform policy makers with strategies for social programs necessary for marginalized communities.

Writing Black life entails difference—ontological difference—where writing through difference calls for recognizing acts of social responsibility. When I teach a graduate class on research methodology in a Canadian university, students often discuss social responsibility and implications for writing; students speak about cultural humility, intellectual humility, and the need to tell one's "Truth." We talk about the need to write through an ethics of humility that is steeped in a history and culture of enslavement, colonization, and disenfranchisement, and how writing through these moments contributes to a theory embodied in Black life, revealing in the process historical and contemporary conditions and their social realities. Such writing calls for a dialogue with the self with respect to understanding the specific contexts and conditions regarding the historical social realities of Black Canadians. I would even say this path to writing calls for heuristic ways of learning. What does it mean to have to write Black life through these incommensurable ways of knowing in which the temporality of colonial histories governs the myriad educational experiences of the past and present? This brings me to my next point concerning heuristic ways of learning and decolonial approaches to educational experiences. Here, I am concerned with what can be achieved by engaging in a dialogue regarding which particular social theories are given currency, how these come to reside within educational institutions, and how they frame our ways of discussing and knowing anti-Black racism. With this dialogue, I am thinking of the historical ways in which education has been conceptualized and concomitantly installed and epistemologically arranged through particular traditions of learning and research.

The pursuit of making sense of Black life has been and continues to be a long road. Over time and place, this pursuit has materialized by way of protest and narratives of resistance, making anew possibilities to go beyond the colonial constraints of Black histories (Maynard, 2017; Walcott & Abdillahi, 2019). Coloniality has created its depository of knowledge, which is presented as immutable. To extricate histories of Black life from these epistemologically secured positions residing within educational institutions demands critical interpretive strategies to retrieve and engender oral narratives embedded in the African diaspora contexts (Simmons, 2020). Though fragmentary, these histories can provide the groundwork for the task. These histories can yield conceptual building blocks to traverse time, place, and colonial signifiers of Black life to convey social entry points to much-needed economic resources. These social entry points are not necessarily commensurable or directly tangible; rather, they are experienced through language, the corporeal, tacit, innate, intuitive, and, as I have said before, heuristic ways of understanding one's social reality.

As I think through this piece, I broach writing as a form of praxis to understand the interconnected workings of how epistemological death (to the extent that fields of knowledge become positioned and inhabited by teachers and learners within educational institutions) and social death become experienced within Black life (Mbembe, 2017). I want to take into account the multiple modes involved, given the historical, cultural, linguistic, and difference residing in Black life, to construct a mode of understanding of the circumstantial and responsive currents specifically relating to social death and epistemological death, be it within educational institutions or the broader society. I often wonder how Black scholars summon the spiritual strength to survive the academy. This summoning, I think, calls for a contextualization that tends to specific periodizations of history in order to make sense of how the persistent epistemological existence of Black life becomes emplaced through the impediments of history.

So entrenched are these historical colonial discourses of Black life that the decolonial project requires rethinking and rewriting processes to understand Black life in this instance of the historical present and in the reification of the political and economic realities of Black life (Sharpe, 2016). Over time, the institutional traditions indebted to colonial histories have come under siege by way of the unparalleled and pointed calls of solidarity from fields such as educational research, including inherent Black epistemologies. Presently, a distinctively increasing push for Canadian Black studies is taking place, with direct insistence on the worthy hermeneutics of decolonial thought and the necessity for different phenomenological approaches to make full meaning of Black life. At the heart of the matter here lie sociological imaginaries with the capacity to traverse place and Black life as emerging from the African diaspora, with the emancipatory project of undoing the colonial legacies inherent within educational research. These social imaginaries conjure decolonial theories necessary to assist with rewriting the narratives of colonial history through the assemblages of the disparate experiences enveloped within Black life. I would also say these rewritten narratives of history tend to have a habitus too, which implicates human action and the meaning-making process.

Conversations concerning Black life and public education have come under discursive surveillance (Browne, 2015), with Black life positioned in ancillary ways within the history of the settler colonial nation-state. Epistemologies emerging from Black life involve forms of thinking of the world that are relational to place, people, and the incommensurability of becoming. They encompass historical engagements with Euro-Enlightenment knowledge constructs that come to situate the terms and conditions of Black life within continuous hegemonic production of anti-Black racism (Wynter, 2001; Wynter & McKittrick, 2015; Wynter & Scott, 2000). Writing through a theoretical framework of Black life entails working with social difference; it necessitates coming to write and dialogue through epistemological forms of resistance, with the pedagogic hope of transformative possibilities to undo anti-Black racism within colonial public spheres, of which educational institutions and contexts are among the most important.

These discussions of Black life confront Eurocentric forms of knowledge and create different ways of knowing Black communities, which make salient the ontologies and epistemologies distinct to Black life, which simultaneously form counterpoints to anti-Black racism. Acknowledging Black communities and places as constitutive elements of Black life undergirds the pedagogical necessity of foregrounding viable epistemological places within Canadian educational settings (Hudson & Kamugisha, 2014). Recognizing place opens pathways for rewriting Black life that can undo colonial narratives of newcomer, immigrant, and transient, which position Black life in anti-Black ways of disposability. Anti-Black racism resides in many forms: discourses of science, music, sport, food, housing, geography, employment, and healthcare. It occupies myriad intersections that propagate unbelonging for Black life as external to what it means to be human and as disengaged from partaking in civic governance within the prescripts of a self-identifying democratic nation-state. Embedded within the cartographies of anti-Black racism are plight-filled assumptions inherent to colonial settler governance that situate educational systems and job markets as being built exclusive of Black life and Black people's aspirations and needs.

If integrating epistemologies emerging from histories of Black life is one of the collective goals of educational institutions, we ought to note how epistemological exclusiveness comes to reside within certain geographies and how epistemological credence becomes produced and contingent on funding. We ought to note how different epistemologies come to enact dissimilar social and political effects regarding civic participation within particular public spheres. Here I want to point out the project of decolonization and the importance to rethink this relationship concerning how Black life partakes in the socializing of thought as governed within educational institutions. I want to consider how histories of science become embodied by way of a particular representation of what it means to be an intellectual within educational institutions, while at the same time forming exclusionary practices that position Black life as intellectually neutral.

So here we are. Could we say educational research is broaching a landmark junction? If so, in provisional terms at least, we also need to think about social science and humanities research grants, and what theories and methodological approaches constitute fundability. Once we ascertain these moments, we can begin to mark the signifying shift regarding where knowledge resides, what counts as knowledge, and how they unfold through historical and current situations. A number of Black scholars from different fields of educational research address the relationship of their scholarship to matters of historical oppression and, in doing so, make bold demands on the academy to put into place concrete policy initiatives resulting in different curricula and programs that address the many social realities, experiences, and injustices faced by Black communities (Hampton, 2020; Hudson & Kamugisha, 2014; Smith, 2019). Perhaps the most pressing moment facing Black scholars is how to design and write our narratives of the historical present that effectively speak to the global context of anti-Black racism as experienced within the different modes of institutional and public spheres and renderings. Anti-colonial scholars have done relevant work to textualize historical terms and conditions of Black life and the concomitant colonial ethics, and this work has been institutionally archived as hegemonic modes of thought and implemented through particular state-imbued practices (Abdi, 2012; Dei, 2017).

Anti-colonial scholars have also reframed historical and contemporary narratives regarding Black and Indigenous people on Turtle Island to better understand what it means to be human, as governed through the terms and conditions of social death, belonging, and expropriation of land. Anti-colonial scholars have written about the historical and political practices of Black life and the myriad social imaginaries necessitating these embodied practices as they come to be enacted through the intimacies of arrivants, settler coloniality, and Indigeneity. Today anti-colonial scholars have given us a world in which higher education has been gripped with recursive arrangements of intellectual practices, which, I think, serve the purpose of reinterpreting our future. Such reinterpreting should also provide us ways to account for how we can reconstruct new possibilities for harmonious forms of living and to relate to one another in ways that respect our ontological differences. From webinars to national and international conferences and community workshops, intimate dialogues have been undertaken around concerns of citizenship; Blackness and belonging; race and queer futurities; Black life; land and Indigeneity; surveillance; policing and Blackness; Black lives in academia; memory; Black Indigeneity and anti-colonial ways of knowing; activism; resistance and reconciliation; and Black masculinity, gender, and intersectionality.

These practices call for a purposeful education that goes beyond the singular goal of obtaining employment within a globalized world. More often in our contemporary times, education, as situated in the university, is positioned in ways to secure interests of the capitalist market and is less interested with colonial forays and questions of morals, ethics, and what it means to belong in a settler nation-state. In particular, universities in Canada have historically been conduits to nurture and condition streams of culture that speak to typifications of a state-imbued nationalism. The problem here lies with the political, economic, and social experiences of Black life, which tend to be expunged from canonized narratives of belonging and contributing to historical and contemporaneous enactments of Canadian history (Brand, 2001).

CONCLUDING REMARKS

In a time when we are surrounded by Black radical thinking, which emerged through resistance to colonization and social, economic, and political struggles, decolonial thought gives us a range of philosophical and cultural threads that converge in various modes of expression that push back on the dominant narratives of conventional education. Decolonial thought necessitates the assemblage of knowledge that is well embedded within the experiences of Black life, as these experiences emerged through histories of resistance, racial oppression, and epistemological injustice as undertaken through colonial modernity (Césaire, 1972; Fanon, 1963; Memmi, 2006; Rodney, 1982; wa Thiong'o, 1986). Decolonial thought allows for epistemological representations that implore ontologies of difference, revealing modes of otherness that have been excluded by way of colonial regimes of knowing and belonging within global societies. Such education provides us with different ways of knowing inspired by struggles nestled within the experiences of Black life, ways of knowing that I position as a distinct field of thought comprised of myriad epistemic sites of shared histories and collective embodiments of enslavement and disenfranchisement.

Given the historical role Canadian universities have played in the ongoing epistemological and social formations of belonging, the question remains: To what extent will writing Black life in the context of Black Canadian studies be supported as an intellectual/academic field? Many Black students are seeking a dialogue regarding race, racialization processes, and Black life, in particular anti-Black racism and the constitutive relations of capitalism and racism. Underpinning these conversations is a search for the self and how Black communities have been colonially positioned in society and what the emerging material outcomes are from such a positioning. To be clear, Canadian universities need to be more serious about addressing coloniality, to move beyond equity and diversity statements of valuing multiculturalism and anti-racism with the aim of including Black life, Indigenous ways of knowing, and histories of racialized communities (Smith, 2019). The precariousness of Black life remains constantly in question and surreptitiously marked within the nation-state through certain forms of surveillance. Black Canadian studies allow for an intellectual field where decolonial ideas of what it means to be human are constantly being reconfigured through different social realities within Black life. Writing Black life provokes thinking about the varied ways to understand these textured diasporic modes of Black sociality. In a sense, writing Black life provides places to trouble historical racial sensibilities of the nation-state to offer ethical questions concerning community and belonging as constituted through difference. Writing a future for Black life involves asking the questions: What types of belonging are made possible, and through which political philosophies are these futures of belonging being materially constructed?

DISCUSSION QUESTIONS

1. What does it mean to say educational research, in particular humanities and social science research, must rethink of its epistemological historicity?

2. How do educators make meaning concerning "What is Black living?" in the contemporary context of the classroom?

3. What are the challenges of writing Black life and decolonial thought whereby colonial histories govern the myriad educational experiences of the past and present?

REFERENCES

Abdi, A. A. (2012). Clash of dominant discourses and African philosophies and epistemologies of education: Anti-colonial analyses. In A. A. Abdi (Ed.), *Decolonizing philosophies of education* (pp. 131–145). Sense Publishers.

Brand, D. (2001). *A map to the door of no return: Notes to belonging*. Vintage Canada.

Browne, S. (2015). *Dark matters: On the surveillance of blackness*. Duke University Press.

Césaire, A. (1972). *Discourse on colonialism*. Monthly Review Press.

Dei, G. J. S. (2017). *Reframing blackness and black solidarities through anti-colonial and decolonial prisms*. Springer.

Fanon, F. (1963). *The wretched of the earth*. Grove Press.

Hampton, R. (2020). *Black racialization and resistance at an elite university*. University of Toronto Press.

Hudson, P. J., & Kamugisha, A. (2014). On Black Canadian thought. *The CLR James Journal, 20*(1/2), 3–20.

Maynard, R. (2017). *Policing black lives: State violence in Canada from slavery to present*. Fernwood Publishing.

Mbembe, A. (2017). *Critique of Black reason*. Duke University Press.

Memmi, A. (2006). *Decolonization and the decolonized*. University of Minnesota Press.

Richardson, L. (2000). Writing: A method of inquiry. In N. K. Denzin & Y. S. Lincoln (Eds.), *Handbook of qualitative research* (pp. 923–948). Sage Publishing.

Rodney, W. (1982). *How Europe underdeveloped Africa*. Howard University Press.

Sharpe, C. (2016). *In the wake: On blackness and being*. Duke University Press.

Simmons, M. (2020). Locating Black life within colonial modernity: Decolonial notes. In S. R. Steinberg & B. Down (Eds.), *The SAGE handbook of critical pedagogies* (pp. 205–217). Sage Publishing.

Smith, M. (2019). *The diversity gap in U15 research intensive universities' leadership after 33 years of equity initiatives (June 2019)*. Academic Women's Association, University of Alberta.

wa Thiong'o, N. (1986). *Decolonising the mind: The politics of language in African literature*. Heinemann.

Walcott, R. (2014). The problem of the human: Black ontologies and the "coloniality of our being." In S. Broeck & C. Junker (Eds.), *Postcoloniality–decoloniality–black critique: Joints and fissures* (pp. 93–105). Campus Verlag.

Walcott, R., & Abdillahi, I. (2019). *Blacklife: Post-BLM and the struggle for freedom*. ARP Books.

Wynter, S. (2001). Towards the sociogenic principle: Fanon, identity, the puzzle of conscious experience, and what it is like to be "Black." In M. F. Durán-Cogan & A. Gómez-Moriana (Eds.), *National identities and socio-political changes in Latin America* (pp. 30–66). Routledge.

Wynter, S., & McKittrick, K. (2015). Unparalleled catastrophe for our species?: Or, to give humanness a different future: Conversations. In K. McKittrick (Ed.), *Sylvia Wynter: On being human as praxis* (pp. 9–89). Duke University Press.

Wynter, S., & Scott, D. (2000). The re-enchantment of humanism: An interview with Sylvia Wynter. *Small Axe*, *8*(September), 119–207.

CHAPTER 5

A Duoethnographic Perspective on Supporting Muslim Children, Youth, and Their Families in Canadian Schools

Antoinette Gagné and Dania Wattar

INTRODUCTION AND CONTEXT

In this duoethnography, intended here as a collaborative research methodology and analysis, we describe and reflect on our experiences working with Muslim students and families in different contexts. We explore our contrasting and sometimes overlapping experiences as parents, teachers, teacher educators, and researchers supporting Muslim families, and we explore promising pathways leading to positive school experiences for Muslim children and youth, and the preparation of teachers to work with diverse students in elementary and secondary schools. We also discuss the danger of the single story as it relates to Muslims and how we can prepare teachers to work with Muslim students. Recognitive justice, "a process model of social justice that includes a positive regard for social differences and the centrality of socially democratic processes" (Mills & Gale, 2001, p. 1), and intersectionality theory (Crenshaw, 1989; Hankivsky, 2014) are central in our critical reflection.

The first recorded Muslims in Canada date back to 1863 (Waugh, 2018). The number of Muslim Canadians has grown significantly since then. In 2011, the National Household Survey counted 1,053,945 Muslims in Canada, or 3.2 percent of the population. This made Islam the second-largest religion, after Christianity. According to the same survey, 7.7 percent of the population in the Greater Toronto Area was Muslim (Statistics Canada, n.d.).

In many cases, the terms *Muslim* and *Arab* are used interchangeably, even though the majority of Muslims worldwide are non-Arabs. For example, there is a high population of Muslims in Indonesia and Turkey, where Arabic is not spoken. Egypt has the largest Muslim and Arabic-speaking population in the world (Sensoy, 2009). In addition to the linguistic and ethnic diversity of Muslims in Canada and worldwide, it is important to note that Muslims belong to different sects and that not all Muslims are equally committed to the faith. They differ in how they observe and practise their faith (Hamdon, 2010).

OUR THEORETICAL FRAMEWORK: RECOGNITIVE JUSTICE AND INTERSECTIONALITY

We draw on the concept of recognitive justice as informed by the work of Nancy Fraser (1995) and Gale and Densmore (2000). Recognitive justice allows us to rethink concepts related to fairness and justice with an emphasis on recognition, positive self-identity, self-development, and self-determination. We use the frame to examine the degree to which Muslim students, their values, and their heritage are recognized in school contexts. Furthermore, we consider practices within schools as part of the overall social context and work toward more just equitable practices within schools. A framework based on recognitive justice invites different members of the community to create new meanings and engage in democratic practices in schools.

Using intersectionality (Crenshaw, 1989; Hankivsky, 2014) as another lens, we have gained a new perspective on our experiences, research, and advocacy work for and with Muslim children and youth and their families. In broad terms, intersectionality can serve as an analytical perspective to understand and critique interconnecting contexts of exclusion, oppression, and power. This framework has helped us to understand religion, culture, socioeconomic status, language(s), and immigration status as just some aspects of the complex and multiple identities of Muslims in Canada. Intersectionality also highlights how problematic it is to reduce any person's identity to a few characteristics often ascribed by "others" to define them.

Figure 5.1 helps us to see how each person's unique circumstances are affected by aspects of their identity. In addition, it shows how various types of discrimination can affect individuals, as well as the way that larger forces and structures work together to reinforce each person's experiences of oppression and/or privilege.

OUR METHODOLOGY—DUOETHNOGRAPHY

Duoethnography has grown from the research traditions of storytelling and Pinar's (1975) notion of *currere*. Duoethnography includes critical conversations where the voices of two people who have experienced similar phenomena can

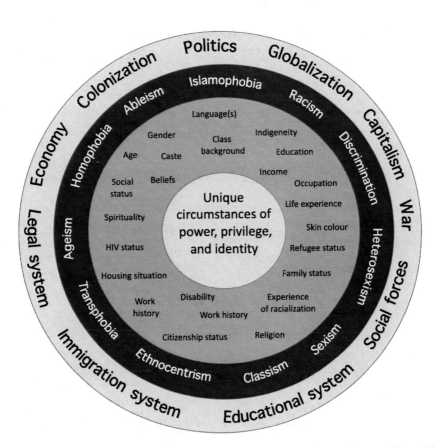

Figure 5.1: Intersectionality graphic adapted from the Intersectionality Wheel in *Everyone Belongs*

Source: Adapted from Simpson, 2009, p. 5.

begin to recognize the influence of their own curriculum of life or personal history. Two researchers work together to critique and question their understanding of social issues and then engage in cycles of interpretation to arrive at new insights (Norris & Sawyer, 2017). The authors are both the researchers and the researched, storytelling is a form of data collection, and discussion is a type of analysis integral to the writing process. It is helpful to share aspects of our life history to help our readers engage in our conversations.

Our duoethnography was shaped by four years of collaborative work that includes more than one hundred hours of conversations via Skype or Zoom. We used Google Drive to store our videotaped conversations and to organize the background readings for this article. We created a folder with our drafts and wrote using different colours to highlight our contributions to each draft. By using a Google Doc draft, we were able to asynchronously access our growing conversations and respond to each other.

Table 5.1: Antoinette and Dania—Background Information

	Antoinette	Dania
Country of birth	Canada	Syria
Languages	English, French, and Spanish	English and Arabic
Countries where we have lived or spent extended periods	Canada Pakistan Chile	Syria Canada United Arab Emirates
Education	• Concurrent BEd, McGill University, Canada • MEd in second language education, McGill University, Canada • PhD in curriculum, University of Toronto, Canada	• BSc, mathematics, Saint Mary's University, Canada • Montessori diploma, North American Montessori Center, Canada • MEd, curriculum studies, Mount Saint Vincent University, Canada • MT, University of Toronto, Canada • PhD, educational policy studies, University of Alberta, Canada
Current position	• Professor and associate chair, student experience, University of Toronto, Canada	• Sessional lecturer, OISE, University of Toronto, Canada • Elementary teacher • Academic consultant
Past positions in education	• K–12 ESL teacher, Montreal and Sherbrooke, Canada • ESL adult educator, Montreal and Toronto, Canada • Teacher educator in four different universities and a number of different programs, McGill University (Montreal, Canada), University of Quebec (Canada), York University (Toronto, Canada), Aga Khan University (Karachi, Pakistan)	• Educational policy specialist, Abu Dhabi Education Council, United Arab Emirates • Instructor, Department of Educational Policy Studies, University of Alberta, Canada • Different teaching and volunteering experiences across Canada as a teacher, and parent council member / vice chair

Table 5.1: Antoinette and Dania—Background Information (*continued*)

	Antoinette	Dania
	• Director of Concurrent Teacher Education Program, University of Toronto, Canada • Associate chair, student experience, Department of Curriculum, Teaching and Learning, OISE (Toronto, Canada)	
Teaching experience	40+ years	14+ years
Current research	The authors have worked together since 2017 on various interrelated research projects to support the integration of students from refugee and immigrant backgrounds in collaboration with community agencies and schools. Some of the "products" of our research can be found at • https://sites.google.com/view/educationofrefugees • https://sites.google.com/view/memapping • https://sites.google.com/view/multilingualmath • https://sites.google.com/view/teachaboutdomesticviolence	
Parenthood	Mother of two daughters and a son aged 25 to 31 years old	Mother of three boys aged 13 to 20 years old

Source: Created by Antoinette Gagné and Dania Wattar.

OUR CONVERSATIONS

To illustrate both our process and our learnings, we offer three dialogues. The first is related to how, as educators, we can counter the danger of the single story as it relates to Muslims. The second explores how we can create inclusive environments for Muslim children and youth attending diverse schools across Canada, with a particular focus on accommodating their religious beliefs and practices. The final conversation explores the recruitment of more diverse teacher candidates and how we can prepare teachers to work with Muslim students.

Conversation 1—Countering the "Single" Story

Antoinette: After reading and discussing how best to support Muslim families and their children, I think that, as educators, we need to explore as many ways as possible to counter the "single story." In 2009, Chimamanda Ngozi Adichie, a Nigerian writer, gave a now-famous TED talk called "The Danger of a Single

Story." Adichie explains what can happen when groups of people, countries, and situations—for example, Muslims—are reduced to a single narrative. The single story leads to stereotypes and critical misunderstandings between people.

As a certified teacher, activist, and mother of three, can you share some of your experiences countering the single story?

Dania: I can think of several instances when I have been able to make connections between my heritage, culture, and religion and what is happening in schools and classrooms. As a Muslim parent and teacher in the post 9/11 era, I have been involved with various initiatives to counter the single story by acknowledging and making space for Muslim students—their heritage, traditions, and practices.

I struggled as a Muslim living in Canada after 9/11 and wanted to make sure that the dehumanizing of Muslims did not continue. I thought the best place to start was in my children's elementary school in Edmonton, Alberta, where I was welcomed by my children's teachers, who viewed my offer to share as a great learning opportunity for them and their students. I brought in and read from picture books that supported the curriculum and illustrated the experiences and traditions of Muslim children, including *Nabeel's New Pants for Eid* (Gilani-Williams, 2010), *The Librarian of Basra* (Winter, 2004), and *1001 Inventions and Awesome Facts from Muslim Civilization* (National Geographic Kids, 2012). Then I continued to share my experiences, resources, and books more broadly with different schools and libraries. These were my first steps in countering the single story and providing humanizing counternarratives of the lives of Muslim children and traditions. Stonebanks (2008) speaks of the transformative potential of narratives to dismantle the dehumanizing stories that intensified post-9/11.

Antoinette: I am pleased to say that there are now many more books in English that feature Muslim characters or have a focus on Islam than in the early 2000s. In fact, I did a search and easily found a number of curated sites where elementary and secondary school teachers can find print and multimedia resources to counter the single story. These included blog posts listing favourite books about Muslims and Islam (Faruqi, 2017; Stepaniuk, 2017).

I also found a number of award-winning films featuring the stories of Muslims in Canada that include detailed guides for teachers. These include (1) *14 & Muslim*, which considers how ideas of diversity play out in the Canadian classroom (Ali & Muir, n.d.); (2) *I Am Rohingya*, which chronicles the making of the play *I Am Rohingya* by a group of Rohingya refugee youth from Kitchener-Waterloo, Ontario, who wanted to find a way to tell the story of their people (Zain, n.d.); (3) *Salaam B'y*, the story of Aatif, the son of Pakistani immigrants who grew up in Newfoundland (Baskanderi, 2018); and (4) *Neglected Voices* (Tessellate Institute, 2016), video stories about Canadian Muslim youth identity.

There are also documentaries with guides for teachers, such as *Islamophobia Is* (Kanji & Kanji, 2020).

Dania: Things have certainly improved in the last decade. However, much is still needed to ensure that Muslim students are respected, valued, and understood. As some teachers have preconceived understandings of Muslim families and their beliefs, it can take a lot of effort to counter those stereotypes and introduce more nuanced understandings of different issues.

For example, a few years ago my son came home requesting that I speak to his health education teacher, as he was uncomfortable with how the teacher presented the unit on human sexuality. After a discussion with my son, I had the sense that the teacher had tried to make the topic relevant to the teens based on his understanding of the experiences of teenagers in Canada. However, it seemed that my son's teacher did not acknowledge or recognize the cultural and religious diversity of his students and that the issues, cases, and stories shared did not resonate with a number of the students. My son insisted on the need for me to talk to the teacher, as my son was becoming increasingly uncomfortable with the conversations in class, so I called the teacher to discuss the issue. During the first few minutes of our conversation, the teacher was defensive and disregarded my son's concerns while assuming that I was opposed to him teaching this unit. It took a great deal of discussion and effort on my part to explain that I was not calling to complain about the topic but requesting that he consider a more inclusive approach to the cases presented and follow-up discussions.

As a teacher myself, I offered to support my child's learning. I suggested some ideas that would allow my son to learn the curriculum expectations in a culturally sensitive manner. By the end of the conversation, the teacher admitted that he was surprised by my request because of his assumption that I had called to say that he should not be teaching this content. He realized that I was trying to find a solution and not to create a problem. Hearing the different suggestions that I offered, the teacher finally acknowledged the issue and was willing to accommodate my request while saying, "I have never done this before, but I will give this a try." My son was happy about the outcome of my conversation with his teacher. In the end, the teacher shared the required content so that my son and I could work through it together in a more culturally sensitive manner, which included a lot of great discussions related to the curriculum. My son learned what was required and then wrote the unit test with his peers.

I don't think this would have happened had I not known how to approach and speak to the teacher and acknowledge his concerns while at the same time explaining my son's perspective. As an educator familiar with the curriculum and accustomed to working across cultures, I was able to navigate the situation and negotiate a solution that worked for everyone. I don't think many parents would have been able to advocate on their children's behalf the way I did.

Antoinette: I agree with you, Dania, that most parents would find it difficult to contact a teacher and negotiate an adequate solution, especially parents of immigrant or refugee backgrounds. Although I am happy that you were able to negotiate a solution that suited your son and the teacher, I worry that this "one-off" solution may have allowed the teacher to continue to teach using a "one-size-fits-all" approach rather than grappling with how to operationalize a more inclusive health education curriculum. It would indeed be ideal if all schools had structures in place to foster parental and community involvement to explore sensitive topics and put in place appropriate accommodations.

Dania: In discussing recognitive justice and conditions of self-determination, Gale and Densmore (2000) describe the issues that parents of marginalized students often face as they try to advocate on their children's behalf. In order to work toward recognitive justice, students' and parents' voices need to be heard and understood. As such, school administrators and teachers should invite parents and students to take part in a dialogue where each group has the opportunity to share their needs and/or experiences and be heard. These conversations are important to ensure that teachers learn and understand the perspectives of Muslims and work toward respecting these voices rather than disregarding them because of assumptions that often correlate to the single story and teachers' own biases and perceptions of Muslim families.

Antoinette: I continually return to intersectionality theory (Crenshaw, 1989; Hankivsky, 2014) as it helps me to remember the diverse experiences and varied needs of Muslim children, youth, and families when it comes to education. The type of schools that Muslim students attend will also impact the nature of their experiences. In the late 1990s, my University of Toronto colleague Linda Cameron and I spent two years in five schools in a large school district in the Greater Toronto Area (GTA) that welcomed many newcomers. Over these two years, we spent four full days with 10 newcomer students in each school; the schools were located in different neighbourhoods. There were a few Muslim students among the 50 students we spent time with. One of my strongest memories is of two Muslim teens who spent an entire day in silence, as their teachers did not call on them or provide any opportunities for small-group work. Although very visible, these girls became invisible to the teacher because they were hard-working and well-behaved. Although we saw commonalities among the experiences of the 50 students as they learned English and the culture of their school, we discovered how the characteristics of the neighbourhood also impacted the nature of their experiences.

As our focus was on newcomers and their "settlement" experiences in schools, we described the various communities surrounding the schools on a continuum from "unsettled" to "settling" to "settled." Many newcomer families, especially those with little income, tended to live in "unsettled" communities when they first arrived and move to "settling" communities once they were somewhat oriented to life in the GTA and could generate a higher family income. We learned that newcomer families who were financially secure usually opted to move to "settled" communities with a less transient population. Table 5.2 shows how various characteristics of newcomer families determine the type of neighbourhood where they are likely to live.

Table 5.2: The "Unsettled" to "Settled" Neighbourhood and School Continuum

Characteristics of Neighbourhood and Newcomer Families	Unsettled Neighbourhoods and Schools	Settling Neighbourhoods and Schools	Settled Neighbourhoods and Schools
The transience of the population	High	Medium	Low
Family income	Low	Medium	High
Knowledge of English upon arrival	Varied	Varied	Likely more knowledge of English upon arrival
Status in Canada	Refugee claimant Refugees Family class Immigrants	Family class immigrants	Economic class immigrants Highly skilled professionals

Source: Created by Antoinette Gagné and Dania Wattar.

Another useful metaphor that emerged from this same study allowed us to capture the diversity of the student population across schools by referencing different types of ribbons, as shown in table 5.3.

Although the unsettled-to-settled school continuum and the ribbon metaphor are likely to help us understand the likely diverse experiences of Muslim children and youth across schools in different neighbourhoods with varied student populations, the continuum and metaphor do not allow us to gauge the variation in religious beliefs of the students and what their needs for accommodation might be. So, Dania, you can begin to see just how complex it is for school administrators and teachers to operationalize inclusive practices and how the pathway to the creation of a learning community where all students feel included may be quite different from school to school.

Table 5.3: The Ribbon Metaphor Provides a Reflection of the School Population

Type of Ribbon	Nature of the Student Population	Examples
Ribbon with a different shade on each side	A fairly equal number of students from two distinct groups	45% Black and 55% white students or 40% white and 60% East Asian students
Ribbon with a rainbow pattern on both sides	An extremely diverse group of students with no one dominant group	15% Black, 15% Middle Eastern or Central Asian, 15% South Asian, 20% white, 15% Southeast Asian, 20% Hispanic students
Ribbon with polka dots	A white-dominant school with a relatively small number of students from one or more different backgrounds	90% white with 2% Black, 5% Southeast Asian, and 3% East Asian

Source: Created by Antoinette Gagné and Dania Wattar.

Dania: Yes, I have had some direct experiences with this in my teaching. In my first week in a "polka dot ribbon" school in a "settled" neighbourhood, I was asked a number of questions about my hijab. Over time, I engaged in dialogue with teachers and shared my experiences as a Muslim educator in Canada, which led some members of the school community to move from perceiving me as "different" to seeing what we have in common. In my social studies class, when teaching about communities across Canada, I used the example of Fort Edmonton Park to teach about how different communities have lived and interacted in Edmonton throughout history. Through a virtual tour, students learned about the Al Rashid Mosque, the first mosque established by Muslims in Canada and one of the earliest in North America (Waugh, 2018). This was an opportunity for students to learn about Muslims, their practices, and their history in Canada.

I have also had the opportunity to teach at a school with a very large population of Muslim students—a "rainbow ribbon" school in an "unsettled" neighbourhood. I was amazed by the teachers' knowledge and understanding of Muslim students and their religious practices. One incident resonated with me: as teachers were trying to find a date for a field trip, one teacher looked at the calendar and asked about Ramadan. Due to the physical demands of a field trip, the teacher wanted to make sure that the field trip would not take place during Ramadan. She wanted Muslim students who fast to be able to participate fully in the trip. This teacher exemplified what it means to accommodate students in school activities.

Conversation 2—Creating an Inclusive Learning Environment for Muslim Children and Youth

Dania: Communicating with parents is crucial to achieve social justice and provide an inclusive learning environment. The laws and policies in Canada and Ontario support inclusion and accommodations. This includes Sections 2 and 15 of the Canadian Charter of Rights and Freedoms (1982), the *Ontario Human Rights Commission Policy on Preventing Discrimination Based on Creed* (2015), and *Policy/Program Memorandum No. 119* regarding implementing inclusive policies in schools (Ontario Ministry of Education, 2013).

Despite these laws, we often see a gap between policy and practice in schools (Mistry, 2018). The implementation of these policies in schools depends on the professional judgments of teachers and principals. However, sometimes tensions arise because parents and school administrators differ in their understanding of religious accommodations. Mistry proposes that principals start by examining their biases and understandings of different religions, then learn more about the social-cultural context of the school community by keeping open lines of communication with students, families, and religious leaders (Mistry, 2018).

Antoinette: In two recent studies (Dunlop, 2017; Miled, 2020), the role of the principal in accommodating religion in Canadian schools was explored. In both studies, the principal is seen as key in setting the tone for the school in terms of the creation of an inclusive environment. The multiple roles of the principal include embracing the policies and taking the lead in facilitating their implementation through communication with religious leaders and families to learn about the needs of their Muslim students and how best to support these students. In Dunlop's study (2017), we learn about the uneven implementation of policies and how this impacts students and their families. Dunlop (2017) also described how the principals in her study managed conflict and "undue hardship" in the accommodation of faith and religion. Here is part of her summary, which shows how open lines of communication between the school and members of the community can lead to conflict resolution:

> It is challenging for principals to reconcile and to balance Ministry and board policies of equity and inclusivity with religious requests that may be violations of the *Code* and the *Charter*. These conflicting rights "open up a ... can of worms" for the principal, as personal and professional experience, board policies and procedures, and sometimes even the law, do not provide "a set answer" for the path to conflict resolution.
>
> To try to counteract religion-based arguments against and conflict about same-sex marriages, principals report they try face-to-face dialogue with parents to promote a common ground—the concept of family in all its forms, for instance—as a rallying point of understanding.... Principals hold the opinion there is always room for compromise and "always somewhere in the middle" in order to reach a mutual understanding. (Dunlop, 2017, pp. 155–156)

Dania: As a teacher and a parent, I know how difficult it can be for schools to develop inclusive practices related to aspects of religion such as prayer, fasting, modesty, or instruction in the arts and physical education. In fact, I have found that several authors and researchers who speak about the importance of partnering with parents to support their children (Gagné, 2007) underline the importance of inviting newcomer parents to share their cultural capital and support students at schools (Ali, 2012; Guo, 2012) and engaging parents in dialogue to achieve inclusion (Mistry, 2018) and social justice (Gale & Densmore, 2000). Moreover, Stonebanks (2008) highlights the positive influence of infusing aspects of every student's heritage in classrooms and schools.

When I was a newcomer myself, I advocated for my children from preschool until the end of high school. In elementary schools, I initiated conversations with teachers, school administrators, and school council members to consider the diversity of students in the classrooms. I often visited my children's classrooms and conducted workshops on different celebrations. I read stories, led art activities, and shared artifacts from different celebrations. Students and teachers often appreciated these workshops and used them as an opportunity to learn and ask deeper questions. When I joined the school council in one of my children's "settled" schools, I advocated for the inclusion of diverse voices in the school. I tried to include the traditions and voices of Muslim families as well as other families in the school community. During my time as a school council member, and later as the vice-chair, the school surveyed families and invited them to get involved in the school and share their experiences. This resulted in the creation of a calendar that acknowledged the different celebrations of families at the school and a week-long celebration of the arts to allow students to experience different traditions and create artifacts. I presented on Islamic arts and architecture, shared examples of different Islamic arts, and invited students to participate in activities that connected art with mathematics.

Antoinette: It is exciting to hear about the many ways that you have been active in your children's schools. In fact, in 2006, I conducted focus groups with immigrant families and the teachers of their children and learned from both groups what a huge gap existed between them (Gagné, 2007). The project also explored how this gap could be mitigated with the help of various community groups working together with school administrators to raise awareness and develop bridging strategies so that parents and teachers could communicate about how best to support the children and youth.

Dania: Another project that we both worked on focused on supporting recently arrived families of refugee background. We invited children and youth of refugee background to take part in "Me Mapping" workshops, in which they had the opportunity to develop their proficiency in English while talking about their experiences, hopes, and aspirations (Gagné et al., 2018). My knowledge of Arabic and Syrian culture helped me to establish rapport with these children and their parents and help them feel comfortable enough to share their stories, challenges, aspirations, and hopes for a better future.

Antoinette: As the impact of these workshops had been so positive, we created a Me Mapping guide for teachers with detailed descriptions of identity-focused activities to help build the self-worth of newcomer children and youth (see figure 5.2).

Dania: One of the most memorable moments was the end-of-program celebration because of the positive impact it had on students and their families. Many parents expressed how respected and valued they felt for the first time since coming to Canada. These families appreciated being "seen" and celebrated at a time when they felt very vulnerable.

Antoinette: As we spent more time with refugee families, we learned about their perspectives, concerns, and questions on different aspects of their children's education.

Dania: In fact, the organization we partnered with invited us to work with parents and talk about different issues that mattered to them as we had become trusted members of the community. We conducted workshops with parents on different issues related to curriculum and schooling in Canada (see figure 5.4). These workshops allowed us to share resources with parents, answer their questions, and learn from their experiences.

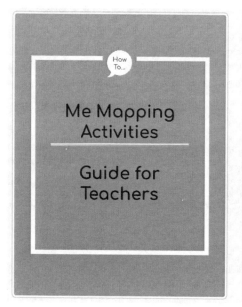
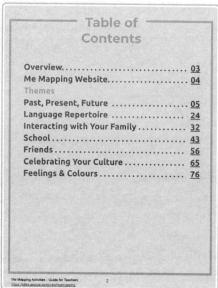
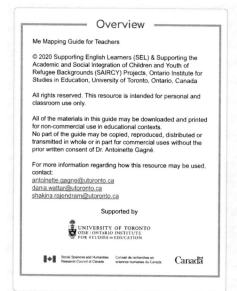

Figure 5.2a: Me Mapping Guide Contents and Overview

Source: https://sites.google.com/view/memapping/guides-for-teachers

CHAPTER 5   A Duoethnographic Perspective on Supporting Muslim Children, Youth, and Families

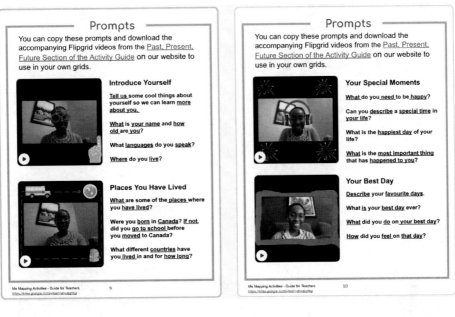
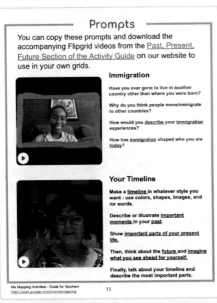
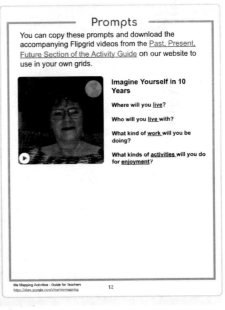

Figure 5.2b: Me Mapping Guide Prompts

Source: https://sites.google.com/view/memapping/guides-for-teachers

Figure 5.3: Me Mapping Program Celebration with Certificates of Completion

Source: Photo credits to Antoinette Gagné and Dania Wattar.

Figure 5.4: Presentation Topics for Newcomer Parents

Source: Created by Antoinette Gagné and Dania Wattar.

CHAPTER 5   A Duoethnographic Perspective on Supporting Muslim Children, Youth, and Families   77

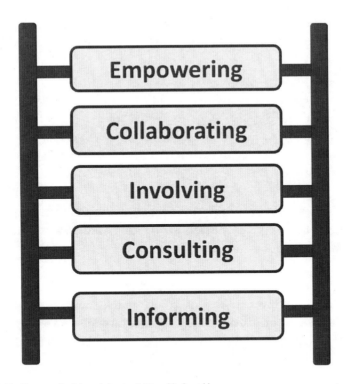

Figure 5.5: Parental Ladder of Participation

Source: Adapted from School-Home Support Services, n.d.

As an educator and teacher educator, I often think of the "ladder of participation" (School-Home Support Services, n.d.), which underlines the importance of informing parents, collaborating with them, and working toward emancipation. This applies to all parents, including Muslim parents, with their diverse backgrounds and range of experiences.

Conversation 3—Teacher Education

Antoinette: As teachers are so central to the mission of ensuring that our schools are truly inclusive, over a number of years, I have been involved with several initiatives that focus on attracting a more diverse group into teacher education programs at the University of Toronto. These initiatives have culminated in very diverse cohorts of students in our teacher education programs. However, there continue to be some groups that are underrepresented. As such, we must continue to work to attract students from all backgrounds so that the teaching force better matches the diversity that exists among students in elementary and secondary schools. For example, it is important to prepare more teachers of Muslim background so that Muslim children and youth have the opportunity to see Muslim teachers working alongside other diverse teachers in their schools. Perhaps a club for students interested in a teaching career could be started in a school with a high number of Muslim students.

Dania: This an interesting idea, Antoinette. In fact, I have been thinking about developing a credit course for minority students interested in teaching. I am quite passionate about this because, as an occasional teacher who continues to supply in schools in the GTA, I often notice students' excitement, smiles, and explicit comments when they see me in their school. Some students ask me questions to confirm my identity and make connections with me. More recently, students in a virtual classroom got excited when they heard me accommodate a language learner and talk to him in Arabic to help him understand the book that others were reading. During the discussion period afterward, several students shared information about their own languages and traditions.

Antoinette: As teacher educators are the teachers of future educators, it is equally important to ensure diversity in this group, as they are tasked with preparing teachers who can be inclusive in their practice. As the knowledge of self is an important foundation for becoming an inclusive teacher, our teacher education program includes opportunities for teacher candidates to take part in various identity-focused activities.

Dania: As a teacher educator in the Master of Teaching program, I have become aware of the importance of creating a safe learning environment where the teacher candidates and I can open up to each other by creating multimedia "Me Maps" modelled on those created by multilingual learners on the Me Mapping website. In my courses, we counter the single story by viewing the "Me Maps" of diverse learners and then sharing our own.

CONCLUSION

Although various factors may affect the experiences of Muslim children and youth in schools, the nature of the relationships they develop are central. Various aspects of the identity of Muslim students may affect their school experiences, including their status in Canada, their housing situation, the size of their immediate family, their age, their proficiency in English, the nature of their journey to Canada, their parents' socioeconomic status, the way their families live their faith, and more. In addition, other factors beyond the individual Muslim learner emerge as influential in their education: (1) the preparedness and makeup of the teachers and the school, (2) the beliefs and practices of the school principal, (3) the number of Muslim students enrolled in a particular school, (4) the nature of the neighbourhood surrounding the school, and (5) the number of supports in place at school and in the community. As such, educators need to take into consideration the intersectionality of learners' lives when they work to create more inclusive spaces for Muslim children, youth, and their families. It is also good to remember the words of Adichie (2009) at the end of her TED Talk, "When we reject the single story, when we realize that there is never a single story about any place, we regain a kind of paradise."

Revisiting the concept of reconstructive justice (Gale & Densmore, 2000; Mills & Gale, 2001), we believe that educators in Canada can create an inclusive environment for Muslim students by acknowledging their diversity and learning more about their religious, linguistic, and cultural backgrounds. Teachers can attempt to use resources with people, places, and events that might resonate with their Muslim students and ensure that their lessons are free of stereotypes and negative language about Muslims. Parents and community members can be invited to support teachers and share their knowledge and help inform schools of accommodations as necessary. We would like to conclude with the words of the *Centre ontarien de prévention des agressions* and the Ontario Teachers' Federation and (2013), which highlight the power of home–school collaboration in the creation of inclusive learning environments:

> When parents and caregivers participate in efforts to ... promote equity and inclusion, it creates a ripple effect, amplifying the outcomes.... Their endorsement of such values and attitudes, in theory and in practice, fosters coherence in students' lives by building a bridge between home and school.

DISCUSSION QUESTIONS

1. Explain the danger of the single story when it comes to the education of Muslim children and youth.

2. Think back to the secondary school you attended and describe it using the "unsettled" to "settled" continuum and the ribbon metaphor.

3. Refer to the parental ladder of participation in figure 5.5 and review this chapter to find examples of different types of participation.

REFERENCES

Adichie, C. N. (2009). *The danger of a single story*. TED Talk. https://www.ted.com/talks/chimamanda_ngozi_adichie_the_danger_of_a_single_story?utm_campaign=tedspread&utm_medium=referral&utm_source=tedcomshare

Ali, M. A. (2012). The Shadow of colonialism on relations between immigrant parents and their children's teachers. *Alberta Journal of Educational Research, 58*(2), 198–215.

Ali, N., & Muir, S. (n.d.). *14 & Muslim: Educator's guide*. Notice Pictures. https://www.14andmuslim.com/classroom-guide

Baskanderi, A. (2018). *Salaam B'y: Educator's companion guide*. https://www.salaamby.ca/educators

Centre ontarien de prévention des agressions and the Ontario Teachers' Federation. (2013). *Working with parents/caregivers*. Safe@School. https://safeatschool.ca/resources/resources-on-bullying/community-resources

Crenshaw, K. (1989). Demarginalizing the intersection of race and sex: A Black feminist critique of antidiscrimination doctrine, feminist theory and antiracist policies. *University of Chicago Legal Forum, 1*, 139–167.

Dunlop, W. A. (2017). *The legal duty to accommodate faith and religion in Ontario's public schools: An exploratory case study* [PhD dissertation]. University of Toronto.

Faruqi, S. (2017). *Top 10 books about Muslims and Islam*. https://www.huffpost.com/entry/top-10-books-about-muslim_b_13872346

Fraser, N. (1995). From redistribution to recognition? Dilemmas of justice in a "post-socialist" age. *New Left Review, 1*(212), 68–93.

Gagné, A. (Ed.). (2007). *Growing new roots: The voices of immigrant families and the teachers of their children. Resource book for educators and immigrant families*. OISE/UT.

Gagné, A., Bakbak, S., Chahrour, G., & Wattar, D. (2018). Re/discovering our teacher identities through digital storytelling with Syrian children and youth: A multi-ethnography of four diverse educators. *Master of Teaching Research Journal, 1*(1), 1–22.

Gale, T., & Densmore, K. (2000). *Just schooling: Explorations in the cultural politics of teaching*. Open University Press.

Gilani-Williams, F. (2010). *Nabeel's new pants for Eid: An Eid tale*. Two Lions.

Government of Canada. (1982). *Charter of Rights and Freedoms*. https://laws-lois.justice.gc.ca/eng/const/page-12.html

Guo, Y. (2012). Diversity in public education: Acknowledging immigrant parent knowledge. *Canadian Journal of Education / Revue canadienne de l'éducation, 35*(2), 120–140.

Hamdon, E. L. (2010). *Islamophobia and the question of Muslim identity: The politics of difference and solidarity*. Fernwood Publishing.

Hankivsky, O. (2014). *Intersectionality 101*. The Institute for Intersectionality, Research & Policy, Simon Fraser University.

Kanji, K., & Kanji, A. (2020). *Islamophobia is: Educator's guide*. https://islamophobia-is.com/wp-content/uploads/2020/10/Islamophobia-Is-Educators-Guide.pdf

Miled, N. (2020). *Beyond men to surveil and women to (un)veil: Muslim youth negotiating identity, home and belonging in a Canadian high school* [PhD Dissertation]. University of British Columbia. https://open.library.ubc.ca/collections/24/items/1.0394732

Mills, C., & Gale, T. (2001). Recognitive justice: Renewed commitment to socially just schooling. In B. A. Knight & L. Rowan (Eds.), *Researching in contemporary educational environments* (pp. 64–83). Post Pressed.

Mistry, H. (2018). Navigating creed, religion and accommodation. In D. Griffiths & J. Ryan (Eds.), *Case studies for inclusive educators & leaders* (pp. 279–289). Word & Deed Publishing.

National Geographic Kids. (2012). *1001 Inventions and awesome facts from Muslim civilization: Official children's companion to the 1001 inventions exhibition.* Author.

Norris, J., & Sawyer, R. D. (Eds.). (2017). *Theorizing curriculum studies, teacher education, and research through duoethnographic pedagogy.* Palgrave Macmillan.

Ontario Human Rights Commission. (2015). *Policy on preventing discrimination based on creed.* https://www.ohrc.on.ca/sites/default/files/Policy%20on%20preventing%20discrimination%20based%20on%20creed_accessible_0.pdf

Ontario Ministry of Education. (2013). *Policy/program memorandum 119: Developing and Implementing Equity and Inclusive Education Policies in Ontario Schools.* https://www.ontario.ca/document/education-ontario-policy-and-program-direction/policyprogram-memorandum-119

Pinar, W. (1975). Currere: Toward reconceptualization. In W. Pinar (Ed.), *Curriculum theorizing: The reconceptualists* (pp. 396–424). McCutchan Publishing Corporation.

School-Home Support Services. (n.d.). *Parental engagement: A Training toolkit.* https://www.schoolhomesupport.org.uk/wp-content/uploads/2015/11/SHS-Parental-engagement-toolkit.pdf

Sensoy, Ö. (2009). Where the heck is the "Muslim world" anyways? In O. Sensoy & C. D. Stonebanks (Eds.), *Muslim voices in school: Narratives of identity and pluralism* (pp. 3–25). Sense Publishers.

Simpson, J. (2009). *Everyone belongs: A toolkit for applying intersectionality.* Canadian Research Institute for the Advancement of Women.

Statistics Canada. (n.d.). *Immigration and ethnocultural diversity in Canada, 2011 National Household Survey.* https://www12.statcan.gc.ca/nhs-enm/2011/as-sa/99-010-x/99-010-x2011001-eng.cfm

Stepaniuk, C. (2017, February 9). *5 great Canadian Muslim books.* Book Riot. https://bookriot.com/five-great-canadian-muslim-books/

Stonebanks, C. D. (2008). An Islamic perspective on knowledge, knowing and methodology. In N. K. Denzin, Y. S. Lincoln, & L. Smith (Eds.), *Handbook of critical and Indigenous methodologies* (pp. 293–321). Sage Publishing.

Tessellate Institute. (2016). *Neglected voices: Stories of Canadian Muslim youth and identity—A video-based curriculum pack for grades 7 to 12.* https://tessellateinstitute.com/wp-content/uploads/2016/06/Neglected-Voices-Curriculum-Pack-June-2016-TTI.pdf

Waugh, E. H. (2018). *Al Rashid mosque: Building Canadian Muslim communities.* University of Alberta Press.

Winter, J. (2004). *The librarian of Basra: A true story from Iraq.* HMH.

Zain, Y. (n.d.). *Teachers kit: I am Rohingya.* https://478e68be-37cc-458d-a90b-0867d4360f36.filesusr.com/ugd/f5f0cd_b04be46f0c0444a4a6572b5ebec9f71f.pdf

CHAPTER 6

The Islamic Call to Prayer as Public Pedagogy in Mississauga, Canada

Sameena Eidoo

> ### *Noise By-Law Suspended—Evening Call to Prayer*
>
> The Mississauga City Council passed a resolution that the enforcement of the Noise Control By-law be suspended to allow for the broadcasting of the evening call to prayer from local mosques and other non-residential buildings regularly used for worship. This resolution is for the period of Ramadan, up to May 24, 2020, provided the "call" is broadcast only once per day in the evening for a maximum of five minutes and that it is not a call for people to physically gather in contravention of Emergency Orders and physical distancing guidelines.
>
> *City of Mississauga, 2020*

INTRODUCTION

On April 29, 2020, Mississauga City Council (Ontario) passed a resolution that the enforcement of the noise control bylaw be suspended to allow for the broadcasting of the evening call to prayer from local mosques and non-residential buildings used for worship for the Islamic holy month of Ramadan during the COVID-19 crisis. The resolution stipulated the call could not invite Muslims to physically congregate in violation of COVID-19 emergency orders. It was proposed by the Muslim Council of Peel, which works on behalf of member

Muslim organizations in the Peel Region (Brampton, Caledon, and Mississauga) to better serve the Muslim community through coordinated efforts to promote public relations and education. The resolution was recognized by some as a compassionate gesture toward Muslim residents of Mississauga preparing to observe Ramadan during an extraordinary moment, when the global pandemic converged with escalating persecution of Muslims worldwide. However, Mississauga City Council's resolution was protested by others, including a registered non-profit, Keep Religion Out of Our Public Schools Incorporated (KROOOPS) (Government of Canada, 2022b). Ottawa, Toronto, Hamilton, London, Edmonton, Calgary, and Vancouver were also among the Canadian cities that made exceptions to noise bylaws during Ramadan 2020.

Three years earlier, a public meeting of the Peel District School Board (PDSB) board of trustees at its headquarters in Mississauga was disrupted by attendees shouting Islamophobic slurs and tearing out and walking on pages from a copy of the Holy Qur'an. They were protesting the PDSB's religious accommodation of Muslim students by providing them with school space for the congregational Friday prayer. Almost one quarter (22.5 percent) of PDSB students identify as Muslim. While this chapter takes a semi–case study perspective on anti-Muslim sentiments in Mississauga, a city of about 800,000 where Muslims represent nearly 12 percent of the population (Statistics Canada, 2011), the insights are certainly extendable, in religious and general spiritual terms, to Canada's Muslim population of 2.5 million. This chapter explores and analyzes the public pedagogy of broadcasting the evening call to prayer, which can serve as a sonic declaration of the spiritual and religious freedoms vital for Muslim children, youth, and families to live and thrive in this pluri-religious society. The exploration is guided by Antonia Darder's (2011) definition of critical public pedagogy "as a deliberate and sustained effort to speak through a critical lens of society in such a way as to inform (and transform) mainstream public discourses and community political practices, in the interest of the disenfranchised" (p. 700).

The chapter begins with an examination of the premise of KROOOPS in relation to legally binding frameworks in Canada and Ontario that protect freedom of religion and prohibit discrimination based on religion or creed. It then takes a closer look at the PDSB's accommodation of Muslim students' religious observances and the experiences of Muslim students in PDSB schools. The chapter concludes with counter-narratives offered by critical Muslim educators and activists in response to the temporary suspension of city noise bylaws to allow for the public broadcast of the evening call to prayer. Throughout the chapter, opportunities for educators and community activists to establish spaces for counter-narratives and alternative public education are noted.

KEEP RELIGION OUT OF OUR PUBLIC SCHOOLS

KROOOPS is registered in Canada as a not-for-profit corporation with the following mandate:

- Keep religion out of Public schools and other Public institutions
- Ensure Provincial Human Rights Codes are abided by in Public Schools and other Public institutions
- Ensure total accountability of Public funds by Public educational institutions and other Public institutions.
- Challenge Parliamentary Motions and Bills that violate the Constitution including and especially the Canadian Charter of Rights and Freedoms
- Carry out activities ancillary and incidental to the attainment of the aforementioned purposes (Subrahmanian, 2020a)

KROOOPS seeks to influence the educational experiences of children and youth in K–12 public schools. Furthermore, KROOOPS attempts to position itself as a human rights monitoring authority while also working against the provision of public education that recognizes religion or creed as a way of being and knowing of some children and youth served by public schools (Zine, 2001; Moore et al., 2012).

In response to Mississauga City Council's unanimous decision to temporarily suspend the noise bylaw so that local mosques could broadcast the evening call to prayer until May 24, 2020, KROOOPS took to Facebook to garner public support for legal action against the City of Mississauga:

> On April 29, 2020, the City of Mississauga amended its Noise By-law to allow houses of worship to broadcast on external loudspeakers. As Canada is a pluralist society embracing people of all culture and religions, it is a fundamental principle that Freedom of Religion must also mean Freedom from Religion. This Facebook Group is a Call for Legal Action against the City of Mississauga for violating this fundamental principle. This lawsuit will be launched by KROOOPS (on behalf of the residents of Mississauga and Ontario as a whole). It is to be noted that this Group is not against any faith or community or members thereof. This group has zero tolerance for hate speech or offensive material. (Subrahmanian, 2020b)

On May 2, 2020, KROOOPS's president, Ramkumar (Ram) Subrahmanian, created the aforementioned Facebook group. It was initially named Mississauga Call to Prayer on LoudSpeaker Unconstitutional. As of May 12, 2020, the name of the Facebook group is "Canadian Call for Legal Action against Charter Violation." Since June 26, 2020, KROOOPS has raised C$47,478.02 of its C$120,000 goal for its lawsuit against the City of Mississauga. KROOOPS states that funds raised exceeding legal costs will be used to pursue its mission.

Shree Paradkar, the *Toronto Star*'s race and gender columnist, publicly tested the Facebook group's disclaimer that "This Group is not against any faith or community or members thereof. This Group has zero tolerance for hate speech or offensive material":

> Mississauga city councillors have felt the ire and pressure of their citizens since April 29 when they passed the motion, and they devoted two hours Wednesday to discussing the decision. In the end, they did not rescind it.
>
> A closed Facebook group named "Mississauga Call Prayer on LoudSpeaker Unconstitutional," that quickly swelled to 6,000 members, offers a glimpse of that anger. "We're not against any religion, we're just against the noise," is the overriding mantra of the founders who live in a city with neighbourhoods around Canada's busiest airport.
>
> It's all about these issues that go unnoticed when it comes to other religions; churches across the country ring their bells on Sundays. (Paradkar, 2020a, paras. 4–5)

Based on her review of the Facebook group's comments section, Paradkar (2020a) describes it as "a fertile meeting ground for Islamophobes of all stripes." She continues,

> In recent years, the fear of "a Muslim takeover" with the forever looming spectre of Shariah has made strange bedfellows out of Hindus with a historical grievance against Muslims (fuelled by the brazen Hindu supremacist ideology in India) and white supremacists who spew nonsensical rhetoric of white genocide at the hands of the other—with Muslims being at the top of that pile of "other." (Paradkar, 2020a, para.7)

Subrahmanian responded publicly to Paradkar's (2020a) article on Twitter: "Several Muslims support our cause. Our mantra 'Freedom of Religion' = 'Freedom from Religion' We oppose charter violation." (Subrahmanian, 2020c). KROOOPS relies on its Muslim supporters to challenge those naming KROOOPS's position as anti-Muslim and Islamophobic. "Islamophobes of all stripes" include Muslim Islamophobes. "Freedom of Religion" is a fundamental human right. "Freedom from Religion" is a false equivalent. Subrahmanian's word choice is worth noting—*mantra* is Sanskrit, and it refers to a sacred word or group of words believed to have religious powers in Hindu and Buddhist traditions.

RELIGIOUS FREEDOM AND ACCOMMODATION

KROOOPS invokes the Canadian Charter of Rights and Freedoms (1982) and the Ontario Human Rights Code (1990) in its claim that the public broadcast of the evening call to prayer constitutes a violation of the Charter. Such a claim can serve as an opportunity for critical educators and community activists to provide public education on the Canadian Charter of Rights and Freedoms, the Ontario Human Rights Code, and other human rights declarations, conventions, and treaties with related provisions. Along with the Canadian Charter of Rights and Freedoms, human rights in Canada are protected in the Constitution of Canada (1867, 1982 [Government of Canada, 2022a]), which sets out the fundamental rules and principles that govern the Canadian settler-colonial state.

Freedom of Conscience and Religion

Section 2 of the Canadian Charter of Rights and Freedoms states,

> Everyone has the following fundamental freedoms: (a) freedom of conscience and religion; (b) freedom of thought, belief, opinion, and expression, including freedom of the press and other media of communication; (c) freedom of peaceful assembly; and (d) freedom of association. (Government of Canada, 2020)

The Charter accords the right to practise religion (e.g., worship, teach, learn, observe) and to change religious beliefs. Related to this, Section 15(1) of the Charter states,

> Every individual is equal before and under the law and has the right to equal protection and equal benefit of the law without discrimination, and, in particular, without discrimination based on race, national or ethnic origin, colour, religion, sex, age, or mental or physical disability. (Department of Justice Canada, 2020)

Similar provisions for religion are found in Canadian and international instruments legally binding in Canada, including Section 1(c) of the Canadian Bill of Rights (1960), Section 3(1) of the Canadian Human Rights Act (1985), Article 18 of the International Covenant on Civil and Political Rights (1966), and Article 14 of the United Nations Convention on the Rights of the Child (1990 [Noel, 2015]). Although not legally binding in Canada, there are similar provisions in Article 18 of the Universal Declaration of Human Rights (1948) and Article 12 of the United Nations Declaration on the Rights of Indigenous Peoples (2007 [United Nations, 2020b]).

Canada is a signatory to the United Nations Declaration on the Rights of Indigenous Peoples but has not ratified it. The Government of Canada has stated that the declaration is "aspirational" and is legally non-binding. This position has been righteously challenged, including by Mi'kmaq lawyer, professor, and activist Pamela Palmater. Palmater points out, "Canada's failure to listen is one of the reasons why Indigenous peoples spent more than 25 years negotiating the *United Nations Declaration on the Rights of Indigenous Peoples* which guarantees the right of Indigenous peoples to free, prior, and informed consent" (2018, para. 2). Article 12 of the United Nations Declaration on the Rights of Indigenous Peoples sets out spiritual and religious freedom:

> Indigenous peoples have the right to manifest, practice, develop, and teach their spiritual and religious traditions, customs, and ceremonies; the right to maintain, protect, and have access in privacy to their religious and cultural sites; the right to use and control ceremonial objects; and the right to repatriation of their human remains. (United Nations, 2020b, p. 11, subarticle 1)

With settlers in Canada living on Indigenous lands, this declaration provides guidance for right relations.

The Convention on the Rights of the Child is a human rights treaty that defines the civil, political, economic, social, health, and cultural rights of children and youth. Under the convention, children are any human beings younger than 18 years of age. The Government of Canada ratified the convention on December 12, 1991, but its implementation is limited due to two reservations entered by Canada relating to Articles 21 and 37(c) (Noel, 2015). Article 21 concerns adoption of children and Article 37(c) concerns children in the criminal justice system (Noel, 2015). The purpose of Canada's reservation to Article 21 is to avoid conflict with customary forms of care of Indigenous people (Noel, 2015); the purpose of its reservation to Article 37(c) is to not separate children and adults where it is not feasible or appropriate to do so (Noel, 2015). Given that KROOOPS seeks to impact the educational experiences of children and youth within the K–12 public educational system, Article 14 of the Convention on the Rights of the Child merits elaboration:

> States Parties shall respect the right of the child to freedom of thought, conscience, and religion. States Parties shall respect the rights and duties of the parents and, when applicable, legal guardians, to provide direction to the child in the exercise of his or her right in a manner consistent with the evolving capacities of the child. Freedom to manifest one's religion or beliefs may be subject only to such limitations as are prescribed by law and are necessary to protect public safety, order, health, or morals, or the fundamental rights and freedoms of others. (United Nations, 2020a)

According to Article 14, children and youth are free to identify or not identify with a religion. Their parents or guardians can provide guidance regarding religion, but they may not force their children to follow or not follow a religion. Furthermore, children and youth who do identify as adherents to a religion should not be subject to discrimination because of their religion. KROOOPS's mandate suggests that children and youth who identify with a religion should not be able to receive religious accommodation to practise their religion in K–12 public schools.

DISCRIMINATION BASED ON CREED AND CORRESPONDING PROTECTIONS

Under the Ontario Human Rights Code, discrimination because of religion (creed) is against the law. The Ontario Human Rights Commission (OHRC, 2015) states,

> Everyone should have access to the same opportunities and benefits, and be treated with equal dignity and respect, regardless of their religion. Religion includes the practices, beliefs, and observances that are part of a faith or religion. It does not include personal moral, ethical, or political views. Nor does it include religions that promote violence or hate towards others, or that violate criminal law.

The OHRC's *Policy on Preventing Discrimination Based on Creed* (2015) clarifies that the impact of the behaviour is more important than whether or not the behaviour was discriminatory. The OHRC explains that where a rule conflicts with religious requirements, there is a duty to ensure that individuals can observe their religion, unless this would cause undue hardship (e.g., cost, health, or safety). Unlawful discrimination because of religion can include refusing to allow individuals to observe periods of prayer at particular times during the day.

The policy (OHRC, 2015) states, "All society benefits when people of diverse creed backgrounds are encouraged and empowered to take part at all levels" (p. 120). It provides the following example of school board–led efforts to facilitate dialogue among educators and parents about religious beliefs or practices requiring accommodation:

> A school board develops detailed guidelines supported by policy, procedure, communications, and designated staff to manage and inclusively design for religious accommodations in schools. At the start of the school year, students,

families, and employees are invited to inform the school of any beliefs or practices requiring accommodation through the proactive use and distribution of religious accommodations invitations forms, and through inquiries during parent–teacher interviews. (OHRC, 2015, p. 120)

The policy recognizes that religion or creed is part of a way of life among some children, youth, and families served by the K–12 public education system. KROOOPS's mandate contradicts the OHRC's *Policy on Preventing Discrimination Based on Creed* (OHRC, 2015).

RELIGIOUS ACCOMMODATIONS FOR MUSLIM STUDENTS IN PDSB SCHOOLS

K–12 public schools in the Region of Peel, which consists of the municipalities of Brampton, Caledon, and Mississauga, fall under the jurisdiction of the PDSB. The PDSB is headquartered in Mississauga. In recent years, the PDSB has become a flashpoint on the issue of religious accommodation in public schools that allow Muslim students to observe congregational Friday prayer.

On the evening of March 22, 2017, the PDSB board of trustees held a public meeting with a heavy security and police presence to discuss, among other issues, religious accommodations for Muslim students. This meeting was attended by supporters of anti-Muslim groups, including Rise Canada and Canadian Hindu Advocacy. Both Rise Canada and Canadian Hindu Advocacy have participated in events organized by KROOOPS (Jovanovski, 2017). Rise Canada advisor and Canadian Hindu Advocacy director Ranendra (Ron) Banerjee delivered prepared remarks at the PDSB board of trustees meeting: "Allowing students to take Islamic prayers may violate Canadian values … Islam is poison" (Bridge Initiative Team, 2019, para. 15). Banerjee has been protesting against religious accommodations for Muslim students in K–12 schools for many years. In July 2011, for example, Banerjee publicly opposed Valley Park Middle School in Toronto for providing Muslim students with access to the school cafeteria for congregational Friday prayer (Bridge Initiative Team, 2019). Lebanese-Canadian businessperson and owner of Paramount Fine Foods Mohamad Fakih brought a defamation lawsuit against Banerjee and Kevin J. Johnston, a Calgary mayoral candidate and anti-Muslim provocateur (Paramount v. Johnston, 2018). In July 2017, Banerjee and Johnston attended a protest, organized by the Jewish Defense League, in front of a Paramount restaurant in Mississauga. The protest was in opposition to the Government of Canada's settlement of Omar Khadr's lawsuit for infringing his rights under the Canadian Charter of Rights and Freedoms (Amnesty International, 2017; Canada v. Khadr, 2010). A Canadian citizen, Khadr was a 15-year-old minor—a child under the Convention on the Rights of the Child—when he was detained by the United States at Guantanamo Bay Detention Centre for a decade (Amnesty International, 2017; Canada v. Khadr, 2010). Banerjee and Johnston said they were not allowed into Fakih's restaurant because "you gotta be a jihadist" and made other hateful comments (Bridge Initiative Team, 2019, para. 19; Paramount v. Johnston, 2018). In June 2018, Justice S. Nakatsuru of the Ontario Supreme Court of Justice noted that "Banerjee is an experienced and prolific speaker of hateful language" and that Banerjee's comments go beyond "hurtful expression" and "involve hallmarks of hate" (Bridge Initiative Team, 2019, para. 20; Paramount v. Johnston, 2018). Fakih was awarded $2.5 million in damages (Bridge Initiative Team, 2019). In response to the court's decision, Fakih stated, "I did this not for me, but for my kids to know that people who bully and spew hate are wrong, and that Canada will defend us" (Nasser, 2019, para. 26). In this case, the court did indeed communicate a strong message against anti-Muslim hate speech. Fakih's determination to seek accountability on the public record, irrespective of the court's decision, could be read as a form of critical public pedagogy. Fakih had the means to pursue a defamation lawsuit and did so to show his kids (and others) that anti-Muslim hate must be resisted and challenged in Canadian society.

When the PDSB board of trustees refused to respond to a petition with six hundred signatories demanding the end of the religious accommodation, the meeting was disrupted. Protestors shouted Islamophobic obscenities. One attendee tore pages from the Holy Qur'an, and others walked on the torn pages. Imam Omar Subedar, of Brampton Makki Masjid, thanked Varsha Naik, the Regional Diversity Roundtable, and the PDSB for gathering the pages torn from the Qur'an and for contacting local imams for guidance on how to take care of it. Subedar buried the Qur'an in an undisclosed location (CBC News, 2017).

Christina Dixon, a Peel Region resident and parent of a child attending a PDSB school, stood up to the protestors:

> They started yelling at the school board.... I heard someone yell, "This is a Christian country." It was a combination of hearing all those different things, and the rage and the anger with which it was being said, that inspired me to stand up.... I've lived in the Peel Region for most of my life ... I never would have expected that this kind of rhetoric and anger and hatred and ignorance ... I never would have expected it in our community to this extent." (quoted in McGillivray, 2017)

Dixon's response exemplified and modelled bystander intervention for those present at the meeting. Her refusal to remain silent and willingness to counter the hateful anti-Muslim and anti-Islam rhetoric is a form of critical public pedagogy. Dixon deliberately spoke through a critical lens of Canadian society and how she imagined the Peel community, in the interest of Peel residents and children attending PDSB schools.

A few hours prior to the meeting, the PDSB had released a 12-point fact sheet on religious accommodation in response to "an effort to counter a clear legal requirement with deliberate misinformation":

- All school boards are required to have a religious accommodation procedure.
- Religious accommodation has been taking place in Peel schools for over 15 years.
- Trustees have heard and continue to listen to the public regarding religious accommodation.
- The board does not favour one faith over another.
- Religion does have a place in secular schools, if accommodations are requested.
- Friday Prayer does not negatively impact student learning.
- There is no cost or undue hardship in providing accommodation for Friday Prayer.
- Accommodation is different depending on the family's faith and beliefs.
- There is also a legal requirement for the board to allow religious clubs at the request of students.
- Although staff will be supervising Friday Prayer, the board cannot interfere with the practice of faith.
- There is a significant difference between the Ontario court removal of the Lord's Prayer and religious accommodation.
- The Ontario Human Rights Code has precedence over any other Code or Act. (PDSB, 2017, pp. 1–2)

Among the facts highlighted in the fact sheet on religious accommodation (PDSB, 2017) is that the congregational Friday prayer has been accommodated in PDSB schools for more than 15 years, as required by the Ontario Human Rights Code. The Ontario Human Rights Code states that only undue burden, such as cost, health, or safety risks, should prevent religious accommodations from being granted. Providing access to school space where Muslim students can observe Friday prayer does not cause undue burden. The PDSB concludes the fact sheet by underscoring the hypocrisy of those protesting against religious accommodation in PDSB schools:

It has been frustrating and disheartening to see what is often hatred and prejudice towards a single faith group disguised in a supposed campaign about religion in schools. No one has expressed concern about school-wide celebration of Diwali, or that we provide vegetarian options in food, or post posters acknowledging all major faith days, including Christmas. This is a campaign against Islam—counter to the laws of the Country, the *Ontario Human Rights Code*, and our board values. (PDSB, 2017, p. 2)

The PDSB's religious accommodation policy first became a flashpoint in September 2016 when it introduced a change requiring Muslim students to read from a set of six preapproved sermons at Friday prayer. Previously, the PDSB's policy said Muslim students could read any sermon that had been approved by an administrator. The PDSB claimed that it had introduced the procedure to promote consistency across PDSB schools. A spokesperson for the PDSB said some of the sermons were written in Arabic and covered topics out of the usual purvey of public school administrators: "What we heard from principals is that that was making them uncomfortable, that they were basically reviewing the faith work of students" (Brian Woodland as quoted in Boisvert, 2016, para. 11).

The PDSB claimed that it had collaborated with 10 local imams to develop the six sermons. Imam Omar Subedar, who is among the collaborators, described the six sermons as a starting point: "It just so happens that six have come through to date" (Boisvert, 2016, para. 13). Other Muslim community members, however, claimed that the process was not transparent. Maleeha Baig, who works with Muslim high school students in Peel Region, stated, "I feel like this [new] policy, this procedure, whatever you want to call it, it really just gives this sort of guilt" (as quoted in Boisvert, 2016, para. 3). Maleeha had reviewed the sermons: "For the most part a lot of the sermons were very much about respecting your parents, being good to your community, being good citizens" (as quoted in Boisvert, 2016, para. 19). Muslim community member Shahmir Durrani remarked, "There's this assumption that Muslim youth aren't promoting a peaceful message.... It's very negative, and it negatively affects the mindset of these youth" (as quoted in Boisvert, 2016, para. 8). In response to pressure from Muslim communities, the PDSB reversed its decision (Alphonso, 2017). This policy change is believed to have galvanized the anti-Muslim groups to organize against the religious accommodation and, ultimately, to disrupt the PDSB board of trustees' meeting on March 22, 2017.

On February 28, 2020, Ontario Ministry of Education–appointed reviewers Ena Chadha, Suzanne Herbert, and Shawn Richard submitted their review of the PDSB to Ontario Minister of Education Stephen Lecce. The report details pervasive anti-Black racism and inequities throughout the PDSB. The report includes two findings specific to the experiences of Muslim children and youth in PDSB schools:

We heard concerns about Islamophobia and were provided with French curriculum materials that were clearly Islamophobic, conveyed blatant hostility to the Muslim community and an ignorance of the basic tenants of Islam. Muslim students, who account for 22.4 percent of the PDSB secondary student community and are the largest religious group within the PDSB community, have been the targets of Islamophobia. Citing conflict referable to prayers in PDSB schools and the presence of White supremacists at a meeting of the Board of Trustees, we heard from students, families, and educators of the real need for an Islamic coordinator to support Muslim students. (Chadha et al., 2020, pp. 5–6)

Students told us that their teachers are not prepared to deal with racism, nor do they have the tools to step up and do what is necessary to improve the culture in schools. Students shared their desire to have "open communication with teachers and students about differences." Muslim students who observe Ramadan, for example, told us that teachers do not understand their experience or respect their need for religious accommodation, noting that although some Muslim students wish to pray five times a day, they do not have the means to do that at school. Despite racialized students being the majority of the population, teachers are predominantly non-racialized. Having a teaching staff that is representative of the students would allow students to focus on learning, rather than having to focus so much of their time and emotional energy navigating an education system where they are made to feel like outsiders. (Chadha et al., 2020, p. 35)

Months after the release of this report, Muslim students, parents, and teachers started to come forward to share their experiences of Islamophobia in the PDSB (Paradkar, 2020b).

THE BROADCAST OF THE ADHAN AS PUBLIC PEDAGOGY

The Islamophobic response to Mississauga City Council's decision to temporarily suspend the noise bylaw to allow the public broadcast of the evening call to prayer (adhan) and the council's refusal to submit to pressure from anti-Muslim groups to reverse their decision are just responses and teachable moments in a city where anti-Muslim sentiment is increasingly visible and volatile. Indeed, the mayor of the City of Mississauga, Bonnie Crombie, wrote in an email to a media outlet, "Since we passed this motion, I have unfortunately received many disturbing emails, calls, and posts on social media in opposition to our decision.... While people are entitled to their own opinion, there is zero place for hate or intolerance in our city" (Zhou, 2020, para. 7). A Canadian elected official's understanding of Islamophobia and refusal to submit to it is another counter-narrative and form of public education, particularly in a country where police-reported hate crime against Muslims is up by 151 percent since 2017 (Moreau, 2020). The noise made by anti-Muslim groups is just noise and cannot drown out the sound responses of critical Muslim educators and community activists for justice.

Sidrah Ahmad Chan, a doctoral student at the University of Toronto who is studying the intersection of Islamophobia and gender-based violence, offers one such critical response. In an essay titled "How the Call to Prayer 'Controversy' Can Build Compassion for Muslims with Spiritual Abuse Trauma" (2020), Chan writes to Muslim communities, creates space for multiple responses to the public broadcast of the adhan, and amplifies the issue of spiritual abuse in Muslim communities. Chan shares that she grew up hearing the adhan five times a day in her home and likens it to "happy childhood memories of the ice cream truck approaching two blocks away" (2020, para. 2). She asks herself, "So why, at the beginning of Ramadan, when I heard the adhan come up through my apartment window, did my heart clench instead of leap? Why did my stomach turn with fear?" (2020, para. 5). The public broadcast of the adhan and subsequent Islamophobic backlash prompted Chan to uncover the answer to that question. Chan describes her initial conflicted responses: deep concern about the rise in hate crimes against Muslims, fear that the adhan would provoke anti-Muslim groups, and even an impulse to blame Muslims for the uproar. Chan holds these conflicted responses and notes that "it is victim-blaming to believe or argue that Muslims are 'provoking' Islamophobia through overt expressions of faith" (2020, para. 8). Chan comes to understand that she heard the person who had harmed her in the past give the call to prayer:

> Now that I have reflected more deeply, I have realized that hearing the adhan broadcast at the beginning of Ramadan didn't just frighten me because of the spectre of Islamophobia. The adhan in this context also, tragically, reminded me of the person who harmed me. In essence, hearing the call to prayer through my window made me feel like the abuser was "coming to get me." Even though I was listening to a completely different muezzin, and even though many years have passed since the harm took place, I felt like he was coming to get me. (2020, para. 25)

Spiritual abuse occurs in different faith and spiritual communities. In a Muslim context, Chan explains, spiritual abuse can be perpetrated by a partner/spouse, family members, friends, chaplains, Qur'an teachers, and imams, among others. Abusers may use Islam to justify abuse and/or blame the person they are abusing. For Chan, speaking out about the spiritual abuse she endured and raising awareness among Muslims about spiritual and other forms of abuse are part of her healing journey. Chan's response to the public broadcast of the adhan is one that Muslim communities need to listen to, particularly as they journey inward and toward community during the month of Ramadan.

Shumaila Hemani, an ethnomusicologist at the University of Alberta and a Sufi singer, believes the sounds of world religions, including the adhan, can cultivate compassion when guided toward expanded understanding. In her essay, "As a Sufi Singer, I Believe the Sounds of World Religions Can Cultivate Compassion during COVID-19" (2020), Hemani describes her teaching experience with Semester at Sea, a study abroad program that takes place on a cruise ship and the port cities it visits: "My students and I discussed the sounds of rituals of the ports that we travelled to as well as soundscapes of political and sacred rituals in people's everyday lives" (2020, para. 8). Hemani observed that her students gained deeper appreciation of the difference and beauty of aural faith practices: "As I watched my students, I saw that that the classroom was enhancing their cultural immersion and giving them tools to understand the sounds of ritual practices they encountered" (2020, para. 10). As part of the program, the ship docked in Port Louis, Mauritius. Hemani had prepared students for the soundscapes of Mauritius, including Islamic sonic markers. She shared information about the five pillars of Islam, different expressions of Islam, and Sufi poetic and musical traditions in Turkey, India, and Pakistan. She invited her students to listen in new ways. Hemani foregrounds "intercultural listening"— "to listen not just to the sound of music of another culture and understand how it is thematically and melodically arranged, but also what makes it meaningful for the people within their respective history and context" (2020, para. 10). Relatedly, she describes the "intercultural ear" as a tool for challenging racism and xenophobia in the pandemic: "In order to save humanity through the global pandemic and to build our social resiliency, we need a greater intercultural awakening through listening. The pushback over the bylaw accommodation to allow Muslims to sound their call to prayer during Ramadan is a case in point" (Hemani, 2020, para. 17).

CONCLUDING OBSERVATIONS

The City of Mississauga's temporary suspension of its noise bylaw to allow the public broadcast of the evening call to prayer for Muslim residents observing Ramadan during the pandemic provides important public pedagogy possibilities. The amplification of the adhan in the Arabic language itself provides access to a sonic marker of Muslim communities. It can create space for Muslims to critically examine their own relationships to Islam, to mosques, and to one another.

The call to prayer is associated with mosques because it is typically issued from minarets built in or adjacent to mosques. However, some Muslims feel neither safe nor welcome in mosques. Chan (2020) offers a necessary intervention for Muslim communities by sharing her own memories of spiritual abuse recalled by the public broadcast of the call to prayer. Her intervention speaks through a critical lens of Canadian society and Muslim communities in Canada, in the interest of Muslims subjected to spiritual abuse.

The sonic marker of Muslim communities is also an opportunity for other communities to practise "intercultural listening," as Hemani (2020) proposes. Arabic is the language in which the Qur'an was revealed and the language in which the adhan is widely recited. Islamophobia extends to the Arabic language (Beydoun, 2016; Suleiman, 2016), which is associated with Islam and Muslims, and there are documented instances of criminalization of Arabic language speakers (Beydoun, 2016; Suleiman, 2016). The amplification of the Arabic language challenges what Hemani (2020) describes as "the socially isolated ear," which she argues is more likely to resist and be intimidated by cultural and religious difference (para. 2).

The Muslim Council of Peel's proposal, the City of Mississauga's response, and ongoing anti-Muslim protests point to the importance of critical media literacy education, political education, and condemnation of and resistance to all forms of hate. KROOOPS, Rise Canada, and Canadian Hindu Advocacy, among other groups opposing Muslim students' religious freedom and accommodation, spread misinformation about Islam, Muslims, and human rights and responsibilities set out in the Canadian Charter of Rights and Freedoms and the Ontario Human Rights Code. Public education must therefore include education about such human rights documents and how they function in the Canadian settler-colonial state. The review of the PDSB (Chadha et al., 2020) reveals that anti-Black racism and intersecting oppressions, including Islamophobia, are pervasive in its schools. The presence of white and Hindu supremacist groups is adversely impacting all children, youth, and families served by PDSB schools. Efforts to speak through a critical lens of Canadian society to inform and transform harmful Islamophobic public discourses and school community political practices must be carried forward into PDSB public schools.

DISCUSSION QUESTIONS

1. What is "public pedagogy"? How does the author use the concept to explore the teaching/learning opportunities of the public broadcast of the Islamic call to prayer in Mississauga, Ontario?

2. The author discusses various Islamophobic responses to the public broadcast of the Islamic call to prayer in Mississauga and to the religious accommodation of Muslim students in Peel District School Board (PDSB) schools. What are the responsibilities of the PDSB toward Muslim students?

3. Practise engaging with the Islamic call to prayer using an "intercultural ear." What emotional response, if any, does it evoke from you? Why? Note: There are numerous recordings of the adhan online. Below are links to two recordings:
    a. A public broadcast of the Islamic call to prayer in Arabic (Jame Masjid, 2020): https://www.youtube.com/watch?v=MQRlKOHLYFE
    b. A British Sign Language interpretation of the Islamic call to prayer, with Arabic audio, and Arabic and English script (Al Isharah, 2019): https://www.youtube.com/watch?v=a4DbNnN6UJ0

REFERENCES

Al Isharah. (2019, May 30). *BSL [British Sign Language] adhaan* [Video]. YouTube. https://www.youtube.com/watch?v=a4DbNnN6UJ0

Alphonso, C. (2017). Peel school board changes controversial decision on Muslim prayers. *Globe and Mail*. https://www.theglobeandmail.com/news/toronto/peel-school-board-changes-controversial-decision-on-muslim-prayers/article33533206/

Amnesty International. (2017, March 8). Canada v. Khadr. *Legal Briefs*. https://www.amnesty.ca/legal-brief/canada-v-khadr/

Beydoun, K. A. (2016, April 20). *Speaking Arabic while flying.* Al Jazeera. https://www.aljazeera.com/opinions/2016/4/20/speaking-arabic-while-flying

Boisvert, N. (2016). *Muslim community slams Peel District School Board over "stigmatizing" Friday prayer restrictions.* CBC News. https://www.cbc.ca/news/canada/toronto/muslim-community-slams-peel-district-school-board-over-stigmatizing-friday-prayer-restrictions-1.3842892

Bridge Initiative Team. (2019). *Factsheet: Ron Banerjee & Canadian Hindu Advocacy*. Bridge: A Georgetown University Initiative. https://bridge.georgetown.edu/research/factsheet-ron-banerjee-canadian-hindu-advocacy/

Canada (Prime Minister) v. Khadr. (2010). Supreme Court of Canada. https://www.canlii.org/en/ca/scc/doc/2010/2010scc3/2010scc3.html

CBC News. (2017, March 30). *Imam thanks Peel school board for gathering pages of Qur'an ripped at meeting.* CBC News. https://www.cbc.ca/news/canada/toronto/brampton-imam-qur-an-1.4047186

Chadha, E., Herbert, S., & Richard, S. (2020). *Review of the Peel District School Board.* Ontario Ministry of Education.

Chan, S. A. (2020). *How the call to prayer "controversy" can build compassion for Muslims with spiritual abuse trauma.* Muslim Link. https://muslimlink.ca/stories/how-the-call-to-prayer-controversy-can-build-compassion-for-muslims-with-spiritual-abuse-trauma

City of Mississauga. (2020, April 29). *City of Mississauga COVID-19 response continues: Keeping our city moving and safe.* https://www.mississauga.ca/city-of-mississauga-news/news/city-of-mississauga-covid-19-response-continues-keeping-our-city-moving-and-safe/

Darder, A. (2011). Radio and the art of resistance: A public pedagogy of the airwaves. *Policy Futures in Education, 9*(6), 696–705.

Government of Canada. (1960). *Canadian Bill of Rights (S.C. 1960, c. 44)*. https://laws-lois.justice.gc.ca/eng/acts/c-12.3/page-1.html

Government of Canada. (1982). *Charter of Rights and Freedoms*. https://laws-lois.justice.gc.ca/eng/const/page-12.html

Government of Canada. (1985). *Canadian Human Rights Act. (R.S.C., 1985, c.H-6)*. https://laws-lois.justice.gc.ca/eng/acts/h-6/

Government of Canada. (2020). *Charter of Rights and Freedoms*. https://www.justice.gc.ca/eng/csj-sjc/rfc-dlc/ccrf-ccdl/check/index.html

Government of Canada. (2022a). *The Constitution Acts, 1867 to 1982*. https://laws-lois.justice.gc.ca/eng/const/index.html

Government of Canada. (2022b). *Federal corporation information—1021888-0*. https://www.ic.gc.ca/app/scr/cc/CorporationsCanada/fdrlCrpDtls.html?corpId=10218880&V_TOKEN=null&crpNm=keep%20religion%20out%20of%20our%20public%20schools&crpNmbr=&bsNmbr=

Hemani, S. (2020). *As a Sufi singer, I believe the sounds of world religions can cultivate compassion during COVID-19*. The Conversation. https://theconversation.com/as-a-sufi-singer-i-believe-the-sounds-of-world-religions-can-cultivate-compassion-during-covid-19-138045

Jame Masjid. (2020, May 4). *Jame Masjid Mississauga first public adhaan* [Video]. YouTube. https://www.youtube.com/watch?v=MQR1KOHLYFE

Jovanovski, K. (2017). *Canadian groups are lashing out about Muslim prayer in schools*. The World. https://theworld.org/stories/2017-05-24/canadian-groups-are-lashing-out-about-muslim-prayer-schools

McGillivray, K. (2017, May 29). *"How dare you say these hateful things?" Woman takes on Islamophobia at school board meeting*. CBC News. https://www.cbc.ca/news/canada/toronto/peel-school-board-meeting-islamophobia-1.4043940

Moore, K., Talwar, V., & Bosacki, S. (2012). Canadian children's perceptions of spirituality: Diverse voices. *International Journal of Children's Spirituality, 17*(3), 217–234.

Moreau, G. (2020, February 26). *Police-reported hate crime in Canada, 2018*. Statistics Canada. https://www150.statcan.gc.ca/n1/pub/85-002-x/2020001/article/00003-eng.htm

Nasser, S. (2019, May 14). *Kevin Johnston ordered to pay $2.5M for "hateful, Islamophobic" remarks against restaurant chain owner*. CBC News. https://www.cbc.ca/news/canada/toronto/kevin-johnston-paramount-2-5-million-mohamad-fakih-1.5134227

Noel, J. (2015). *The Convention on the Rights of the Child*. Canada Department of Justice. https://www.justice.gc.ca/eng/rp-pr/fl-lf/divorce/crc-crde/conv2a.html

Ontario Human Rights Commission. (2015). *Policy on preventing discrimination based on creed*. Ontario Human Rights Commission.

Palmater, P. (2018). *True test of reconciliation: Respect the Indigenous right to say No*. Canadian Dimension. https://canadiandimension.com/articles/view/true-test-of-reconciliation-respect-the-indigenous-right-to-say-no

Paradkar, S. (2020a). A small gesture of compassion for Muslims during the pandemic unleashes ugly torrent of intolerance in Mississauga. *Toronto Star.* https://www.thestar.com/opinion/star-columnists/2020/05/06/a-small-gesture-of-compassion-for-muslims-during-the-pandemic-unleashes-ugly-torrent-of-intolerance-in-mississauga.html

Paradkar, S. (2020b). Students, teachers, parents feel the sting of Islamophobia in Peel schools. They share their stories. *Toronto Star.* https://www.thestar.com/opinion/star-columnists/2020/06/16/students-teachers-parents-feel-the-sting-of-islamophobia-in-peel-schools-they-share-their-stories.html

Paramount v. Johnston. (2018). Ontario Superior Court of Justice. https://www.canadianlawyermag.com/staticcontent/AttachedDocs/Paramount%20Fine%20Foods%20et%20al.%20v.%20Kevin%20J.%20Johnston%20et%20al.%20June%2020,%202018.pdf

Peel District School Board. (2017). *Religious accommodation: Key facts.*

Queen's Printer of Ontario. (2022). *Human rights code, R.S.O. 1990, c. H.19.* https://www.ontario.ca/laws/statute/90h19

Statistics Canada. (2011). *National household survey bulletin for Peel Region—ethnic diversity & religion.* https://www.peelregion.ca/planning/pdc/data/nhs/pdfs/Ethicity_Religion_Bulletin_letter.pdf

Subrahmanian, R. (2020a). *Canadian call for legal action against Charter violation* [Facebook Group]. https://www.facebook.com/groups/1140885932926954

Subrahmanian, R. (2020b). *A community initiative against broadcast of prayers in public.* https://www.nobroadcastprayers.com/ (Site accessed on March 13, 2022; site inactive on July 25, 2022)

Subrahmanian, R. (2020c, 7 May). @ShreeParadkar brazenly biased article. Several Muslims support our cause. Our mantra 'Freedom of Religion' = 'Freedom from Religion'. We oppose Charter violation. If u have a shred of honesty amend ur article. @TarketFatah @munirpervaiz [Twitter post]. https://twitter.com/r_subrahmanian/status/1258400612066222081

Suleiman, Y. (2016, March 20). *After Islamophobia comes the criminalisation of Arabic.* Al Jazeera. https://www.aljazeera.com/opinions/2016/3/20/after-islamophobia-comes-the-criminalisation-of-arabic

United Nations. (1948). *Universal Declaration of Human Rights.* https://www.un.org/en/about-us/universal-declaration-of-human-rights

United Nations. (2020a). *Convention on the Rights of the Child.* United Nations Treaty Collection. https://treaties.un.org/pages/ViewDetails.aspx?src=IND&mtdsg_no=IV-11&chapter=4&clang=_en

United Nations. (2020b). *United Nations Declaration on the Rights of Indigenous Peoples.* https://www.un.org/development/desa/indigenouspeoples/wp-content/uploads/sites/19/2018/11/UNDRIP_E_web.pdf

United Nations Human Rights Office of the High Commissioner. (1966). *International Covenant on Civil and Political Rights*. https://www.ohchr.org/en/instruments-mechanisms/instruments/international-covenant-civil-and-political-rights

Zhou, S. (2020). Mosques face backlash for broadcasting evening prayers during Ramadan. *Vice*. https://www.vice.com/en_ca/article/z3ebmw/mosques-face-backlash-broadcasting-evening-prayers-ramadan-mississauga

Zine, J. (2001). Muslim youth in Canadian schools: Education and the politics of religious identity. *Anthropology & Education Quarterly*, *32*(4), 399–423.

CHAPTER 7

Social Justice through Indigenization and Anti-Oppressive Teaching

Anna-Leah King

INTRODUCTION

Social justice in education has been a challenge for Indigenous people since white encroachment. Historically we had our own learning ways. These have never been valued and, in fact, have been discredited by the settler colonials whose goals were assimilation and control of Indigenous people. Indigenous leaders and educators made significant changes in the province of Saskatchewan after Indian Control of Indian Education. Indigenizing and decolonizing efforts have taken place visibly since the 1970s and even before that. These visionaries went as far as founding the First Nations University of Canada (FNUniv). The efforts made by Indigenous people put to shame the rest of the country, which often seems to be 50 years behind. The Truth and Reconciliation Commission (2015) also impacted social justice education with the challenge sent out to educators from the 94 Calls to Action in its multi-volume report. Indigenization and decolonization have been the new focus at the universities, with many mistakes made. Saskatchewan is also a very racist province, and anti-oppressive, anti-racist courses have become mandatory in education at both the University of Regina and the University of Saskatchewan, although their impact on students remains to be seen. Indigenous people have always had their own way of teaching. To instill our ways of knowing and being in academe is a possibility and is certainly embraced by FNUniv. Our collective Indigenous dream for higher education has yet to be fully actualized, but the vision has always been there, and the hope right now is great. In the following pages, I focus on such salient issues as decolonization and Indigenization; perspectives from the Truth and Reconciliation Commission, especially on the Calls to Action sections, which selectively concern education; possibilities of Indigenization in the universities; and teaching anti-oppressive education. Finally, I recommend in the conclusion a brief forward-working proposal, ending with seven important principles that guide the lives of the Anishnaabe people.

DECOLONIZING AND INDIGENIZING LONG BEFORE ACADEME'S RECENT NEW TERMINOLOGIES: HISTORICAL OVERVIEW

I have spent my entire teaching career Indigenizing curriculum from the perspective of an Anishnaabe kwe. I have always only taught Indigenous children. It is not that I was determined to teach in schools populated with Indigenous children, but the school board had other plans. Any Indigenous teachers they could grab from the Indian Teacher Education Program (ITEP) and the Saskatchewan Urban Native Teacher Education Program (SUNTEP) were relegated to teach in schools populated fully with Indigenous children and youth. I was trained as a reading teacher, and I acquired the French language while at university. I had hopes of teaching in a French immersion school. In my current position teaching in academe, this colonial-modelled university "sits on our head" in the sense that just when we Indigenous scholars thought we had some authority to make great changes to the system, we found the hierarchal power structure is set in place, and universities are the same as any school system. It is still a top-down system with the same old people around who have never had to think about what racism is and who have no understanding of what Indigenous or Indigeneity is, or what poverty is with regard to education. In addition, school boards are steeped with white-haired male colonial settlers and their stereoscopic view of education that has remained the same. Not a lot has changed in the time that I have been in schools. Throughout the time that I was teaching, teachers complained they could not facilitate any Indigenous inclusion as there were no resources. As we increased acceptable teacher resources after pulling books of stereotypes and negative imagery and colonial biases from all Saskatchewan libraries, the settler teachers complained that unless there was some curricular development, they would not make the effort by reading Indigenous literature and texts to add to curricular content. An advisory council to the minister was created in 1984 and was referred to as the Minister's Advisory Committee on Native Curriculum Review. This became one of the first initiatives in education to reflect First Nations and Métis values, beliefs, and worldviews. It was later renamed the Métis Education Advisory Council (IMEAC). Indigenization and/or decolonization among Indigenous educators has taken place since Indian Control of Indian Education and even before that. The province's Indigenous education history with regard to curriculum development and the formulation of IMEAC is as follows:

> The history of Indigenous education in Saskatchewan has been strongly influenced by a variety of provincial policies, practices, and partnerships. In the 1980s, the Department of Education's Core Curriculum initiative endorsed the integration of First Nations and Métis content and perspectives as a foundation for provincial curriculum and resources for all students. Subsequently the 1989 framework, *Indian and Métis Education Policy from Kindergarten to Grade 12*, charted curriculum integration of First Nations and Métis content and perspectives across all required areas of study.... In 1984 the Minister's Advisory Committee on Native Curriculum Review was established, and renamed the Indian and Métis Education Advisory Committee (IMEAC) in 1989. (Simpson, 2003, para.1)

Formulating partnerships became vogue in the early 1990s in Saskatchewan, when the province was producing an increasing number of First Nations and Métis teachers and administrators through highly regarded teacher education programs that include the First Nations University of Canada (formerly known as Saskatchewan Indian Federated College, established in 1972). This was the initial vision before the First Nations University of Canada was founded, which came from the Kiteyak (old ones), First Nations leadership, educators, and visionaries of the time. Saskatchewan Indian Cultural College, an institution of the Federation of Saskatchewan Indian Nations (FSIN; now Federation of Sovereign Indigenous Nations), was established in 1972 and recently became Saskatchewan Indigenous Cultural Centre (SICC). The SICC became the premiere First Nations–controlled education institution for the entire province. It holds a significant resource base for school systems of culture and language and continues research on First Nations' culture and heritage. The SICC includes an Elders Council, a board of governors, and a languages and cultures program (SICC, 2020, p. 1). The Indian Teacher Education Program, or ITEP, was founded by André Renault, Aldrich Dyer, and Cecil King at the University of Saskatchewan in 1972. ITEP alumni now take up leadership roles in education and government, and the teachers ensure that culturally appropriate education fulfills the goal of Indian Control of Indian Education. The Northern Teacher Education Program (NORTEP) was created in 1976 via the Northern School Boards (which later became the Northern Lights School Division). This was to allow students to acquire their Bachelor of Education degree without leaving the North. The Gabriel Dumont Institute was formed in 1980, and eventually, the institute established the Saskatchewan Urban Native Teacher Education Program (SUNTEP).

The creation of all these Indigenous education–centred efforts, with IMEAC serving as an advisory body to the minister of education, was instrumental in creating Indigenous curriculum development resources for Saskatchewan Learning and making them available for teachers to use as supplemental materials to advance Indigenous education and Indigenous perspectives. Teachers will still complain they do not have time to refer to these resources. The government established a curriculum-writing team at the ministry to weave Indigenous perspectives throughout the curriculum, but this rewrite of Indigenous perspective only lasted a small number of years until the new government stepped in and dismantled the Indigenous curriculum–development team. In addition, NORTEP, the Northern teachers' college, was shut down in 2017. The government seems bent on cost-cutting measures all around, with no consideration for the impact on the Indigenous population.

THE TRUTH AND RECONCILIATION COMMISSION

For over one hundred years, Indigenous children were taken away from their homes to government-funded, church-run residential schools. These institutions were set up by the government to assimilate Indigenous children. Many students experienced brutal abuse, both physical and sexual, at the hands of nuns and priests in these schools. The impact of these experiences resulted in the intergenerational trauma that is still playing out today. The legacy of this trauma passed on from one generation to the next, and also tragically amplified by the finding of Indigenous children's unmarked graves on the lands of former residential schools, has affected the relationship between Indigenous people and the rest of Canada. In the efforts to revitalize this relationship, reconciliation became an important goal. The Truth and Reconciliation Commission (TRC) began to hear testimonials of residential school survivors beginning in 2008 as part of the Indian Residential Schools Settlement Agreement (IRSSA). After seven years of witnessing testimonials of Indian residential school survivors across Canada, a comprehensive report came out. The TRC's final comprehensive report in December 2015 included 94 Calls to Action, as delineated by the commission, that will guide all Canadians in working toward reconciliation. Of these 94 Calls to Action, four (62–65) relate to education.

In the past five years, Murray Sinclair, former TRC commissioner, became disappointed with the slow momentum of the reconciliation efforts. In a CBC interview, he states,

> We need to ensure that we never, ever let Canada forget what they have done, and the situations that we are now facing that are the responsibility of this history, of the losses that have been experienced by Indigenous communities

and Indigenous Peoples ... systemic discrimination still carries on today in 2020 (Littlechild) with the Mi'kmaw lobster fishery in Atlantic Canada, and Joyce Echaquan's recording of racist slurs by staff prior to her death in a Quebec hospital. (Sinclair, 2015, para. 3)

Sinclair (2015), Wilson (cited in Sinclair, 2021), and Littlechild (cited in Sinclair, 2021) worked tirelessly over the seven-year period it took to collect the testimonials of survivors. Sinclair claimed the horrific experiences of the survivors of the government- and church-run residential schooling process was evidence of a "genocidal" practice. Canadian educators have witnessed the slow and brutal devastation of a people over generations and yet have seen nothing. Far too many colonial educators outside the "ghettoized" Indigenous school feel nothing for Indigenous children but annoyance or indifference, as I have experienced myself and witnessed in my teaching career. In an effort to eliminate ignorance about the plight of Indigenous people in Canada, the TRC's Calls to Action are crucial. Education also calls upon the compassion of these colonial educators—a factor yet to be seen.

Indigenization at Universities

The response to Indigenization at universities has happened in a few different ways. According to Gaudry and Lorenz (2018), there are three distinct uses of the term *Indigenization*: Indigenous inclusion, reconciliation Indigenization, and decolonial Indigenization. Indigenous inclusion policy is about increasing the number of Indigenous students, faculty, and staff. Reconciliation Indigenization lies somewhere between Indigenous and Canadian ideals and creates debate for what counts as knowledge. And decolonial Indigenization is about an overhaul of the academy, reorienting knowledge production on the basis of balancing power relations (Gaudry & Lorenz, 2018). The authors go on to state that higher education institutions have only started with introducing the least transformative of these three visions. In general, the Canadian academy has rhetorically adapted an inspirational vision of reconciliation Indigenization, but it is, in fact, largely committed to Indigenous inclusion; in essence, postsecondary institutions are attempting to merely increase the number of Indigenous people without making broader changes (p. 219). Many Indigenous academics rally for drastic change through decolonial Indigenization, which university administrators have failed to embrace so far.

A former Indigenous Lead for the Office of Indigenization at the University of Regina, Shauneen Pete, wrote *100 Ways to Indigenize and Decolonize Academic Programs and Courses* (2015). There is no real system in place to monitor cross-campus efforts to Indigenize or decolonize. Although there have been Indigenous research weeks, an Indigenous ethics symposium, various events around the buffalo, with Indigenous authors featured, the effort and support needs to start at the top. In 2021, one of five pillars of the University of Regina's strategic plan is Truth and Reconciliation, which is a good start. Within the Faculty of Education, a small number of faculty can be counted on to attend the Education Indigenous Council (on Indigenizing efforts), composed predominantly of settlers, one SUNTEP/GDI representative, and myself as Indigenous Chair. The same small group are the ones willing to make curricular additions to Indigenize their syllabus with Indigenous historical content and literature and/or invite an Elder or Knowledge Keeper to speak in the classroom. There are no mandated goals to work toward at this point. Lewis (2020), as an administrator for the Faculty of Education, suggests that the systems and structures of white settler society tend to be neither answerable nor responsible to the discourse of decolonization and Indigenization. He further states that should we choose to decolonize, reconciling and Indigenizing, there is a significant amount of work that will come along with it (Lewis, 2020). In light of there being no checks and balances or monitored efforts, the invested crew will remain small and change will be slow.

Although there are no checks and balances, I feel that the members of the Faculty of Education at the University of Regina are generally more conscientious and aware of the issues First Nations people face with regard to racism within education and outside of education than other education faculties I have worked with or have been a student of. The faculty who do not attend the Education Indigenous Council meetings do take time to speak to me about the curricular and pedagogical efforts they are making in their subject areas. I feel hopeful that some of our faculty have moved beyond "awareness to action" (Tuck, 2018, p. 160) with the inclusion of Indigenous literature, activism for Indigenous causes, welcoming of Knowledge Keepers in courses, developing and participating with Indigenous languages initiatives, and occasionally even joining us in participating in ceremonies. I believe the University of Regina is an exception considering the context of where we are positioned. The province of Saskatchewan has been labelled the most racist province in Canada (Elliott, 2004). Racism is the greatest hurdle to overcome in order for reconciling to take place. In the words of Anishnaabe Elder Mary Deleary: "Our relatives who have come from across the water [non-Aboriginal people], you still have work to do on your road.... The land is made up of the dust of our ancestors' bones. And so to reconcile with this land and everything that has happened, there is much work to be done ... in order to create balance" (Regan, 2018, p. 222). Reconciling is also about restoring the balance of the land and its peoples to what it once was. Indigenous people have great respect for the lands and ancestral teachings, which guide them today. Indigenous knowledges have only recently found resonances in policy frameworks of the universities and colleges in Canada (Battiste, 2018, p. 125). Now is certainly the time to create the policies that ensure that Indigenous knowledges, Indigenous languages, and Indigenous histories are required components of any degree. It is high time to work on colonial ignorance of Indigenous people in collaborative efforts to inspire a keen understanding that we could only hope ignites compassion to turn things around for Indigenous children's education.

Teaching Anti-Oppressive Education as Indigenization

In my current role as teacher of anti-oppressive education in an institution of higher learning, my ideal goal for students is a journey of self-discovery through an anti-oppressive course titled Social Justice Education: Self and Other. Students are encouraged to challenge their own biases and assumptions through literature study, documentaries, and class discussion in order to understand who they are as human beings and work on who they want to become as future teachers. Anti-oppressive education is just one of many subjects they will cover, and only a minimal understanding can be delivered due to limited time. Although they do have a mandatory senior-level course, I am unsure as to whether or not we really reach them and motivate them to turn away from the biases and preconceived notions that create their racialized thinking.

I am the teacher for this compulsory first-year anti-oppressive education course, Social Justice Education: Self and Other. It covers social justice issues for Indigenous people, including anti-racist education, 2SLGBTQQIAAP, poverty, and eco-justice at the intersections of race, class, gender, disability, and sexuality. It is an interesting teaching assignment in that the students are not sure what to expect and are slightly subdued in the initial classes. The students in my anti-oppressive course are predominantly from small towns in Saskatchewan. Regina is the big city to a lot of them. They write about being from farming families or small-town businesses. One student wrote of her pride in being part of a farming family and revealed a tattoo of a wheat sheaf on her forearm. Often their impression is that the course may be about learning about the other in multicultural perspective with regard to culture, as they have from K to 12. They learn the first day that it is not about that but is focused on social justice issues and anti-racism education for Indigenous people often operating from the depths of despair as a resultant effect of the genocidal practice of residential schooling in Canada. These students have only been told the conquerors' story, and many arrive with a superior standpoint. They believe this country to be theirs and believe that education will continue to deliver the conquerors' story and ideology of superiority.

When they learn of the real treatment of Indigenous children in residential schooling and the story of historical trauma experienced by Indigenous people, they "become unsettled" (Regan, 2011, p. 13). They also learn the concept of white privilege, and there are times when I feel they could walk out the door just a bit taller based on what they are learning. Things can backfire if 17- and 18-year-old white students learn about white privilege when they are too immature or unwilling to understand its real impact on Indigenous people. They cannot seem to connect the dots to hegemony and their future position as teachers to commit to its deconstruction; still, we need to find ways to open their hearts and minds. This is rarely the case, though. In Anishnaabe culture, understanding the connection of the mind and heart is part of social upbringing and is embedded in the language and defines truth speaking. For us, Naanaagdewendimowin is thinking not only with the heart but with both hemispheres of the brain as well, that is, emotion and logic (J. Wemigwans, personal communication, 2021). It reveals three places of thinking: heart, logic, and emotion. In Anishnaabe culture, we think with three mindsets at once. Every thought is filtered through heart and emotion. We are known as the heart people. Our midewewin lodge is about acquiring the spirit of lightheartedness. In spite of all the historical hurts and wrongs, we can always find a way to be happy. It is our greatest strength as a people, yet that is considered a weakness by the colonial guards that are centred on greed. I never share any aspects of our worldview or cultural teachings with students. I could not handle any negative response or lack of respect for the beauty and love I have for my people, even if understanding a bit of our philosophy would enhance their learning. I, therefore, introduce Willie Ermine's Aboriginal Epistemology, found in Battiste and Barman's (1995) work *First Nations Education in Canada: The Circle Unfolds*. Ermine reveals Aboriginal epistemology as defined by an Indigenous scholar relative to the expectation for future Indigenous teachers in our collective hope for our future.

I am never quite sure if I have succeeded in teaching these students that racism is unacceptable if you are choosing to be a teacher. The students write and say the right things or what they think they need to, in order to get a good mark, but I feel they are no less racist than when they entered the class. I do tell them that if they cannot let go of the biases that they learned at the family dinner table, teaching is not for them. I am only compelled to say this if I witness subtle forms of racism expressed to my face, to the delight of the students who are trying to make a mockery of the course due to their discomfort and unwillingness to let their racist platforms be challenged. Such behaviours can be a way of expressing their resistance to what is being taught. Resisters are a big part of this course, and they show their racialized opinions in different ways, such as racialized comments in Zoom classes. One student, in reference to Tasha Hubbard's film *nîpawistamâsowin: We Will Stand Up* (2019), stated, "I think Hubbard's film is really biased." Interesting observation when "the shoe is on the other foot." In the case of Hubbard's film, as an Indigenous filmmaker, she deliberately featured the all too often silenced side to speak their truth in this unbelievably sad and unjust story. In another show of resistance, a student wrote in his paper, "Indigenous people should not be given educational funding." This was exclaimed by a student who paid his own tuition with his "hard-earned money" but somehow remained ignorant of the literature presented in class. I am in disbelief that, having read all the literature and viewed all documentaries provided, a person could still remain unchanged.

These statements based on racialized thinking and privilege are a form of student resistance. St. Denis and Schick (2003) affirm that students' resistance to anti-racist courses is based on three ideological assumptions they have, namely that race does not matter; a belief of meritocracy; and that through goodness and innocence by individual acts of good intentions, one can secure innocence as well as superiority (St. Denis & Schick, pp. 61, 63, 65). This brings to mind the day my daughter came home from elementary school to inform me that the students were telling her that she was one of the brown people (Indigenous) and that she gets a free education. I said, yes, we do get education funding for university, but it is by the blood of our ancestors that we get it. Mindful of the mass slaughter with germ warfare, war, starvation, land relocation, and genocidal practices, we managed a Treaty clause to education to ensure a decent future. My daughter was surprised by my defensive and politically charged reaction. I had been waiting for the comments and racial jabs that would come from school. Fortunately, they were minimal from her group of friends whom she went to daycare with before school started and who remained her friends throughout elementary school. It was her teachers and the administrative staff that became the bigger concern, as they proved to be increasingly racially biased throughout her elementary schooling.

As an anti-racist educator, I find it all disheartening to say the least. First, there is a government that is seemingly against any progress for Indigenous people in education, with the elimination of Indigenous curriculum writers for the ministry and, more recently, the closing of NORTEP. I am never sure whether I have made racist students more secure in their racism and made them feel more superior by learning they have "white privilege" working for them or if I reached them through classroom discussions about the seriousness of the consequences of a racist teacher in a classroom with Indigenous children and children of colour. I have to hope that I reached most of them, and as they progress through courses that touch on similar anti-racist content, I can only hope that I have influenced the minds of the majority of them. Our schools cannot continue as they are with an all-white teaching staff and board office members—and, more than likely, board trustees. I feel trepidation for the Indigenous students and the influx of new immigrants into these schools wherein they must fit into a hegemonic curriculum and lack of acceptance.

WHERE TO FROM HERE?

How do we devise a socially just university? Is that even a possibility? Indigenous knowledges have never been considered or respected until just recently, with the Canadian Deans of Education's Accord on Indigenous Education (2010). Indigenous Knowledge is now being sought after, and Elders are the current norm for the university setting. The recent Calls to Action through the Truth and Reconciliation recommendations (2015) have prompted the Indigenization/decolonization impetus in universities. Battiste (2018), drawing from her research-intensive years with the Canadian Council on Learning, found that Indigenous pedagogies and Indigenous content–based curricula are having a positive effect on Indigenous learners (Battiste, 2013). We know that this knowledge reaches our youth. It resonates with them through their ancestral heritage and blood memory. In my experience, it makes more sense to them than any colonial offering. The question is how do we translate this into the classroom context and then to university courses without further appropriation by the competitive mindset of the colonial who is headstrong on self-aggrandizement? And what do we consider sharing at an academic institution when our Indigenous knowledges are tied to our heart?

A true depiction of Indigenous learning has been defined by the aforementioned Cree scholar and traditionalist Ermine (1995), who is also a Cree speaker from Sturgeon Lake First Nation, Saskatchewan. Aboriginal epistemology is defined as "those who seek to understand the reality of existence and harmony with the environment by turning inward and have a different, incorporeal knowledge paradigm that might be termed Aboriginal epistemology" (Ermine, 1995, p. 103). In essence, tapping into the "all encompassing" life force and connecting with it is where knowing becomes possible. Ermine refers to this as the inward journey, a voyage our ancestors took part in since the dawn of human existence. He sees this as the goal of future Indigenous educators. Anishnaabe have similar cultural practices to gain knowledge. I believe this is a serious consideration for our youth and university students. But how can we implement this at the universities for Indigenous students? The exception, of course, is First Nations University of Canada. First Nations University centralizes Indigenous teachings and ceremonies, and students are required to fully participate. Here the student body is predominantly Indigenous, with the exception of graduate students. Settlers find a place here to attend graduate classes and ceremonies and become quite at home in the Indigenous community. We still have to be aware of what will be shared and to what degree when settlers are in the teaching ceremonies. They will often take from these ceremonies to write in their papers, and in settler crowds, they usurp expertise. One of the primary challenges surrounding the resurgence of Indigenous philosophies of relationality emerges from the ever-evolving problem of how to revitalize without having them further marginalized, appropriated, or distorted by the Western world (Starblanket & Kiiwetinepinesiik Stark, 2018). Navigation is always careful when Indigenous knowledge is being shared with colonials. We are cognizant that further reconciliation efforts will have to embrace and include colonial settlers to the circle, whether it be a ceremonial circle, sharing circle, or engagement circle, and it cannot happen without both parties present. Maybe we need to assert policy with regard to the protection of Indigenous knowledge and intellectual property rights before settlers register for a course at our Indigenous institutions or participate in Indigenous ceremonies and gatherings.

Ermine speaks to the ethical space of engagement, drawing on the theoretical work of Poole, who looks at the space between two disparate peoples in the hopes of creating a dialogue between Indigenous people and colonial settlers in every discipline at the universities so they may come to a better understanding of each other's perspective. For the most part, I do not believe these dialogues are taking place. In considering reconciliation with regard to ethical engagement, Ermine questions: How do we reconcile worldviews wherein one tradition is written and one tradition is oral? Further, Ermine contends that cultural encounters require shifting our perspectives to recognize that the Indigenous–Western encounter is about thought worlds and that frameworks or paradigms are essential to reconcile these disparate solitudes. The theory of ethical space is one such framework, and configuring ethical/moral/legal principles in cross-cultural cooperation, at the common table of the ethical space, will be a challenging and arduous task (Ermine, 2007). It is only through these ethical space dialogues that we can advance Indigenous education to a more socially just place.

Waawyezendimowin is a term in Anishnaabemowin that refers to striving for enlightenment (J. Wemigwans, personal communication, 2021). Light measure refers to a concept used by Indigenous people that comes out of the language but is never spoken or necessarily thought of as a concept to consider in the professional fields, and particularly education. Could we see this as a goal: consciousness as step one? A goal is to strive to be more aware of issues that affect Indigenous people: historical racism and genocidal practices that have brought us to the brink of self-destruction. Could the colonial settlers look inward to see their immediate judgmental, distrusting, racialized notions that guide them and challenge their own thinking to be mindful of oneself and then work at self-challenge to be more loving in their approach to teaching—more tolerant and more guiding, maybe even becoming brotherly or sisterly figures? Is it asking too much to have teachers who are more spiritually focused? We have a greeting out West from the Saulteaux Anishnaabe, *Anin sikwe kin*, which loosely translates to "Hello, how are you?" But many Elders remind us of its proper translation: "I see your light" (Brass, 2018). My dream for Indigenous people is to restore the ability to see one's light, to recognize that we are spiritual beings, and to design our education with the spiritual focus first. The term *Anishnaabe* is said to mean "man who was lowered," meaning man was lowered here from the spirit world. One little boy was chosen to impart spiritual knowledge, ceremony, and guidance to the people. He learned from the grandfathers of the star world first. He brought these teachings to us as guiding principles to live by.

I refer to Tanya Talaga's prologue for *Seven Fallen Feathers* (2017), a non-fiction novel depicting the lives taken from seven Indigenous high school students who attended high school in Thunder Bay, Ontario. I use it to teach in my anti-racist course, and I am sharing it here as a suggested way to move forward in Indigenous education. The Anishnaabe are guided by seven principles:

> **Zah-gi-di-win** (love): To know love is to know peace.
> **Ma-na-ji-win** (respect): To honour all of creation is to have respect.
> **Aak-de-he-win** (bravery): To face life with courage is to know bravery.
> **Gwe-ya-kwaad-zi-win** (honesty): To walk through life with integrity is to know honesty.
> **Dbaa-dem-diz-win** (humility): To accept yourself as a sacred part of creation is to know humility.
> **Nbwaa-ka-win** (wisdom): To cherish knowledge is to know wisdom.
> **De-bwe-win** (truth): To know of these things is to know truth.

I have always believed that these seven grandfathers' teachings are good enough to build a school around, with language teachers and Kiteyak (old ones) who live by these principles and students who will learn them as they grow through a positive education to carry them forward with strength and dignity; and as they enter academe, they will make it a better place than it ever was.

DISCUSSION QUESTIONS

1. How can the Indian Teacher Education Program (ITEP) and similar teacher education programs shape the way forward for Indigenous educational development and anti-racism work?

2. Some universities in Canada have not yet made any effort toward Indigenization; what could be the reason for that?

3. Indigenization is not a straight pathway to success with regard to its implementation in Canadian universities; how can this complex instillation be improved by universities' leadership?

4. What would be the beneficial outcomes of settlers and newcomers learning more about the truth of Indigenous history in Canada and Indigenous ways of knowing and being?

REFERENCES

Archibald, J., Lundy, J., Reynolds, C., & Williams, L. (2010). *Accord on Indigenous education*. Association of Canadian Deans of Education. https://csse-scee.ca/acde/wp-content/uploads/sites/7/2017/08/Accord-on-Indigenous-Education.pdf

Battiste, M. (2013). *Decolonizing education: Nourishing the learning spirit*. Saskatoon and Purich Publishing and UBC Press.

Battiste, M. (2018). Reconciling Indigenous knowledge in education. In M. Spooner & J. McNinch (Eds.), *Dissident knowledge in higher education* (pp. 123–148). University of Regina Press.

Battiste, M., & Barman, J. (1995). *First Nations education in Canada: The circle unfolds*. UBC Press.

Brass, D. (2018). All my relations. In D. J. Clandinin, V. Caine, & S. Lessard (Eds.), *The relational ethics of narrative enquiry* (pp. 153–162). Routledge.

Elliott, J. (Director). (2004). *Indecently exposed* [Film]. Blue Eyes Productions.

Ermine, W. (1995). Aboriginal epistemology. In M. Battiste & J. Barman (Eds.), *The circle unfolds* (p. 101–123). UBC Press.

Ermine, W. (2007). The ethical space of engagement. *Indigenous Law Journal, 6*(1), 194–203.

Gaudry, A., & Lorenz, D. (2018). Indigenization as inclusion, reconciliation, and decolonization: Navigation the different visions for indigenizing the Canadian Academy. *AlterNative: An International Journal of Indigenous Peoples, 14*(3), 218–227.

Hubbard, T. (Director). (2019). *Nîpawistamâsowin: We will stand up* [Film]. Downstream Documentary Productions & National Film Board of Canada.

Lewis, P. (2020). Still stumbling toward Indigenization, reconciliation, and decolonization: We acknowledge the land, now what? In N. K. Denzin & M. D. Giardina (Eds.), *Collaborative futures in qualitative inquiry* (pp. 93–103). Routledge.

Pete, S. (2015). *100 ways to Indigenize and decolonize academic programs and courses*. https://www.uregina.ca/president/assets/docs/president-docs/indigenization/indigenize-decolonize-university-courses.pdf

Regan, P. (2011). *Unsettling the settler within: Indian residential schools, truth telling and reconciliation in Canada*. UBC Press.

Regan, P. (2018). Reconciliation and resurgence: Reflections on the final TRC report. In M. Asch, J. Borrows, & J. Tully (Eds.), *Resurgence and reconciliation: Indigenous settler relations and earth teachings* (pp. 209–228). University of Toronto Press.

Saskatchewan Indigenous Cultural Centre. (2020). *SICC history*. https://www.sicc.sk.ca/about-sicc

Simpson, M. (2003). *Indigenous education*. Indigenous encyclopedia, University of Saskatchewan. https://teaching.usask.ca/indigenoussk/import/Indigenous_education.php

Sinclair, M. (2015, December 15). *5 years after report, Truth and Reconciliation commissioners say progress is "moving too slow."* CBC News. https://www.cbc.ca/news/indigenous/trc-5-years-final-report-1.5841428

Sinclair, M. (2021, January 27). Sen. Murray Sinclair urges Canadians to reckon with systemic racism. *The Current*. https://www.cbc.ca/radio/thecurrent/the-current-for-jan-27-2021-1.5888592/sen-murray-sinclair-urges-canadians-to-reckon-with-systemic-racism-1.5888597

St. Denis, V., & Schick, C. (2003). What makes anti-racist pedagogy in teacher education difficult? Three popular ideological assumptions. *The Alberta Journal of Educational Research, 49*(1), 55–69.

Starblanket, G., & Kiiwetinepinesiik Stark, H. (2018). Towards a relational paradigm—Four points for consideration: Knowledge, gender, land, and modernity. In M. Asch, J. Borrows, & J. Tully (Eds.), *Resurgence and reconciliation: Indigenous settler relations and earth teachings* (pp. 175–208). University of Toronto Press.

Talaga, T. (2017). *Seven fallen feathers: Racism, death, and hard truths in a Northern city*. House of Anansi Press.

Truth and Reconciliation Commission. (2015). *Honouring the truth, reconciling for the future: Summary of the final report of the Truth and Reconciliation Commission of Canada*. https://irsi.ubc.ca/sites/default/files/inline-files/Executive_Summary_English_Web.pdf

Tuck, E. (2018). Biting the hand that feeds us. In M. Spooner & J. McNinch (Eds.), *Dissident knowledge in higher education* (pp. 149–167). University of Regina Press.

CHAPTER 8

Postsecondary Education's Chronic Problem (or, It's About Time)

Alison Taylor and Robyn Taylor-Neu

INTRODUCTION

Discussions about social justice raise questions about aims, means, and beneficiaries. Proponents of a "recognitive approach" suggest that social justice involves an open-ended process of challenging oppressive institutional conditions and practices that impede the development of marginalized groups (Gale, 2000). Within universities, such conditions and practices are related to access (including tuition costs), how different forms and kinds of knowledge are valued, and how degree programs are organized. A less obvious element of this oppressive infrastructure is *time*: universities' structures and processes are underpinned by capitalist time logics.

This chapter explores how the time logic of capitalism permeates university students' discourse around the relation between schoolwork and paid work. Through this exploration, we demonstrate the extent to which institutions of higher education are coextensive with the market economic domains that they inhabit; the university is thoroughly permeated by the political-economic logics of its milieu. Although the imbrication of postsecondary education and economy has been analyzed and critiqued from various angles, our discussion suggests that this association has become thoroughly normalized. Indeed, the "marketization" of higher education has been normalized to the degree that it is difficult to imagine how it could be otherwise. By focusing on students' narratives about the links between school and work, we demonstrate the banality of this co-implication—a banality that masks the real, pernicious effects of the marketization of education. By the same stroke, we suggest why attempts to reimagine a "socially just" university without confronting the logic of market exchange leave the fundamental structures unchanged.

In what follows, we first examine how students' conceptions of time recapitulate the time logics ingredient to industrial and post-industrial modes of production. We tease out the ways that such conceptions are imbricated in commonplace idioms that depict time as a concrete, divisible resource: an object to be budgeted and parceled out strategically. Through this analysis, we show how linguistic structures and practices support, reinscribe, and naturalize dominant political economic structures. Yet perhaps things could be otherwise.

Language shapes our reality and values, and different sociocultural linguistic structures articulate different conceptions of time. Likewise, we might imagine alternative political economies of time. Accordingly, in this chapter's concluding section, we sketch one such alternative: a vision in which time is not a finite resource but, rather, a gift. The vision of an academy that embraces the gift of Indigenous epistemes has been proposed by Kuokkanen (2007). Our analysis takes a slightly different tack. In addressing the affinity between university and capitalist time logics before presenting an alternative temporal frame rooted in the logic of the gift, we highlight the radical changes necessary for human flourishing.

I. LIKE CLOCKWORK: TIME IN STUDENTS' DISCOURSE

In discussing their schoolwork and paid work, students depict time as a finite resource: to be conserved, invested, spent judiciously, or wasted. Their discourse reflects the time logics (*qua* chrono-logics) that E. P. Thompson (1967) identifies with the industrial capitalist modes of production. Moreover, such forms of time-talk are inscribed in linguistic practice and structure: English and other Indo-European languages facilitate certain conceptions of time and preclude others. On the one hand, a dominant political economy of time at once presumes and entails corresponding linguistic frames and scaffolds. On the other hand, these linguistic formations serve to naturalize their political economic milieu.

For students, this political economic milieu is characterized by precarious work and competing demands. Following the notion of the "double shift" experienced by women who balance paid labour with unpaid domestic labour (see, e.g., Hochschild & Machung, 1989), we suggest that contemporary working students juggle triple or quadruple "shifts." This sense of competing demands on time—construed as a finite resource—emerges through students' frequent references to "wasting time," "eating time," and "losing time." Likewise, students' remarks about "investing" in future careers reflects a sense that "time is money" (to a degree unanticipated in this oft-cited quip). These renditions of time resonate with E. P. Thompson's analysis of the time logics of capitalism.

Thompson (1967) historicizes predominant time logics by attending to their material bases—their rootedness in historically specific relations of production.

A task-orientation to time was evident in rural fishing and farming communities, where the required tasks influenced by nature (e.g., tides, weather) shaped the length of the workday. Before the advent of large-scale machine-powered industry, and where people were in control of their working lives, a common work pattern involved alternate "bouts of intense labour and of idleness" (p. 31). This idea is echoed by Bataille (1988), who describes the rhythm in a general economy as the "alternation of austerity, which accumulates, with prodigality, which dissipates" (p. 87).

Some commentators associate the emergence of a "clock time" orientation with puritanism and industrial capitalism in western Europe (see, e.g., Bataille, 1988, p. 125). As more workers entered industrial employment, employers began to control labour time to ensure it would not be "wasted." In the mid-18th century, American Founding Father Benjamin Franklin expressed the spirit of capitalism succinctly:

> Remember that time is money. He that can earn ten shillings a day by his labour, and goes abroad, or sits idle, one half of that day, though he spends but sixpence during his diversion or idleness, ought not to reckon *that* the only expense; he has really spent, or rather thrown away, five shillings besides. Remember that money is of the prolific, generating nature. Money can beget money, and its offspring can beget more, and so on. (Cited in Bataille, 1988, p. 126)

Schools played (and continue to play) an important part in habituating children to constant employment. Throughout the 18th century, although workers fought over time (for a reduced workweek and hours), the new time discipline prevailed (Thompson, 1967). Leisure—and especially the leisure of the masses—came to be seen as a problem. By the 19th century, in mature capitalist society, "all time must be consumed, marketed, put to use; it is offensive for the labour force merely to 'pass the time'" (Thompson, 1967, p. 35).

Thompson (1967) concludes by contrasting two alternative futures for a society with more time for leisure. One maintains a commodity-valuation orientation to time and preserves a focus on how time is used or exploited; the other involves a relearning of more "natural" work rhythms. The latter, for Thompson, might include how to "fill the interstices of [one's] days with enriched, more leisurely, personal and social relations" (p. 37). In the postscript to a book on the politics of contemporary working life, Haug (2009) echoes Thompson's concern with recreating the art of living. Her discussion of the need to redistribute human activities into spheres that include socially reproductive work and political life, as well as wage labour and lifelong development, recognizes that time is enacted in social practices that are marked by gender and race, as well as social class. Therefore, a redistribution of human activities with social justice aims would require different areas of activity, in particular social-reproduction and economic production, to be more equally valued, with societal members being able to participate in all (Fraser, 2016). We elaborate a similar vision below, in terms of a "gift of time."

In the more than 50 years since Thompson was writing, economic life has continued to transform, as Ogle (2019) describes as involving

> the de-standardization of working hours and work rhythms since the 1970s, with the gradual introduction of work from home (again, with important gendered implications) and other schemes emphasizing flexibility, but also, with the impact of instant communication technologies that make the geographical location (or rather, time zone) of a workplace less relevant, the waning and replacement of certain socio-temporal and even natural rhythms such as day and night. (pp. 317–318)

For many workers, economic transformations since the 1970s translate into more part-time, temporary, flexible forms of work or unemployment as opposed to the full-time, lifelong employment associated with Fordist large-scale mass production. From Fordism to post-Fordism and globalized capitalism, "capital kept its stranglehold over time well within its tightened grip" (Palmer, 2021, p. 33), leaving workers with few options other than to try to outsmart or control time (Walker, 2009).

Modernist narratives of linear progress toward a better future have therefore been unsettled in a number of countries, with unfortunate consequences for many youth (Allison, 2012). Post-Fordist labour is defined by its "irregular and uncertain temporalities," which are evident in studies of precarious work and unemployment (Millar, 2015, p. 30). Time discipline in flexible production systems is more multifaceted than Fordist factory discipline (Glennie & Thrift, 1996). Sennett (2006) observes that "unlike the self-disciplined worker who is dedicated to working his or her way up the bureaucracy, the kind of worker required in the 'new economy' is one who manages short term relationships and themselves, while migrating from task to task, job to job, place to place" (p. 4). While Sennett appears to be nostalgic for a more stable past, Thompson's historical work suggests the extent to which precarity is bound up with capitalism—"the very condition of having to depend on a wage to sustain one's life is what makes a worker precarious" (Millar, 2017, p. 6). Precarity and the temporal structuring of time more generally are bound up with patriarchy and racism too (Colley, 2007).

An examination of the relationship between time and the lived experiences of work for diverse groups is thus important. The study referenced here examines undergraduate students' experiences of "balancing" work and studies. Over half of university students work while studying, often in retail and accommodations, food and beverage, or teaching sectors (Taylor et al., 2020). Average wages are slightly above the minimum wage, and work schedules are often unpredictable. However, there is significant variation in students' working conditions. While most working students experience some degree of time pressure throughout the year, this pressure is particularly intense for those who are financially insecure and who have caring responsibilities for themselves and others. While most undergraduates have some financial support from parents, a small proportion relies primarily on work income and student loans. For such financially insecure students, working while studying is often less stressful than accumulating yet more debt as they struggle to make ends meet. Consequently, they are often less willing to take risks in decisions around work and studies.

For example, Jenny is a white student who comes from a low-income, single-parent family and has been reliant on student loans and income from working to pay her living costs. She has worked at various cleaning, retail, and food services jobs since she was 13 years old and comments that she was reluctant to apply for research assistant positions at the university because of the "insecurity of knowing if I'm gonna get them." At the same time, she acknowledges that her employer at a grocery store exerts pressure on students to work certain hours while not providing training: "You're kind of disposable. You just are, as a student. And I know that even my old manager just didn't invest as much time in me, in training me, than, like, as she did with the full-time employees. Yeah, like I was considered an asset, but not the priority, I guess." The willingness to put up with such precarious work is common for many college students, who are often more preoccupied with future professional careers than immediate workplace problems (Tannock & Flocks, 2003). Yet Jenny is afraid she will "burn out" by the time she graduates because she is working year-round in addition to studying. She plans to delay applying to graduate school for a few years so that she can pay down her debt and "find a healthier balance."

In contrast, Anil is a South Asian international student who is primarily supported financially by his family while he takes an applied degree and has made the decision (with parental input) to accept only career-related work. He recounts a conversation with his father when he discussed taking a job at Tim Hortons to "maybe get the kind of experience which North American kids have since high school and maybe become a better speaker, better server." And his father said, "Why do you want to do that?" To which Anil replied, "Yes, it doesn't apply to anything." Instead, he has found jobs on campus that are directly related to his studies and where employers are attuned to and accommodate the busy schedules of full-time students.

Anil's academic journey is described as a family investment, and this investment influences his relationship to time (and space), for example, the decision about whether or not to apply for cooperative education (which extends the duration of students' degrees). He shares

> North American kids, their parents' savings work different from their savings. They have their own savings. But for us, it doesn't work like that. My savings are my parents' savings and those are my sister's savings as well.... I would do what is the best for the family, for having more money in the family. Because ... if I do a cheaper co-op now, I would spend the same time for earning less money while my father can support me right now. But it's the same money, right?

Anil's comments demonstrate the extent to which transitions (defined as a process of change over time) include social expectations that vary across cultures. Further, the time value of money differs for students like Anil, who are moving from countries where the cost of living and tuition is much lower, where they often have greater access to scholarships and would not need to work while studying. This was Anil's situation before he transferred to a Canadian university. Further, his story reveals the invisible labour involved as international students prepare for admission tests and applications, work to attain and demonstrate English language proficiency, and spend months trying to transfer credits. While Anil has been quite successful in finding work on campus related to his studies, his adjustment to life in Canada also took time and energy, as he learned how to take care of himself (learning how to cook and clean), gained comfort operating in English, and developed a peer support network.

Not surprisingly, Anil is unwilling to consider switching programs at this point: "I would be stupid ... and my parents won't allow it." Although he enjoys taking arts electives, he believes his opportunities are mostly driven by the pay he will get and "the working conditions," which he believes are the best in North America right now. He also believes that 20 to 30 "is the prime age of gaining knowledge" and plans to take a graduate program after completing his undergraduate degree.

Mandy is also an international student, but Canadian tuition and living expense costs are less than what she would pay in her home country, and she has parental support. Still, she faces other challenges that impede her ability to engage in the kind of short-term and long-term planning undertaken by peers. For example, in a focus group conversation where participants were asked for one word to describe their university experience she responds to another student, Jocelyn:

Jocelyn: A marathon.
Mandy: Overwhelming.
Interviewer: Do you want to expand on that? Marathon?

Jocelyn: So, like I, so many people burn out halfway through the first semester 'cause they're like, "Go, go, go, go, go—get those grades." ... I know the secret.... Like I have a calendar that is visible every day when I wake up that has all my deadlines on it. And then if I have a particularly busy time coming up, I have all my deadlines on sticky notes and I put like the date on it, like this is the 28th, I have a paper due.

Mandy: Sometimes, I find like, all the deadlines slightly suffocating and in order to [*pause*] cope with it, I put myself in a little bit of a state of denial.... you [Jocelyn] definitely do know the secret, the secret is to you know, be able to look at that calendar and to break things up and to do [a] few things at a time.... But sometimes, I like look at the lists of all the things I have to do and I'm just like, that cannot possibly be right. I'm just like, I need to cover myself in piles of blankets and hide from it and hope it will go away, and it never does.

Mandy has considered leaving university and explains her response as follows:

It's really discouraging to see myself do poorly in things that I'm really invested in. You know, like when I put off some work or something, it's not out of laziness, it's out of like the inability to be in like the emotional state to tackle it right now. And that's definitely hard because like [*pause*] there is so much competition on the [university] campus and there are so many people that do so well, if not flawlessly.... So, you know, trying to compete with people who may not have the same obstacles as I do. And you know, consistently seeing like those shortcomings in my grades and in my resume and in my inability to find research positions, makes it really hard to keep it up.

Mandy is well aware that "there is definitely like a system around like building a resume and prioritizing your GPA, and I think if you do that really well, then there are a lot of doors that just kind of open." However, she feels unable "to compete" because her grades and relationships with professors are impacted by her learning disability and mental health challenges. Her relationship to time is impacted by the hours and energy required to maintain her well-being, including mindfulness and fitness activities, medical appointments, the need to take frequent breaks from schoolwork, adapting to changing medications, and the ongoing work required to seek accommodations from the university and professors.

Although she knows what it takes to "succeed" within the system, Mandy also expresses concern about a system that perpetuates a culture of overwork: "I definitely think there's a reward system around people who, you know, can't say no and maybe some have some unhealthy [laugh] working habits, but are really, really hard working." Mandy did not want to specialize too early in her degree because she enjoys the "act of learning"; in her first two years, she took electives in anything that interested her. She sees her undergraduate degree as "just like pursuit of knowledge" and would like to pursue graduate studies. Mandy adds that she would like her paid jobs to align with her values, although her work has been "draining" (care work) and "exhausting" (fundraising). Because she is unable to handle a full course load, she takes courses year-round in order to graduate "on time" and reduce the financial burden on her parents. Mandy's discourse exposes both the extent to which expectations have been normalized as well as the anxiety that results from tensions in time logics as activities that are not easily time bound (e.g., learning) become governed by clock time.

Jenny, Anil, and Mandy demonstrate the diversity of students' constructions and experiences of time in its different dimensions. Their stories suggest that each has experienced time pressures because of their individual situations—Jenny needs to work all year to survive economically, and Anil's labour of trying to integrate into Canadian society is invisible, as is Mandy's work in addressing her mental health and learning challenges. Yet university schedules and programs tend to assume a student with few outside commitments or constraints. Mandy expresses gratitude for the opportunity to talk about the normalization of the student juggling act:

> I think it's really important because like there is a dehumanization of all these people doing all this work. Because we're all killing ourselves to get our GPA and like why does it matter that one person is killing themselves. It's not an individual experience anymore. We're just like a collective group of tortured souls [*laugh*], not to be dramatic or anything.

It is common for people in Western societies to think about time as equal units divided into past, present, and future. Time is seen as linear and irreversible (Colley, 2007). However, it is a mistake to assume that this way of thinking about time is universal. For example, time in traditional African thought consisted of actual events experienced in human relations and contexts (Parratt, 1977). As we suggest above, ideas about time are also related to economic changes that occurred from the 17th century to the present (cf. Millar, 2015; Thompson, 1967).

Linguist Benjamin Whorf (1944) further argues that linear conceptions of time are related to the structure of western European languages. Whorf posits that members of a linguistic community inherit a particular structure of language that shapes their life habits and social institutions. In comparing western European languages with an Indigenous language (Hopi), Whorf notes that the grammar of each language system bears a clear relation to culture. For example, the three-tense system of language used in western European languages (past, present, future) encourages us to imagine time as an "objectified configuration of points on a line" (Whorf, 1944, p. 204). We tend to estimate the future in the same way that we record the past, "producing programs, schedules, budgets," and the impact of the way we fit our behaviour to our temporal order is evident also in the way we use watches, clocks, and calendars to "measure time ever more precisely" (p. 211). Likewise, European languages objectify non-spatial situations using physical metaphors. For example, we "grasp the thread" of others' arguments even when they are "over our head" (p. 205).

In contrast, Hopi concepts of time and space are constructed quite differently. For example, in the Hopi language, time is not a motion on a space but instead "a relation between two events in lateness" (Whorf, 1944, p. 201). While Hopi nouns are very concrete, its grammatical tenses can be quite abstract. Unlike western European languages then, holistic and relativistic views of reality can be talked about in ways that appeal to the common sense of speakers. Language thus shapes our thought worlds, and people tend to "*act about* situations in ways which are like the ways they *talk about* them" (Whorf, 1944, p. 207; emphasis added). For example, if we emphasize "saving time," this objectification leads to the "high valuation of speed." The term *fast capitalism*, commonly used to describe the global economy today, suggests the persistent valuation of speed, aided by advances in technology (Agger, 2004).

Despite this hegemonic construction, working students' comments reveal tensions in industrial and post-industrial time logics and, to varying degrees, concerns about the institutional normalization of the super-student. It is apparent that the constructions of time as money and education as investment are problematic for different students in different ways. More generally, such constructions are intertwined with a social order that privileges competition, hyperindividualism, profit, and the externalization of social responsibility (Kuokkanen, 2007).

II. LEAKY CHRONO-LOGICS: GIVEN TIME

Yet there are other ways of talking about time that articulate other chrono-logics and suggest alternative political economies of time. In this section, we draw out these other possibilities. By identifying tensions and contradictions within students' discourses of time, we have illustrated that the dominant logics of time are "leaky"; the cracks and fissures in these chrono-logics afford glimpses of other possible political economies of time. One such economy is that of the gift, which gives insofar as it gives *time*. In revisiting conceptual and ethnographic discussions of gift economy, we trace out a logic of "general economy" within which time ceases to be a commodity to be partitioned, managed, and parsimoniously spent and instead becomes an "unsecured investment" in the social good.

It is unsurprising that students feel the need to be future-oriented and to engage in calculations about how they spend their time given the messages they receive from politicians and parents. Bataille (1988) observed in 1949 that capitalist society reduces what is human to the condition of a thing—a commodity. This reduction continues to be perpetuated through the discourse of human capital, which has been a defining feature of neoliberalism and a dominant subjective form since the 1980s (Feher, 2009). Human capital discourse refers to the development of skills that are expected to yield future returns in the labour market through investments in formal education and training. Still, young people are also told that secure jobs and lifetime employment are passé. With increasing educational attainment, competition for professional jobs has intensified, and a university parchment is viewed as but one part of the graduate's portfolio (Brown et al., 2010). Investing in one's human capital involves not only earning a credential but also gaining employability skills. In this section, we address the problematic aspects of "time is money" and "education for developing human capital" discourses by exploring an alternative perspective rooted in the logic of gift exchange.

The concept of the gift has attracted a host of writers, including Mauss, Derrida, and Bourdieu, who have been concerned about political questions related to how human beings treat each other and how to encourage an ethic of generosity (Schrift, 1997). While commodity exchange constructs quantitative relationships among the objects transacted, "the gift functions mainly as a system of social relations, for forming alliances, communities, and solidarity" (Kuokkanen, 2007, p. 23). In gift exchange, the actual objects transferred are less important than the value of the relationships between subjects. Such exchange implies obligation and creates a cycle of reciprocity (Schrift, 1997). This being said, writers do not always treat gift exchange and commodity exchange as if they are diametrically opposed.

For both Derrida and Bourdieu, the time lapse "between the gift and the counter-gift ... makes it possible to mask the contradiction between the experienced (or desired) truth of the gift as a generous, gratuitous, unrequited act, and the truth that emerges from the model, which makes it a stage in a relationship of exchange that transcends singular acts of exchange" (Bourdieu, 1997, pp. 231–232). The logic of gift exchange, as a social act, leads to the establishment of durable relationships, unlike commodity exchange, which promotes calculation and the pursuit of material interests. In a similar vein, Bataille (1988) argues that the economy should be conceived in terms of excess and the need to share wealth instead of scarcity and the need to be parsimonious with time and resources. While a *restrictive* economy calls for utilitarian calculation, the economic logic of a *general* economy calls for expenditure of excess. A general economy mimics the radiation of the sun, which gives the gift of energy without reciprocation (Bataille, 1988).

Kuokkanen (2007) concurs that while markets are founded on the principle of scarcity, a gift exchange assumes abundance. She highlights the importance of a gift economy for many Indigenous people, "for whom giving entails an active relationship between the human and natural worlds, one characterized by reciprocity, a sense of collective responsibility, and reverence toward the gifts of the land" (p. 23). Gift-giving challenges competitive individualism, instead fostering values related to cooperation and care. For Kuokkanen, the act of embracing the disruptive idea of Indigenous epistemes as gift would serve to move universities toward the long-term goal of redressing epistemic dispossession, exclusion, and marginalization. The concept of the gift, in her view, can form the basis for an alternative paradigm that acknowledges responsibility and interdependence.

Such a paradigm would productively include alternative ways of constructing time. The fact that justice is often depicted using the image of balanced scales reminds us that "contractarian notions of equal exchange inform our most fundamental model of human interaction" (Schrift, 1997, p. 19). This image recalls the idea of retributive justice, which is primarily concerned with fairness in the competition for goods (Gale, 2000). This paper adopts a position that is closer to recognitive justice; we argue for an alternative logic that prioritizes values of care, cooperation, and bonding—gift logic. Kuokkanen (2007) argues that adopting this logic in higher education is an essential part of the process of decolonizing education by recognizing the value of Indigenous epistemes. We argue that adopting this logic in higher education requires a collective societal investment in institutions in order to produce the economic and social conditions for virtue and generosity. Such an investment requires critical awareness of people's sociopolitical and cultural locations, needs, and expectations (Fraser, 2009).

An obvious "gift of time" would mean that governments offer university education freely as a public good and help support students through the kind of student finance regimes that are provided in some Nordic countries (Garritzmann, 2016). The disparities in costs for international and domestic students and between professional and other programs, for example, would also need to be addressed so that all students have opportunities to participate fully in university education. Most importantly, the gift of time would expand the aims of education and curricular knowledge to become more respectful of the diversity of students and the unpredictability of their transitions. While there are still likely to be schedules and timetables, the priority on *clock time* (where time is the measure of labour) would give way to a new emphasis on *process time* (where the duration of social practices, tasks, and processes is the measure of time) (Colley et al., 2014). Such changes in the temporal and, by extension, spatial contexts would make it acceptable for university students to be "lost in transition" as they seek to realize their learning needs and form aspirations that give direction to their lives (Colley, 2007).

DISCUSSION QUESTIONS

1. What form of time logic did E. P. Thompson identify with industrial capitalist modes of production?

2. Why is this time logic problematic, according to the authors?

3. What alternative conceptions of time do they suggest are worth consideration?

4. What are possible implications of gift logic for postsecondary education?

REFERENCES

Agger, B. (2004). *Speeding up fast capitalism*. Routledge. https://doi.org/10.4324/9781315631967

Allison, A. (2012). Ordinary refugees: Social precarity and soul in 21st century Japan. *Anthropological Quarterly*, *85*(2), 345–370. https://doi.org/10.1353/anq.2012.0027

Bataille, G. (1988). *The accursed share: An essay on general economy, vol. 1*. (R. Hurley, Trans.). Zone Books.

Bourdieu, P. (1997). Marginalia—some additional notes on the gift. In A. Schrift (Ed.), *The logic of the gift: Toward an ethic of generosity* (pp. 231–241). Routledge. https://doi.org/10.4324/9780203760369

Brown, P., Lauder, H., & Ashton, D. (2010). *The global auction: The broken promises of education, jobs, and incomes*. Oxford University Press. https://doi.org/10.1093/acprof:oso/9780199731688.001.0001

Colley, H. (2007). Understanding time in learning transitions through the lifecourse. *International Studies in Sociology of Education*, *17*(4), 427–443. https://doi.org/10.1080/09620210701667103

Colley, H., Henriksson, L., Niemeyer, B., & Seddon, T. (2014). Putting time to "good" use in educational work: A question of responsibility. In T. Fenwick & M. Nerland (Eds.), *Reconceptualising professional learning: Sociomaterial knowledges, practices and responsibilities* (pp. 198–212). Routledge. https://doi.org/10.4324/9781315813714

Feher, M. (2009). Self appreciation; or, the aspirations of human capital. *Public Culture*, *21*(1), 21–41. https://doi.org/10.1215/08992363-2008-019

Fraser, N. (2009). *Scales of justice: Reimagining political space in a globalizing world*. Columbia University Press. https://doi.org/10.1111/j.1467-8675.2012.00674.x

Fraser, N. (2016). Contradictions of capital and care. *New Left Review*, *100*, 99–117. https://newleftreview.org/issues/ii100/articles/nancy-fraser-contradictions-of-capital-and-care

Gale, T. (2000). Rethinking social justice in schools: How will we recognize it when we see it? *International Journal of Inclusive Education*, *4*(3), 253–269. https://doi.org/10.1080/13603110050059178

Garritzmann, J. L. (2016). *The political economy of higher education finance: The politics of tuition fees and subsidies in OECD countries: 1945–2015*. Springer. https://doi.org/10.1007/978-3-319-29913-6

Glennie, P., & Thrift, N. (1996). Reworking E. P. Thompson's "Time, work-discipline and industrial capitalism." *Time & Society*, *5*(3), 275–299. https://doi.org/10.1177/0961463X96005003001

Haug, F. (2009). A politics of working life. In T. Seddon, L. Henriksson, & B. Niemeyer (Eds.), *Learning and work and the politics of working life: Global transformations and collective identities in teaching, nursing and social work* (pp. 217–225). Routledge. https://doi.org/10.4324/9780203863121

Hochschild, A. R., & Machung, A. (1989). *The second shift: Working parents and the revolution at home*. Viking.

Kuokkanen, R. (2007). *Reshaping the university: Responsibility, indigenous epistemes, and the logic of the gift*. UBC Press.

Millar, K. M. (2015). The tempo of wageless work: E. P. Thompson's time-sense at the edges of Rio de Janeiro. *Focaal*, *2015*(73), 28–40. https://doi.org/10.3167/fcl.2015.730103

Millar, K. M. (2017). Toward a critical politics of precarity. *Sociology Compass*, *11*(6), e12483. https://doi.org/10.1111/soc4.12483

Ogle, V. (2019). Time, temporality and the history of capitalism. *Past & Present*, *243*(1), 312–327. https://doi.org/10.1093/pastj/gtz014

Palmer, B. (2021). The time of our lives: Reflections on work and capitalist temporality. *Socialist Register*, *57*, 14–49. https://socialistregister.com/index.php/srv/article/view/34946

Parratt, J. (1977). Time in traditional African thought. *Religion*, *7*(2), 117–126. https://doi.org/10.1016/0048-721X(77)90019-7

Schrift, A. (1997). Introduction. In A. Schrift (Ed.), *The logic of the gift: Toward an ethic of generosity* (pp. 1–24). Routledge. https://doi.org/10.4324/9780203760369

Sennett, R. (2006). *The culture of the new capitalism*. Yale University Press.

Tannock, S., & Flocks, S. (2003). "I know what it's like to struggle": The working lives of young students in an urban community college. *Labor Studies Journal*, *28*(1), 1–30. https://doi.org/10.1353/lab.2003.0028

Taylor, A., Raykov, M., & Sweet, R. (2020). *Hard working students report of 2018 and 2019 survey findings*. https://hdl.handle.net/2429/73374

Thompson, E. P. (1967). Time, work-discipline, and industrial capitalism. *Past & Present*, *38*, 56–97. https://doi.org/10.1093/past/38.1.56

Walker, J. (2009). Time as the fourth dimension in the globalization of higher education. *The Journal of Higher Education*, *80*(5), 483–509. https://doi.org/10.1353/jhe.0.0061

Whorf, B. L. (1944). The relation of habitual thought and behavior to language. *ETC: A Review of General Semantics*, *1*(4), 197–215.

CHAPTER 9

Critical Pedagogy in Teacher Education: Disrupting Teacher Candidates' Deficit Thinking of Immigrant Students with Origins in the Global South

Yan Guo

INTRODUCTION

> I think that for the most part, immigrant students are seen as immigrants first and students second—that their being is defined principally in terms of difference.... I think that the wider societal perception of immigrant students is that these students are in some way deficient in being fully able to participate in the dominant culture—that there is an implicit "disconnect" with the nuances of native spoken language; while I know this is not the case for these students, I have seen evidence of this perception. (online reflection by a teacher candidate)[1]

The above quote illustrates the identification by a teacher candidate of deficit thinking, evident in dominant social, cultural, and institutional narratives that underpin the representations of immigrant students in the literature, media, curriculum documents, and teachers' daily interactions with immigrant students.

Drawing from critical and postcolonial theoretical perspectives and examples from my earlier research (Guo, 2012a, 2012b) and teaching practice, this chapter demonstrates how I, a teacher educator in Canada in the past 20 years, have implemented some experiential strategies in order to encourage teacher candidates to challenge their largely unexamined deficit thinking regarding their English as an Additional Language (EAL)[2] students. Teacher educators preparing teachers to work effectively and equitably in a linguistically, culturally, and racially diverse context can employ teaching strategies described in this chapter. Sato and colleagues (2017) note that critical pedagogy does not just promote reflection, but encourages active engagement in society so that students "can recognize and transform the unfair and unjust situations around them" (p. 58).

CONTEXT: NATIONAL AND LOCAL SNAPSHOTS

Immigration is now the main source of Canada's population growth. This has significant implications for Canadian school systems and for the preparation of teachers. According to the 2016 census, about 21.1 percent of the population (7.3 million) speaks a language other than English or French as their mother tongue in Canada (Statistics Canada, 2017). Moreover, the long-term prospect for this population trend is continued growth. Calgary is the largest recipient of immigrant and EAL students in Alberta and the fourth-largest urban area in Canada, after Toronto, Vancouver, and Montreal. Foreign-born and Canadian-born EAL students have a strong presence in Canadian society. In Alberta, the number of EAL students rose from 60,000 in 2007 to 128,000 in 2017, which currently represents more than 17 percent of the student population in the province (Alberta Education, 2017), a typical enrolment pattern that is found in other provinces, such as British Columbia (Ilieva, 2016). In the Calgary Board of Education, a large urban school board, more than 25 percent of students were identified as EAL, and they spoke 140 different languages.

Given the increasing linguistic and cultural diversity of the Canadian population, existing teacher education programs cannot prepare sufficient numbers of teacher specialists for the EAL school population. This strongly suggests that all teachers need to be prepared to teach EAL students. Teacher candidates tend to be white, middle-class, female, and monolingual (Hodgkinson, 2002). Today's immigrant students are mostly from Asia, Africa, the Middle East, Central and South America, and the Caribbean (Statistics Canada, 2017). This cultural, racial, and linguistic divide between teachers and students has major implications for appropriate teacher education. Indeed, many classroom teachers have not received the preparation required to help EAL learners achieve their best (Garnett, 2012).

CRITICAL EXAMINATION OF DEFICIT THINKING: A SYNTHESIS

EAL students bring their languages, cultures, religions, and educational backgrounds to our schools, enriching our educational environments. However, many teacher candidates use deficit-oriented discourses, highlighting EAL students' inability to speak English and their difficulties in communicating in schools. Deficit thinking includes making overgeneralizations about students' family backgrounds, having low expectations of students' achievements, creating caring classroom environments at the expense of students' academic successes, and, importantly, holding mainstream monocultural views of appropriate childrearing practices and criteria for school success. Many teacher candidates believe that many EAL students' educational risks and vulnerabilities could be linked to adverse sociocultural factors such as poverty, limited English proficiency, and racial or ethnic minority status. These generalizations perpetuate the traditional missionary perspective that EAL children and families are deficient and in need of remediation. Deficit thinking about immigrants and their children permeates mainstream society and is largely mirrored in schools.

It is important for teacher educators to engage teacher candidates to actively resist deficit perceptions of EAL learners, whereby "the inability to speak standard English is oftentimes equated with low levels of cognitive functioning" (Goodwin & Macdonald, 1997, p. 212). In my classes, we discuss how *difference* is perceived as *deficit* and how that leads to the *devaluation* of EAL children's and their families' knowledge (Guo, 2009). Accordingly, the rich cultural, linguistic, and religious knowledge of EAL students is often unrecognized by teachers and school administrators (Cummins et al., 2005). Deficit thinking can be attributed to misconceptions of difference and lack of knowledge about different cultures (Guo, 2009). A deficit model of difference leads to the belief that difference is equal to deficiency and that the knowledge of others—particularly those from developing countries—is incompatible, inferior, and hence invalid (Abdi, 2007). If teacher candidates hold these attitudes, even tacitly, they may fail to recognize and make use of EAL students' prior knowledge.

Feeling Unprepared

Some teacher candidates were shocked to see the large number of EAL students in their practicum schools (Guo, 2012b). They commented that there was not enough training offered in teaching EAL in their on-campus courses. They felt overwhelmed and helpless because they did not know how to support EAL children (Guo, 2012b). Some teacher candidates chose to ignore EAL students and perceived the difficulties faced by EAL students as evidence that there is something wrong with these students. In my teaching, I often used a language shock activity. The students were asked to follow my directions in Chinese in an activity. They were also asked to observe their peers' physical reactions and share their emotional responses at the end of the activity. I noticed that some of them quickly became frustrated. This language shock activity provided an opportunity for the teacher candidates to experience firsthand what it was like to be an

EAL student. Students commented, "I didn't truly feel what it was like for EAL students to sit and learn in class until she [Yan] forced us into that situation." Another student commented, "we really feel the exclusion that the [EAL] students feel." I also hoped that they would become more sensitive to their students' affective needs in their future teaching.

Challenging Discrimination of Southern Accents

One of the major dilemmas teacher candidates reported is that some EAL children speak English with non-traditional accents. Accordingly, despite significant differences in regional accents in Canada, the United States, and the United Kingdom, such differences are allowed. Interestingly, accents from the countries of the Global South are highlighted and perceived to be different from the standard Canadian English accent spoken on the Canadian Broadcasting Corporation (CBC). Perhaps more problematically, difference is, unfortunately, perceived to be a marker of unintelligence, as made evident in this reflection by a teacher candidate: "For example, if I am teaching a student with a strong accent, I find myself generalizing that the students' English comprehension may in some way lack fluency. I know that this is not the case, but I cannot help changing the way in which I speak to these students."

In challenging the notion that accents are equated with unintelligence, I invited the teacher candidates to read the essay "Mother Tongue" by Amy Tan (1990), a well-known American writer. In this essay, Tan recalls that when she was young, she felt ashamed of her mother's English. She was embarrassed because she usually had to accompany her mother to her appointments and translate for her. Much later she realized that her mother's "broken" English was not a marker of unintelligence. On the contrary, her "simple" English revealed "her intent, her passion, her imagery, the rhythms of her speech and the nature of her thoughts" (Tan, 1990, p. 8). Eventually, Tan claimed her mother's linguistic and cultural heritage with pride. She realized that it was not her mother who was unintelligent, but the false stereotype of immigrants held by the larger society. I used this essay to raise the following questions with the class: Why was Tan ashamed of her mother's English when she was young? In your field experience, did you think that EAL students felt ashamed of their English accents? What did you do to support EAL students? What made Tan change her perception of her mother's English? Explain what Tan means by "different Englishes." Describe the differences between the way Tan viewed her mother's "simple" English, in contrast with the way the rest of society viewed her mother's "broken" English. How did Tan struggle with these conflicting views? How did Tan claim her mother's linguistic and cultural heritage with pride? Why is it important to build on EAL students' pride in their own linguistic and cultural resources? How are you going to build on EAL students' linguistic and cultural resources in the classroom?

I also read a part of Amy Tan's (1989) novel *The Joy Luck Club* with the class. Rose, an American-born woman, sacrifices her own desires in order to make her husband, Ted, happy. Gradually Ted becomes tired of her and decides to divorce her. Rose, without her husband, the decision-maker, does not know what to do. She goes to a psychiatrist for help, which her mother thinks is quite foolish. Rose's mother tells her that "a mother is best. A mother knows what is inside you ... a psyche-atricks will only make you *hulihudu* [or *hulihutu* 糊里糊涂], make you see *heimongmong* [or *heimengmeng* 黑蒙蒙]" (p. 210). Rose's mother uses Chinese expressions not only to preserve her right to speak Chinese but also to suggest to her daughter that her Chinese way of thinking is better than that of Rose's American-trained psychiatrist. The Chinese expressions also enable an important cultural connection between mother and daughter. To her surprise, Rose realizes that "it was true. Lately I had been feeling *hulihudu*. And everything around me seemed to be *heimongmong*. These were words I had never thought about in English terms. I suppose the closest meaning would be 'confused' and 'dark fog'" (p. 210). Rose's mother has thus been able to point out what is wrong with her daughter, namely, that Rose is disoriented because she has lost her polestar, her husband. In order to help Rose learn to make a choice for herself, Rose's mother tells her daughter how she learned to speak back to those who tried to silence her. She simply asks Rose, "Why do you not speak up for yourself?" (p. 216). After having learned her mother's story, Rose comes to understand the significance of finding one's voice. I used this dialogue as an example to demonstrate how the Chinese mother's playful and creative pun, "psyche-atricks," and the use of her Chinese words explicitly reveal her intent, her sense of humour, and her wisdom. This effectively dispels societal stereotypes that link intelligence to one's accent.

English-Only Policy and Resultant Devaluation of Students' First Language

As stated earlier, more than 25 percent of the student population of the local public school board were identified as EAL students, and they spoke 140 different languages. Despite multilingual realities, one teacher candidate noted, "our school system, from curriculum to assessment to teacher preparation is predicated on a monolingual bias." Several schools adopted an English-only policy, as evidenced by another teacher candidate's comment:

> One of the school rules is ENGLISH ONLY throughout the entire building. Students have received lectures from various members of administration for not speaking English in the common areas or in classrooms or on their break time. Teachers also receive lectures for enforcing this rule.

The teacher candidates stated that even though in some schools "English only" was not publicly promoted, in practice their partner teachers appeared to have a fear of different languages. Some parents also supported the "English only" policy and practice. They believed that their children should speak only English and discouraged the use of the first/home language.

In my class, we critiqued the monolingual principle, which emphasizes "instructional use of the target language (TL) to the exclusion of students' home language (L1), with the goal of enabling learners to think in the TL with minimal interference from the L1" (Cummins, 2009, p. 317). Some teachers firmly believe that the students' first language interferes with effective second language learning and school achievement. They believe that students should be taught exclusively in English in schools (Garcia-Nevarez et al., 2005), although the efficacy of this practice has been refuted by many scholars (Cummins, 2009; Garcia & Li, 2013). However, the English-only policy adopted in some schools suggests that many administrators and teachers still strongly hold a belief in this practice. For example, one teacher candidate wrote, "I saw the English-only policy being enforced several times, and it became this taboo to be caught even whispering in any language other than English." There is no empirical evidence to support the claim that English is best taught monolingually. Educators must abolish the damaging view that stamping out immigrant students' languages will somehow ensure educational success. They need to recognize students' first languages as an important component of their identity, a useful tool for thinking and learning, and a valuable medium for effective communication in the family and the community.

Critiquing the "dominant discourses of schooling as an English monolingual ... space" (Giampapa, 2010, p. 416), I invited teacher candidates to examine their own attitudes toward EAL students' first languages. Some teacher candidates reported that they were blind to EAL students' multilingual abilities. One wrote, "I don't view my students as bilingual or multilingual speakers. I view them all as children. I can't say that it crosses my mind to think of them in that way." Others offered a good critique of the English-only policy in their practicum schools but did not take sides in the ongoing debate in Canada and the United States. Some wanted to use students' first language but were discouraged by their partner teachers, who were not comfortable with the students' first language. Some bilingual teacher candidates related to their own experience with how they felt their cultural identity was devalued when they were discouraged from speaking their first languages. Their own experience in school helped them identify with EAL students. As students, it was obvious to them that their first languages were seen as inferior. They were caught in a situation of coercive power relations that traditionally oppressed minorities by subordinating the first languages of EAL students (Cummins, 2000).

From Monolingualism to Multilingualism

It is important for teacher educators to help teacher candidates shift their perceptions from viewing multilingualism as a problem to viewing it as a valuable resource. Concerns often expressed by teachers regarding the use of students' first languages in classrooms may, indeed, reflect their ideological beliefs (Karathanos, 2010). As Auerbach (1993) notes, "whether or not we support the use of learners' L1 is not just a pedagogical matter: It is a political one, and the way that we address it in instruction is both a mirror of and a rehearsal for relations of power in the broader society" (p. 10). Accordingly, teacher educators need to guide teacher candidates to challenge their existing and often unacknowledged beliefs and assumptions about students' first language use (e.g., the students' first language interferes with second language learning). A critical reflection via journaling processes, as well as other means, including the use of dual-language books, can be implemented. In my class, I demonstrated how to use dual-language books. I chose *Story of the Chinese Zodiac* (十二生肖的故事) by Monica Chang (1994) to read in English and in Chinese. Most of my students were unfamiliar with the story. It was a good opportunity to demonstrate how to provide background information and culturally relevant materials. This example illustrates how teachers can reconceptualize pedagogies that build on students' multilingual resources (Giampapa, 2010).

I was aware that some teacher candidates felt overwhelmed by the number of languages in the classroom. Ideally teacher candidates should learn a second language. Even if they do not understand a second language, it is important for them to develop translingual dispositions (Lee & Canagarajah, 2019) and to create a classroom environment that is open to different languages. I shared a story of a kindergarten teacher—a former graduate student—who invited parents who spoke 11 different languages to be part of a family reading program in her classroom. Every Friday, she allocated 25 minutes for parent volunteers to read to small groups of children, often from dual-language books, on their own or with a partner parent reading the English text (Guo, 2012a). The teacher reported the children's increasing appreciation of their classmates' multilingual abilities as well as the fact that the parents of these children valued the opportunity to share their first languages and be part of the learning community. This example validates the students' first language within the classroom. Furthermore, it challenges the colonial ideology associated with the superiority of speaking only one language, English, over speaking multiple languages (Yu, 2010). Validating students' first languages also challenges the ascribed subordinate status of many minority groups and affirms students' identities as being competent learners (Cummins, 2009).

In addition to dual-language books, we also explored the use of bilingual "identity texts" (Cummins et al., 2005). Identity texts are the product of students' creative works or performances in which their identities are reflected in a positive light. In the identity text project, EAL students who were often quite disengaged from writing in English became so engaged that they did not want to leave the classroom for recess. Through the demonstration of the effectiveness of dual-language books and identity texts, I sought to engage teacher candidates to challenge monolingual and monocultural perspectives in education and, hopefully, to foster multilingual and multicultural approaches to teaching and learning that draw from the linguistic and cultural forms of capital and include the identities of students and their families (Bourdieu, 1991). Some bilingual teacher candidates became role models for their students. Some teacher candidates started to consider incorporating the first language of their students. Others expressed the desire to use students' first language in their future teaching but were uncertain how to do so. Some shared experiences of how their partner teachers used their students' first language in math classes. In my own classes, I encouraged students to share different math games. One teacher candidate brought a math card game from Italy. She showed us how to play the card game and taught us how to say simple Italian words. In my teaching, I invite the teacher candidates who speak different languages to count from 1 to 10. This year, we counted in 11 different languages: Cantonese, Mandarin, Spanish, Italian, German, Vietnamese, Dutch, Urdu, Punjabi, Nepali, and Japanese. I recorded these different languages with the expectation that the teacher candidates could use the recording as a resource for their future teaching. I also hope that they will encourage their own students to do the same thing in their future teaching.

Unlearning Cultural Privileges

In response to the question about how teacher candidates see their own culture, some wonder whether they have a distinctive culture:

> My family and my husband's family are all from the United Kingdom. We are all Caucasian, and we all speak English. We are part of the perceived majority group culture in Canada. So in that sense, I do sometimes feel that I don't have much of a culture because it is so common and accepted.

Others revealed their attitudes of resentment:

> I sometimes feel my culture is overlooked as the focus is on minority groups and maintaining their culture.... There are cultures where Canadian companies will allow certain clothing of different cultures ensuring they are respected for that part of their culture ... but then people are saying Happy Holidays

during Christmas. That spirit of saying Merry Christmas is being pulled away and a part of my culture is disappearing to suit all cultures. I'm saddened inside as my culture is not being respected, it's just being taken away.

This statement revealed a belief in "reverse racism" and some loss of cultural, social, and religious power. They feel their unearned privileges are challenged. This white teacher candidate, for example, expressed the discrepancy of different sets of expectations for people from racialized groups and those from the mainstream. She complained that the spirit of saying Merry Christmas is being taken away without realizing the significant influence of Christian holidays in the school in which Christianity's attitudes, practices, procedures, policies, and very structures privilege the dominant white Euro-Canadian groups and at the same time disadvantage members of racialized groups who may not be Christians (hooks, 1995).

Other teacher candidates observed that diversity was not valued beyond a surface recognition of students' cultures. As a result, some teacher candidates recognized that EAL students were struggling with their cultural identity but found it difficult to support their students' quests because they did not know how to do so: "This grade 2 student felt ashamed to be publicly identified as being Chinese. She rejected her own cultural characteristics, including her Chinese lunch, and chose to distance herself from her ethnic group." Another teacher candidate related this story to her own schooling experience: "During my school years, I never told anyone about my father or my Turkish heritage as I was afraid that I would be ridiculed." Goodwin (1997, p. 126) referred to this behaviour as internalization: "it is a consequence of rejection whereby people who are marginalized and excluded begin to see themselves in those terms and to define others of colour in those terms as well." The incident with the grade 2 student made the teacher candidate think about how she will explore the concept and reality of identity in her own classroom. In my teaching, I invited teacher candidates to see beyond the "heroes and holidays" approach to culture to recognize that culture embraces language, identity, relationships, beliefs, and ways of knowing and learning (Lee et al., 2007). I used a case study collected from my research on immigrant parent engagement, in which I interviewed 38 immigrant parents from 15 countries (Guo, 2012a). Here is an example from one of the interviews. Tyrone reported an incident that happened to a Sudanese family in Calgary:

> One day, a 6-year-old child opened the fridge, got some food out, and played with the food. He went back to the fridge several times and got more food out and played with the food. His mother was tired of this and told the kid and his two siblings, if you guys go again to the fridge, there is a lion there. Her purpose was not to let the kids touch the fridge.... It came out in a classroom

conversation. The 6-year-old told his teacher he could not get food from the fridge because there was a lion there. So automatically, the teacher reported this incident to social services. Social services took it seriously, and they took the kids away. A legal battle dragged the parents to the courts. (Tyrone, Sudan)

I created the following questions: (1) From the Sudanese parent's perspective, what was she trying to do when she said, "There is a lion in the refrigerator"? (2) How did the teacher interpret this incident? Why? (3) As a teacher, how would you deal with the case differently?

It is important for teacher candidates to critically examine the cultural contexts that influenced the development of their own attitudes and beliefs (Solomon & Levine-Rasky, 2003). Some teacher candidates are able to understand their own privileges. One stated that "much of my culture is based on European traditions brought over to Canada years ago. This has largely focused on Christian holidays, values, and beliefs that have strongly influenced how I think." They are able to understand their own biases, such as "my way of doing things was normal." Hopefully, such self-awareness helps them to "challenge Eurocentric beliefs and practices and move from a position that assumes a singular, monocultural reality, to adopting a worldview that is respectful of multiple belief systems" (Guo et al., 2009, p. 574).

Naming Racism

In addition to being linguistically and culturally diverse, the students in the local school board came from different racial backgrounds. However, many teacher candidates were reluctant to engage in discussion of race and racism, a phenomenon also noted by other researchers (Egbo, 2011; Milner, 2006). Being mindful that how teachers construct race significantly impacts their practice and their interactions with students, I invited teacher candidates to pay attention to racial discrimination in their practicum. Some teacher candidates noticed that EAL children were excluded by their peers in the classroom. Other teacher candidates chose to remain silent about racist remarks. They were uncomfortable disrupting the racialized statements because they did not want to "rock the boat." Egbo (2011, p. 32) referred to this behaviour as "engaging the discourse of silence" about racism. Keeping silent about issues of race will make these teacher candidates complicit in the perpetuation of individual and institutional racism.

One teacher candidate blamed the EAL students' failure on their lack of effort. Many of the teacher candidates shared a similar attitude: individual merit, ability, and effort meant success. They failed to recognize that possession of "non-merit"—inherited factors such as wealth, social and cultural capital, and other social conditions—gives some groups privilege over others (Dei, 2008). They failed to recognize that the school generates its attitudes, practices, and structures, which can privilege the dominant white group and may disadvantage members of visible minority groups (hooks, 1995). By not realizing the impact of school culture and other sociocultural conditions, some teacher candidates effectively removed themselves from the systemic change process.

Other teacher candidates noticed that there was a lack of systemic support for EAL students. One noted, "In my practicum school, 70 percent of the children are from another country. At the beginning of the year [the school] had a funding cutback, and the first thing they did was to eliminate the ESL teacher" (focus group). In my classes, we discussed systemic racism toward EAL students. For example, coded EAL students in Alberta receive EAL funding for a maximum of five years. This funding cap for additional support is the "most recent example of a systemic, structural barrier to equitable treatment" (McCarthy & Foxx, 2001, p. 6). EAL learners present a wide range of needs, such as refugees who may have never attended school prior to immigration and who take more than five years to acquire academic English. With no knowledge on caps in the situation, the current fiscal provisions privilege some groups and create inequalities (Young, 2008).

Summary of Strategies
The following strategies and activities can be used to support and encourage teacher candidates to work effectively and equitably in a linguistically, culturally, and racially diverse school context.

- Adopting a language shock activity to challenge teacher candidates to better understand what it feels like to be an EAL student
- Discussing the essay "Mother Tongue" by Amy Tan (1990) in order to challenge accent discrimination and the limited perceptions of "broken English"
- Discussing Amy Tan's (1989) novel *The Joy Luck Club* to gain a better understanding of immigration experiences and, as importantly, the value of immigrant parents' aspirations for their children
- Inviting teacher candidates to examine their own attitudes toward EAL students' first language in order to challenge their monolingual assumptions
- Demonstrating how to use dual-language books by reading, for example, the *Story of the Chinese Zodiac* by Monica Chang (1994) in English and Chinese to illustrate multilingual practices

- Sharing the experience of the teacher who invited parents, grandparents, and community members to their classroom to read dual-language books to students in order to demonstrate multilingual practices and parent engagement
- Inviting teacher candidates to count in different languages to validate the multilingual abilities of their future students
- Incorporating a student's original identity text in English and Urdu in order to build on their future students' linguistic capital and validate their identities
- Inviting teacher candidates to share math games from different cultures to demonstrate how to integrate some aspects of their future students' cultures into different subjects

CONCLUSION

Ways of working with linguistically and culturally diverse learners should be woven throughout teacher education programs (Vanthuyne & Clark, 2015). Accordingly, teacher education programs in today's highly diverse immigration contexts must be reconceptualized. Addressing what it means to teach in multilingual, multicultural, and multiracial schools is essential. Further to the development of interlinguistic and intercultural competencies, we argued elsewhere (Guo et al., 2009) how it is necessary to implement anti-racism education in teacher education so as to overcome an underlying but pervasive fear of difference. The label of difference should be deconstructed and reconstructed. There is a need to move from viewing differences as deficits to understanding and appreciating differences as the most fundamental trait of humanity. Such differences are positive and enrich our lives (Abdi et al., 2012). From this perspective, educators need to see immigrant and all other EAL students as capable of achieving their potential, which is crucial for their overall well-being. From this perspective, it is important to understand the significant knowledge possessed by many EAL students, including their linguistic and cultural backgrounds. It is important for teacher educators to help teacher candidates shift their representations of multilingualism from being "a problem" to seeing students as intelligent and resourceful learners who know how to navigate and survive difficult life challenges. Teacher candidates need to unlearn their privileges. They need to recognize and make use of the knowledge of immigrant students. It is also important for teacher educators to support teacher candidates in developing a critical awareness of cultural and racial discrimination and the deep-seated school policies, attitudes, and beliefs that perpetuate it.

DISCUSSION QUESTIONS

1. How does this chapter challenge or expand your thinking about difference?

2. Why is it important to use students' first languages in the classroom? In your current or future teaching, how do you or plan to use your students' multilingual abilities in the classroom?

3. How can teachers connect with EAL students' home cultures and out-of-school experiences?

4. From the Sudanese parent's perspective, what was she trying to do when she said, "There is a lion in the refrigerator"? How did the teacher interpret this incident? Why? As a teacher, how would you deal with the case differently?

5. Have you witnessed an EAL student who was discriminated against in school based on their name, accent, ethnicity, race, religion, language proficiency, or other factors? Who were the key players? How did it happen? How was it resolved? How does this experience inform your future teaching? Or, as a teacher, how do you deal with racism that your students experience?

NOTES

1. The quotes are taken from a larger research project, funded by Social Sciences and Humanities Research Council, in which the research methodology and research findings are fully documented (see Guo, 2012a, 2012b). All quotes by teacher candidates used in this chapter are taken from their online reflections unless noted as being taken from focus groups.
2. Also called English as a Second Language (ESL) in some provinces.

REFERENCES

Abdi, A. (2007). Global multiculturalism: Africa and the recasting of the philosophical and epistemological plateaus. *Diaspora, Indigenous and Minority Education, 1*(4), 251–264.

Abdi, A., Shultz, L., & Purton, F. (February 23, 2012). *Do we know our new students? Social justice, global citizenship and the dignity of difference.* Workshop conducted at the Conference of the Western Canadian Association for Student Teaching, University of Calgary.

Alberta Education. (2017). *Results analysis 2016/17 Alberta Education*. https://education.alberta.ca/media/3615900/results-analysis.pdf

Auerbach, E. R. (1993). Reexamining English only in the ESL classroom. *TESOL Quarterly, 27*(1), 9–32.

Bourdieu, P. (1991). *Language and symbolic power* (G. Raymond & M. Adamson, Trans.). Polity Press.

Chang, M. (1994). *Story of the Chinese zodiac*. Yuan-Liou Publishing.

Cummins, J. (2000). *Language, power, and pedagogy: Bilingual children in the crossfire*. Multilingual Matters.

Cummins, J. (2009). Multilingualism in the English-language classroom: Pedagogical considerations. *TESOL Quarterly, 43*(2), 317–321.

Cummins, J., Bismilla, V., Chow, P., Cohen, S., Giampapa, F., Leoni, L., Sandhu, P., & Sastri, P. (2005). Affirming identity in multilingual classrooms. *Educational Leadership, 63*(1), 38–43.

Dei, G. J. S. (2008). *Racist beware: Uncovering racial politics in the postmodern society*. Sense Publishers.

Egbo, B. (2011). What should preservice teachers know about race and diversity? Exploring a critical knowledge-base for teaching in 21st century Canadian classrooms. *Journal of Contemporary Issues in Education, 6*(2), 23–37.

García, O., & Li, W. (2013). *Translanguaging: Language, bilingualism and education*. Palgrave Macmillan.

Garcia-Nevarez, A. G., Stafford, M. E., & Arias, B. (2005). Arizona elementary teachers' attitudes toward English language learners and the use of Spanish in the classroom instruction. *Bilingual Research Journal, 29*(2), 295–317.

Garnett, B. (2012). A critical review of the Canadian empirical literature: Documenting generation 1.5's K–16 trajectories. *TESL Canada Journal, 29*(6), 1–24.

Giampapa, F. (2010). Multiliteracies, pedagogy and identities: Teacher and student voices from a Toronto elementary school. *Canadian Journal of Education / Revue canadienne de l'éducation, 33*(2), 407–431.

Goodwin, A. L. (1997). Multicultural stories: Preservice teachers' conceptions of and responses to issues of diversity. *Urban Education, 32*(1), 117–145.

Goodwin, A. L., & Macdonald, M. B. (1997). Educating the rainbow: Authentic assessment and authentic practice for diverse classrooms. In A. L. Goodwin (Ed.), *Assessment for equity and inclusion: Embracing all our children* (pp. 211–228). Routledge.

Guo, S. (2009). Difference, deficiency, and devaluation: Tracing the roots of non-recognition of foreign credentials for immigrant professionals in Canada. *Canadian Journal for the Study of Adult Education, 22*(1), 37–52.

Guo, Y. (2012a). Diversity in public education: Acknowledging immigrant parent knowledge. *Canadian Journal of Education / Revue canadienne de l'éducation, 35*(2), 120–140.

Guo, Y. (2012b). Exploring linguistic, cultural, and religious diversity in Canadian schools: Pre-service teachers' learning from immigrant parents. *Journal of Contemporary Issues in Education, 7*(1), 4–23.

Guo, Y., Arthur, N., & Lund, D. (2009). Intercultural inquiry with pre-service teachers. *Intercultural Education*, *20*(6), 565–577.

Hodgkinson, H. (2002). Demographics and teacher education: An overview. *Journal of Teacher education*, *53*(2), 102–105.

hooks, b. (1995). *Killing rage, ending racism*. Henry Holt.

Ilieva, R. (2016). EAL in public schools in British Columbia: Reconsidering policies and practices in light of Fraser's social justice model. *International Journal of Bias, Identity and Diversities in Education*, *1*(2), 67–81.

Karathanos, K. A. (2010). Teaching English language learner students in the US mainstream schools: Intersections of language, pedagogy, and power. *International Journal of Inclusive Education*, *14*(1), 49–65.

Lee, E., & Canagarajah, A. S. (2019). Beyond native and nonnative: Translingual dispositions for more inclusive teacher identity in language and literacy education. *Journal of Language, Identity & Education*, *18*(6), 352–363.

Lee, E., Menkart, D., & Okazawa-Rey, M. (Eds.). (2007). *Beyond heroes and holidays: A practical guide to K–12 multicultural, anti-racist education and staff development*. Teaching for Change.

McCarthy, V., & Foxx, V. (2001). ESL: Time to remove the funding cap. *Teacher*, *13*(May/June), 6.

Milner, H. R. (2006). Preservice teachers' learning about cultural and racial diversity: Implications for urban education. *Urban Education*, *41*(4), 343–375.

Sato, D., Hasegawa, A., Kumagai, Y., & Kamiyoshi, U. (2017). Content-based instruction (CBI) for the social future: A recommendation for critical content-based language instruction (CCBI). *L2 Journal*, *9*(3), 50–69.

Solomon, R. P., & Levine-Rasky, C. (2003). *Teaching for equity and diversity: Research to practice*. Canadian Scholars.

Statistics Canada. (2017). *2016 Census (updated version, 31 August)*. Census in Brief series. https://www12.statcan.gc.ca/census-recensement/2016/dp-pd/prof/index.cfm?Lang=E

Tan, A. (1989). *The joy luck club*. Ivy Books.

Tan, A. (1990). Mother tongue. *The Threepenny Review*, *43*, 7–8.

Vanthuyne, A., & Clark, J. (2015). Teaching for change and diversity. In L. Thomas & M. Hirschkorn (Eds.), *Change and progress in Canadian teacher education: Research on recent innovations in teacher preparation in Canada* (pp. 525–549). Canadian Association for Teacher Education.

Wild, J., Helmer, S., Tanaka P., & Dean, S. (2009). *A "crisis in ESL education" in BC schools*. http://boards.amssa.org/ancie/members/viewPost/post_id:71

Young, I. M. (2008). Justice and the politics of difference. In S. Seidman & J. C. Alexander (Eds.), *The new social theory reader* (pp. 261–269). Routledge.

Yu, H. (February 1, 2010). Vancouver's own not-so-quiet revolution. *Vancouver Sun*.

CHAPTER 10

Cultural Capital Re/constructions and the Education of Minoritized Youth

Dan Cui and Ali A. Abdi

INTRODUCTION

> Roulette, which holds out the opportunity of winning a lot of money in a short space of time, and therefore of changing one's social status quasi-instantaneously, and in which the winning of the previous spin of the wheel can be staked and lost at every new spin, gives a fairly accurate image of this imaginary universe of perfect competition or perfect equality of opportunity, a world without inertia, without accumulation, without heredity or acquired properties, in which every moment is perfectly independent of the previous one, every soldier has a marshal's baton in his knapsack, and every prize can be attained, instantaneously, by everyone, so that at each moment anyone can become anything. (Bourdieu, 1986, p. 241)

Roulette is the metaphor that Bourdieu used to discuss his central concept of capital. The social world implicated and analyzed in Bourdieu's (1986) oft-referenced focus on capital should not be understood as a roulette game, in which the very chance of winning is equally possible or impossible. Rather, it is important to understand the social world as an accumulated history and capital as accumulated labour that has a potential capacity to generate profits and reproduce itself in objectified or embodied forms across generations. It is an (in)visible force that is inscribed in or, to be more exact, hidden behind the objectivity of things so that meritocracy, namely, everyone having an equal opportunity to participate in a fair and just educational competition in which the chances of success depend on one's innate "ability" or "potential," is an *illusion*. Bourdieu's capital theory, especially the concept of cultural capital, has been widely deployed in educational and sociological research to explain cultural and social reproduction across generations and in different socioeconomic and educational possibilities.

From this, the existing scholarship on cultural capital tends to either overwhelmingly focus on class-based inequality or unwittingly affiliate this concept with whiteness. Limited research is available to examine how this concept can be used to examine racial and related inequalities and inequities in the Canadian context, particularly in relation to some non-traditional racialized minority groups such as Chinese Canadian students. In this chapter, we aim to extend the explanatory power of this concept into exploring the racism that Chinese Canadian students experience at school. To do that, we first review two major interpretations of the role of cultural capital in educational research: traditional versus expanded. Then we discuss the academic debate on how to use cultural capital to examine ethno-racial differences, in other words, contrasting a Bourdieusian approach and a non-Bourdieusian approach. Finally, we draw on a case study of Chinese Canadian youth to call for an epistemic reconstruction of cultural capital by challenging teachers' racialized habitus and the racist logic of the educational field from a Bourdieusian perspective.

TRADITIONAL VERSUS EXPANDED INTERPRETATION OF CULTURAL CAPITAL

In understanding and analyzing cultural capital and its affiliated social and educational contexts, we start with a few relevant questions. What does cultural capital tell us about educational inequality? Or how we should use cultural capital as an explanatory framework in educational research? Answers to these and similar questions would depend on the researcher's unique understanding of the concept itself. In reviewing English-language literature, Lareau and Weininger (2003) identified two interpretations of cultural capital: dominant or traditional interpretation and expanded or alternative interpretation. Particularly, a dominant interpretation rests on two critical premises. First, it defines cultural capital as knowledge of, or participation in, prestigious "highbrow" aesthetic culture, such as fine arts, classical music, and related societal privileges. Second, it distinguishes the effects of cultural capital from educational skills, abilities, or achievements. Putting these two premises together results in a series of studies in which "the salience of cultural capital is tested by assessing whether measures of 'highbrow' cultural participation predict educational outcomes (such as grades) independently of various 'ability' measures (such as standardized test scores)" (Lareau & Weininger, 2003, p. 106). DiMaggio's (1982) article "Cultural Capital and School Success" has been regarded as setting the stage for much of this type of research (Dumais, 2002; Kalmijn & Kraaykamp, 1996).

More specifically, students' cultural capitals are defined and measured in terms of their attitudes/interests, activities, and information in the areas of art, music, and literature. The effects of cultural capital on students' educational performance are believed to be restricted only in some non-technical subjects, such as English, history, and social studies, where the evaluation of students' performance is relatively subjective, but not in technical subjects, such as mathematics, which require special skills that can be objectively measured. In this way, cultural capital is interpreted as conceptually distinct from "measured ability" (p. 112). The dominant interpretation and its specific application based on this assumption in educational research, for Lareau and Weininger (2003), is inadequate.

A closer reading of Bourdieu's own work renders the association between cultural capital and highbrow interpretation ambiguously warranted, which may be more applicable in the social context of France than those of other countries. Students' highbrow competence and its associated power status may indeed impact their educational processes and outcomes, but it is only one dimension of their overall competence, and teachers rewarding students' highbrow competence is only one possibility among others. Therefore, the dominant interpretation based on such assumption has not exhausted the explanatory potentials of cultural capital. Further, the attempt to separate cultural capital from technical skill or ability is to "fall into [a] trap," in Bourdieu's words, as the "ability and talent is itself the product of an investment of time and cultural capital," and thus the two are "irrevocably fused" (Lareau & Weininger, 2003, p. 118). Based on their critiques of the dominant interpretation of cultural capital, Lareau and Weininger (2003) aligned themselves with an alternative account of cultural capital, which they believe extends the inherent potentials contained in this concept. Indeed, all subjects of study, whether in the social and/or physical and mathematical sciences, are cultural outcomes created in specific tempo-spatial societal contexts. On the study of mathematics especially, Steinthorsdottir and Herzig (2014) cogently note that it is not just that this area of study is culturally located and undertaken, but success in it also has cultural meanings and expectations.

In contrast to the dominant interpretation, Lareau and Weininger (2003) emphasize the socially determined character of cultural capital in the sense that it is not fixed but should be understood in the dynamic micro interactions. Its recognition, value, and power depend on a strong social consensus that may vary across institutions and is also subject to the manipulation of social agents. Their conceptualization of cultural capital shifts the research focus from highbrow culture to socially and culturally constructed *institutionalized standards*, which educators use to evaluate students on the one hand, and with which students and parents either comply to or challenge for educational outcomes and profits on the other hand. The emphasis on *evaluative criteria* is also central to Bourdieu's own understanding of how cultural capital works in educational markets, that is, "the educational norms of those social classes capable of imposing the ... criteria of evaluation which are the most favourable to their children" (Lareau & Weininger, 2003, p. 126). Indeed, this is where cultural power and competence, in their complexity and structured manifestations, but also via normalized knowledge claim exclusivities, construct and shape educational policies that privilege specific physical, linguistic, and relational designs that endow the learning success of some while suppressing that of others. Based on the broader interpretation of cultural capital, therefore, Lareau and Weininger point out that empirical studies in education should identify both formal and informal expectations that school personnel use to evaluate students on the one hand, and how the different abilities, dispositional skills, and knowledge that students and parents possess affect them to meet, influence, or change these institutional expectations or standards for evaluative purposes on the other hand. Cultural capital research should capture these dynamics at the micro-interactional level.

A number of qualitative studies on the sociology of education fit this expanded conception of cultural capital despite their differences (Lareau & Weininger, 2003). For example, Reay (1998), in her research on mothers' involvement in their children's primary schooling in London, England, defines parents' cultural capital as a kind of confidence to assume an educational expert role and ability to effectively express their concerns to teachers. Lareau and Horvat (1999) examined the micro-interaction dynamics between parents and teachers in a Midwestern school in the United States where African American parents had more difficulties than their white counterparts in complying with institutionalized expectations of appropriate parent–school relationships due to the local history of racism. Particularly, when African American parents expressed frustration with educators' racial insensitivity, their attitudes and behaviours were unfortunately interpreted as problematic and difficult. Cultural capital in this regard could be defined as parents' cultural and social resources that facilitate their compliance with school standards and communication with teachers. More specifically, it refers to the language they use as related to or divergent from the teachers' official linguistic dispositions and their sense of entitlement in terms of being treated as equals to teachers.

In our research with racialized minority students in Canada, we find the expanded interpretation of cultural capital (as interactively located in all aspects of learners and their families' lives) appealing because it highlights the direct or indirect imposition of evaluative norms that favour particular groups of students and their families at school. These evaluative norms, based on dominant Western values or the white middle-class standard, marginalize immigrant students as the Other or inferior (Abdi, 2009). Furthermore, the expanded interpretation stresses the micro-interactional process whereby social agents use different knowledge, skills, and strategies to respond to institutionalized expectations and norms. Particularly, racialized minority students from immigrant families may be disadvantaged in engaging in an "effective or appropriate" interaction with school personnel, due to systemic, institutional, or individual racism. The question arising here is this: How should we apply what we would like to reconstruct as critical cultural capital to research, beyond the prevalent cultural realities, on racialized minority students? The addition of the term *critical* here is intended to connote, as it should be operationalized in the critical pedagogy tradition, inclusively expanding the situation to robust and equally ongoing interrogations of inter-school-student, inter-school-family, and inter-school-community power relations that need to be transformed for the well-being of all learners. It can procure for learners and their families the needed critical consciousness (Freire, 1985/2013) to contextually acquire the necessary relational capital to effectively respond to the exigency of both ongoing and emerging school-community issues. Topically related to the different and, especially for our purposes here, expanding definitions and possible practices of cultural capital, we focus here on important debates on the main *approaches*, which could be categorized as "Bourdieusian" and "non-Bourdieusian."

BOURDIEUSIAN VERSUS NON-BOURDIEUSIAN APPROACH

Extending Bourdieu's concept of cultural capital, as we implicate above, to study how students' racial and ethnic backgrounds affect their school performance is only a recent phenomenon. Wallace's work (2017, 2018) represents a Bourdieusian approach to address this theoretical and analytical gap. It has been argued that Bourdieu's work only focuses on class-based cultural capital and social reproduction without considering racial inequality (Go, 2013). In reading "race" in Bourdieu, Wallace (2017) points out that such misunderstanding is due to people's limited readings of Bourdieu's work. Race indeed matters to Bourdieu, although it may not be a steady feature of his work (Rollock, 2007). In his early work, *The Algerians* (Bourdieu, 1962), Bourdieu used a more contextualized word, *caste*, which is a typology of race or ethnicity, to describe the socially constructed hierarchy and segregation of mid–20th century Algeria. Bourdieu sharply points out that it would be "useless to hope to abolish racism without destroying the colonial system of which it is the product" (p. 50). For Bourdieu, anti-racism and anti-colonialism are two inextricably intertwined parts of the goal of social justice and equality. In this sense, the contemporary extension of Bourdieu's theory in relation to race is not "an imposition" on his scholarship but something that he initiated himself in his early work (Wallace, 2017, p. 911). Particularly, in extending Bourdieu's cultural capital to address racial and ethnic differences, Wallace proposes a concept of Black cultural capital, which for us is also intentionally extractable from the critical cultural capital noted above. In studying a group of young, middle-class Black Caribbean students in a multicultural school in south London, England, Wallace illustrates the strategies, scripts, and styles that this group uses to elevate their status in school. Cultural capital is defined as "dominant tastes and expressions adopted and adjusted by the Black middle classes to signal class status and racial identity simultaneously" (Wallace, 2017, p. 908). More specifically, Black middle-class students use embodied class scripts such as codes of walking, speaking, dressing, and behaving to improve their social and academic performance at school. For example, Akilah, a year 10 student, revealed that, before he started going to school, his mother taught him how to shake hands with teachers, look them in the eye, and answer at least one question on the first day of class:

> Like if my teacher is talking about British history, I can raise my hands and tell her what I know about Henry VII and Queen Elizabeth II, and also add what I have learned about Black people in British history.... I also know how to answer them all the time with "yes, Miss," "no, Sir." You can't just say yes or no.... That's how you get ahead ... my time at Newton is proof that this works. (Wallace, 2017, p. 915)

Obviously, the Black cultural capital demonstrated by Akilah is characteristic of a combination of traditional embodied middle-class cultural capital with an assertion of his Black heritage and identity "in pursuit of recognition, respect, and upward social mobility" (Wallace, 2017, p. 915). The enactment of Black cultural capital is based on the knowledge that the rules of the field are often over-determined by the white middle classes, and this over-determination exerts symbolic violence on racialized minorities who have to modify their ways of expression to avoid marginalization and exclusion. Wallace's study demonstrates that middle-class Black Caribbean students are aware of the rules of the game and strategically employ middle-class interactional codes, aesthetic values, and speech styles to forge a positive relationship with their white teachers. Acquiring and embodying such reconstructed and critical Black cultural capital seems beneficial to racialized minority students, especially those from middle-class backgrounds. However, those Black working-class students who lack this type of Black cultural capital may be further disadvantaged when teachers compare them with their middle-class counterparts. More importantly, the concept of Black cultural capital does not seem to be applicable to new immigrant students from racialized minority groups who are struggling with language and cultural barriers. Understanding white middle-class cultural norms and "the rules of the game" based on these norms at school would be very challenging for them and their immigrant parents. Not to mention they could strategically assert their racial and ethnic identity while at the same time conforming to these norms.

Moreover, Wallace's (2017) Black cultural capital, despite its delicate racial twists, is based on maintaining the status quo by "conforming to" the white middle-class norms to some degree rather than completely challenging them. Wallace summarizes the benefits of Black cultural capital as including

> *the awareness* of how informal relational skills influence teachers' perspectives of Black pupils, *the ability* to marshal social networks and economic resources to garner recognition from teachers, and *the agentic practices* of Black middle-class students to deploy their class advantages based on parental instructions amidst social inequalities. (p. 917)

When students form good relationships with teachers through their individual awareness, ability, and agentic practices, such understanding tends to overemphasize the possible positive outcomes from students' one-sided efforts, while ignoring the role of teachers' racialized habitus in influencing the social interaction between the two sides (Cui, 2017). After all, good relationships depend on more than racialized minority students' own willingness and efforts, especially when they are in different positions of racial and power hierarchy with white teachers. On some occasions, no matter how respectfully Chinese Canadian students act toward teachers, such as with the Black Caribbean youth did in Wallace's study (e.g., "not to shout, not to roll my eyes, not to be late, not to avoid my teachers, not to talk back, and not to develop a bad relationship" [Wallace, 2017, p. 917]), they may still be unfairly and unequally treated when teachers hold stereotyped assumptions about Chinese students (Cui, 2015, 2017). In this sense, we need to identify and acknowledge the specificity of oppression that Chinese students encounter in the educational field and theoretically reconstruct the concept of cultural capital in relation to this particular population.

Similarly, Yosso (2005) also challenges the dominant interpretation of Bourdieu's cultural capital, which treats it as synonymous with whiteness, but she does so from a non-Bourdieusian approach. Particularly, she criticizes setting white middle-class culture as the norm against which all other forms and expressions of culture are assessed and judged. Particularly, the privileged groups are regarded as culturally wealthy when their specific knowledge, skills, and abilities are valued as "cultural capital," whereas those of marginalized groups are perceived as culturally poor or lacking in cultural capital. By asking "whose culture has capital," Yosso attempts to epistemologically reconstruct the concept itself by introducing an alternative concept, "community cultural wealth," from a critical race theory (CRT) approach. Yosso's concept of community cultural wealth consists of six forms of reconstructed cultural capital: aspirational capital, linguistic capital, familial capital, social capital, navigational capital, and resistant capital. Rather than elaborating on each of these six forms, we highlight three of them that showcase the idea of "reconstructing cultural capital," especially in relation to racialized minority students. We start with *aspirational capital*, which refers to "the ability to maintain hopes and dreams for the future, even in the face of real and perceived barriers" (Yosso, 2005, p. 77). This form of cultural capital is often what motivates immigrant parents to settle down in Canada in the hope of better life opportunities for their children. It is also the foundation of resilience that enables marginalized students and their parents to look beyond current barriers and hold dreams for a better future. In our study of the identity construction of Chinese Canadian youth in Alberta, we found that many first-generation Chinese immigrant students possess this type of cultural capital to varying degrees. They acknowledge the sacrifices that their parents made for them by deciding to immigrate, which meant starting everything from scratch in a new environment. They express a responsibility, desire, and hope to lead a successful life despite various difficulties. In the literature on education and hope, David Halpin (2001) described what he called *absolute hope*—that is, a limitless aspiring for a goal that can be transformative—which could be connected to immigrant families from China or elsewhere, as enacting upon their aspirational capital.

The second is *linguistic capital*, which refers to "the intellectual and social skills attained through communication experiences in more than one language and style" (Yosso, 2005, p. 78). Chinese Canadian students may develop two or more languages as well as communication skills through speaking English at school and speaking Mandarin, Cantonese, or Chinese local dialects (e.g., Taishan) with their immigrant parents or grandparents at home. They can help translate phone calls, mail, and legal documents from English to Chinese while still acquiring "multiple tools of 'vocabulary,' audience awareness, cross-cultural awareness, and 'real world' literacy skills" (Yosso, 2005, p. 79). For first-generation Chinese immigrant students especially, linguistic capital also means two systems of cultural references (e.g., Chinese and Canadian/Western beliefs, values, proverbs, life wisdom, etc.), which they can draw on in critically assessing educational or real-world problems, making good decisions, and looking for reasonable solutions. For example, Chinese Confucian quotes—such as "do not impose on others what you yourself do not desire"—which are usually taught within immigrant families, educate Chinese students on how to appropriately interact with people. Similarly, the Confucian quote "Even when walking in a party of no more than three, I am sure I can learn something from the other two" teaches Chinese students to be open-minded and humble, because everyone has some good qualities for them to imitate and bad ones to allow them to realize their own shortcomings. These linguistic cultural capitals are usually not recognized by mainstream discourses on cultural capital, which tend to simplistically treat immigrant students, from a deficit perspective, as lacking language or cultural capital.

The third form of reconstructed cultural capital, *resistant capital*, is "knowledge and skills fostered through oppositional behavior that challenges inequality" (Yosso, 2005, p. 80). Many Chinese immigrant students do not have any experience of racial discrimination until they come to Canada, where they realize they are officially categorized as a "racialized minority" and treated as inferior to their white counterparts due to the ideology of white supremacy. Through their everyday contact with major social institutions, such as school and media (Cui & Worrell, 2019), they are gradually exposed to some popular discourses that they come from an authoritarian and backward country in comparison to Western democracy and civilization. However, not all Chinese students automatically accept this ideological construction about culture, community, and country of origin. Some indeed fight back by voicing their opinions against any biased and derogatory representation of China and Chinese culture (Cui, 2017). In this sense, these Chinese students demonstrate a kind of resistant capital by challenging the status quo and constructing a positive racial and ethnic identity.

Yosso's concept of community cultural wealth can epistemologically dismantle the dominant discourses regarding who has cultural capital and whose capital is valued in the educational field. By criticizing the deficit thinking that racialized minority groups are deficient in cultural capital, she reconstructs the concept itself by highlighting the multiple forms of cultural wealth among subordinated groups. Despite the select merits of Yosso's epistemological reconstruction of cultural capital, it has also incurred some critiques, which mainly focus on her non-Bourdieusian approach that isolates culture capital from habitus and field and that overextends cultural capital as all kinds of resources, thereby diluting its explanatory power (Bennett & Silva, 2011; Wallace, 2018). Our empirical study with Chinese Canadian youth further supports the critique that a narrow focus on cultural capital reconstruction without addressing its interaction with habitus and field will make us lose some important theoretical insights in addressing racism that Chinese Canadian students encounter at school and in wider societal situations.

RETHINKING CULTURAL CAPITAL RECONSTRUCTION IN PING'S CASE

Ping is a first-generation Chinese Canadian youth who immigrated to Canada with her parents from mainland China at the age of 10. At the time of her interview, she had already lived in Canada for five years. Theoretically, Ping possessed all three forms of reconstructed cultural capital previously discussed. Although her English was not good, Ping held high aspirations for her future. She enacted this aspirational capital theorized in Yosso's study (2005) in her junior high school choice. As she noted,

> At that time, I only came for a short while, and my English is not good. I want to challenge myself to see how far I could go. I heard G is the best junior high in Edmonton, and it has some academic program, so I went there to take entrance test. After the test, they decided to accept me.

In addition, receiving her primary education in both China and Canada enables Ping to accumulate *linguistic capital* by speaking two languages when straddling two different cultural worlds—Mandarin at home and English at school. Most importantly, the earlier educational and lived experiences in China provided Ping with capacities and skills to confront Western-biased knowledge construction about China at school. Ping recalled an unpleasant incident in her grade 6 social studies class when they studied the topic of China:

> The textbook was written many decades ago. It doesn't have a real and good description of China; [it is] very terrible … so some students said, "oh, look, China looks so bad, streets are very dirty, their currency is not valuable. Pollution is everywhere." At that time, I told them, China does not look like that because I am from China.

By challenging the biased dominant discourses about China, Ping demonstrated her resistant cultural capital. However, doing so did not put Ping in an advantageous position in that specific educational field, as her cultural capital on China was not recognized and valued by her white social studies teacher. Instead of giving Ping an opportunity to voice her opinion of what China "really" looks like and share her lived experiences and knowledge about China, the teacher insisted on criticizing China as a background country, inferior to Western democracy and civilization. As Ping mentioned, her teacher had never been to China, and all her knowledge about the country was based on Western dominant discourses that have consistently vilified China as a "problematic" country, both historically and in current contexts. On this point, the white teacher's cultural capital on China conflicted with Ping's. To better understand this conflict, we should not focus on the cultural capital itself but examine its interaction with field and habitus.

Field, according to Bourdieu (1998), is a structured social space consisting of people who dominate and who are dominated. A field may value particular forms of capital while rejecting others, depending on the rules of the field. Individuals' relative positions and power within the field depend on the types of capital that they possess. Habitus can be understood as individuals' internalized social structures, or a system of durable social dispositions. It is structured by one's past experiences and circumstances; at the same time, it is not fixed but evolving, structuring individuals' present and future practices (Maton, 2008). For Bourdieu, to understand individuals' social practices, we need to analyze the interplay between capital, habitus, and field. Particularly, as Bourdieu (1990) argues, compared with the present field, the past field is more significant in producing social agents' habitus; "It is just that we don't directly feel the influence of these past selves precisely because they are so deeply rooted within us" (p. 56). Therefore, to understand the white teacher's biased knowledge construction about China, we need to briefly explore the historical field where the teacher's racialized habitus evolved.

Historically, China was regarded as stagnant and backward, and fundamentally different from Western civilization. Asians were described as "the antithesis of Europeans" in popular textbooks, such as "Canadian Readers," and China was "the land of oddities and contrarieties" in which "everything seems to be the exact opposite of what we have in this country" (Stanley, 2011, p. 108). An elementary school textbook used in British Columbia between 1911 and 1923 described the white race as "the most active, enterprising, and intelligent race in the world" and the yellow race as "some of the most backward tribes of the world" (Stanley, 2011, p. 108). As Stanley (2011) points out, "By indoctrinating younger generations with white supremacist forms of knowledge, school textbooks made it as difficult for students in British Columbia to question the idea of innate differences between racialized groups as it would have been for them to question that the earth revolved around the sun" (p. 112). The constructed historical dichotomy between the West and the East, the civilized and the uncivilized, the superior and the inferior, so cogently analyzed by Edward Said (1978), did not disappear with the emergence of Canada's multiculturalism policy. Eurocentric curricula continue to regard Western culture, capitalist economies, and forms of government as the global gold standard (Henry et al., 2006). As Bourdieu (1990) argues, "The habitus, a product of history, produces individual and collective practices—more history—in accordance with the schemes generated by history" (p. 54). The continuity of the racist social order, in both historical and contemporary fields, contributes to the evolution as well as the continuity of a kind of racialized habitus among social agents within these fields, especially in their ways of thinking and treating Chinese people.

Specifically, by denying and silencing Ping's opinions and not providing her a chance to speak, Ping's teacher manifested this kind of racialized habitus toward China and Chinese people, which tends to perpetuate the racist past into now, continually activating past racist discourses in school knowledge constructions and provision. Although Ping demonstrated resistant capital in challenging such dominant Western discourses against China, this cultural capital conflicts with that of her teacher, leading to lack of recognition and devaluation. As Taylor (1995) affirmed in his seminal analysis on recognition, lack of recognition or an externally imposed recognition, which usually carries negative connotations, is damaging to our being and social status. Laughed at by her classmates and criticized by her teacher's remarks, Ping was upset and angry in recalling this school experience. In other words, Ping became the victim of the symbolic violence brought about by such conflict. On this account and in relation to Ping's experiences, reconstructing cultural capital involves more than just recognizing the racialized community's cultural wealth and contributions to the field. More than that, and most importantly, it requires deconstructing the dominant cultural capital embodied by white teachers as well, especially their epistemological assumption of what kind of cultural capital should be valued and whose criteria this should be based upon. It means challenging the white supremacy–constructed knowledge and going beyond reconstructing cultural capital itself, transforming white teachers' racialized habitus, their ways of thinking and doing toward racialized minority students. It also means, on a wider platform, changing the racist order of the field and, by extension, the sociocultural, educational, and political public spaces that sustain the supremacist ideology and its affiliated practices.

CONCLUSION

> The notion of cultural capital initially presented itself to me, in the course of research as a theoretical hypothesis which made it possible to explain the unequal scholastic achievements of children originating from the different social classes by relating academic success ... to the distribution of cultural capital between classes and class fractions. (Bourdieu, 1986, p. 243)

With the concept of cultural capital, Bourdieu intends to challenge the common sense understanding that perceives one's academic success or failure "as an effect of natural aptitude" (Bourdieu, 1986, p. 243). In our discussion of Ping's experience, this is obviously not the case. Ping's knowledge of China was not recognized and valued by her white teacher. The evaluation criteria based on the Western perspective and norms put Ping in a disadvantaged position. The teacher's racialized habitus produced from historical and contemporary fields negatively affected her micro-level social interaction with Ping and, consequently, her evaluation of Ping's performance in the class. In other words, Ping's academic success or failure cannot be simplistically reduced to her "natural aptitude" but closely related to the deeply rooted racism in Canadian society. It has been argued that when Chinese students share indigenous knowledge in the Western/English classroom, they often encounter indifference and impatience from peer students and professors (Zhou et al., 2005). As a result, Chinese students usually choose to remain silent when they find their cultural capitals are devalued. Razack (1998) explains that Chinese students' behaviour, such as passivity with authority figures, may not be based on so-called Chinese culture but a response to an unfriendly and racist environment. In order to achieve academic success, Chinese students have to follow the rules of the field that assume Western perspectives and knowledge as superior.

This means they have to learn to criticize their parents' homeland and devalue the "Chinese" knowledge and beliefs that their immigrant parents hold dear and pass on to them. Acquiring dominant cultural capital means these students must develop a dominant Western perspective and cognitive skills that aim to destroy their cultural roots and criticize the community where they come from (Cui, 2017). Such education, when imposed on Chinese students, is seriously problematic. In this sense, we call for epistemologically reconstructing the dominant cultural capital that continuously constructs the "Other" and vilifies China and the Chinese Canadian community. By doing so, we do not mean to cultivate a "Chinese cultural capital" that assumes middle-class cultural norms as Wallace's Black cultural capital (2017). Neither is it so simple to focus on reconstructing cultural capital itself, as advocated by Yosso (2005). We call for a complete, transformative, and epistemic reconstruction of what should be regarded as valued cultural capital in terms of knowledge on China and the Chinese people in the Canadian educational field. By reconstructing, we mean to challenge the racist order of the field and interrogate racist habitus that is both structured by and structuring the field. We do so from a Bourdieusian approach, but we share the same tenets as the CRT approach (Solorzano, 1998; Yosso, 2005). That is, we believe that racism is one fundamental and sizable block that can explain how Western societies function in relation to racialized minorities, which, with its dominant discourses of white supremacy and distorting epistemologies (especially in relation to racialized minorities), needs to be challenged. Obviously, in a roulette game, racialized minority students, particularly Chinese Canadian students, do not enjoy equal opportunities to win compared with the dominant groups when their indigenous cultural capitals are not recognized or valued in an educational field whose rules of the game are based on white supremacy.

DISCUSSION QUESTIONS

1. What is your understanding of the location as well as the function of cultural capital in the education of all students?

2. How are minority students' experiences and knowledges marginalized in schooling contexts?

3. What steps should teachers and schools take to create equitable spaces of learning for all students regardless of their racialized, linguistic, and/or socioeconomic backgrounds?

REFERENCES

Abdi, A. A. (2009). Recentering the philosophical foundations of knowledge: The case of Africa with a special focus on the global role of teachers. *The Alberta Journal of Educational Research, 55*(3), 269–283.

Bennett, T., & Silva, E. (2011). Introduction: Cultural capital—histories, limits, prospects. *Poetics, 39*(6), 427–443.

Bourdieu, P. (1962). *The Algerians*. Beacon Press.

Bourdieu, P. (1986). The forms of capital. In J. G. Richardson (Ed.), *Handbook of theory and research for the sociology of education* (pp. 241–258). Greenwood Press.

Bourdieu, P. (1990). *The logic of practice*. Polity Press.

Bourdieu, P. (1998). *On television and journalism*. Pluto Press.

Cui, D. (2015). Capital, distinction, and racialized habitus: Immigrant youth in the educational field. *Journal of Youth Studies, 18*(9), 1154–1169.

Cui, D. (2017). Teachers' racialised habitus in school knowledge construction: A Bourdieusian analysis of social inequality beyond class. *British Journal of Sociology of Education, 38*(8), 1152–1164.

Cui, D., & Worrell, F. C. (2019). Media, symbolic violence and racialized habitus: Voices from Chinese Canadian youth. *Canadian Journal of Sociology, 44*(3), 233–256.

DiMaggio, P. (1982). Cultural capital and school success: The impact of status culture participation on the grades of U.S. high school students. *American Sociological Review, 47*(2), 189–201.

Dumais, S. A. (2002). Cultural capital, gender, and school success: The role of habitus. *Sociology of Education, 75*(1), 44–68.

Freire, P. (2013). *Education for critical consciousness*. Bloomsbury. (Original work published 1985)

Go, J. (2013). Decolonizing Bourdieu: Colonial and postcolonial theory in Pierre Bourdieu's early work. *Sociological Theory, 31*(1), 49–74.

Halpin, D. (2001). The nature of hope and its significance to education. *British Journal of Educational Studies, 49*(4), 392–410.

Henry, F., Tator, C., Mattis, W., & Rees, T. (2006). *The color of democracy: Racism in Canadian society* (3rd ed.). Nelson.

Kalmijn, M., & Kraaykamp, G. (1996). Race, cultural capital, and schooling: An analysis of trends in the United States. *Sociology of Education, 69*(1), 22–34.

Lareau, A., & Horvat, E. (1999). Moments of social inclusion and exclusion: Race, class, and cultural capital in family-school relationships. *Sociology of Education, 72*(1), 37–53.

Lareau, A., & Weininger, E. B. (2003). Cultural capital in educational research: A critical assessment. *Theory and Society, 32*(5/6), 567–606.

Maton, K. (2008). Habitus. In M. Grenfell (Ed.), *Pierre Bourdieu: Key concepts* (pp. 49–65). Acumen.

Razack, S. H. (1998). *Looking white people in the eye: Gender, race, and culture in courtrooms and classrooms.* University of Toronto Press.

Reay, D. (1998). *Class work: Mothers' involvement in their children's primary schooling.* Routledge.

Rollock, N. (2007). Legitimizing Black academic failure: Deconstructing staff discourses on academic success, appearance and behaviour. *International Studies in Sociology of Education, 17*(3), 275–287.

Said, E. (1978). *Orientalism.* Vintage.

Solorzano, D. G. (1998). Critical race theory, race and gender microaggressions, and the experience of Chicana and Chicano scholars. *International Journal of Qualitative Studies in Education, 11*(1), 121–136.

Stanley, T. (2011). *Contesting white supremacy: School segregation, anti-racism, and the making of Chinese Canadians.* UBC Press.

Steinthorsdottir, O. B., & Herzig, A. (2014). Cultural influences in mathematics education. In S. Lerman (Ed.), *Encyclopedia of mathematics education* (pp. 129–132). Springer.

Taylor, C. (1995). *Philosophical arguments.* Harvard University Press.

Wallace, D. (2017). Reading "race" in Bourdieu? Examining Black cultural capital among Black Caribbean youth in south London. *Sociology, 51*(5), 907–923.

Wallace, D. (2018). Cultural capital as whiteness? Examining logics of ethno-racial representation and resistance. *British Journal of Sociology of Education, 39*(4), 466–482.

Yosso, T. J. (2005). Whose culture has capital? A critical race theory discussion of community cultural wealth. *Race Ethnicity and Education, 8*(1), 69–91.

Zhou, Y. R., Knoke, D., & Sakamoto, I. (2005). Rethinking silence in the classroom: Chinese students' experiences of sharing indigenous knowledges. *International Journal of Inclusive Education, 9*(3), 287–311.

CHAPTER 11

Challenging Normalized Ableism in/through Teacher Education

Bathseba Opini and Levonne Abshire

INTRODUCTION

From COVID-19 to racial violence, current events have brought to light challenges that individuals with disabilities experience in accessing education. Ableism, the conscious and unconscious prejudicial attitudes, actions, policies, and discriminatory behaviours directed at individuals with disability by able-bodied people (Dunn, 2019), is rife in educational institutions. Ableism is often unrecognized and, as Baglieri and Lalvani (2019) observed, is largely outside of the public consciousness.

Society is never built for or structured on people with disabilities in mind; the same is true of the education system. Across Canada, students with disabilities in K–12 and postsecondary settings experience ableism at both individual and institutional levels. In 2018, the Ontario Human Rights Commission (OHRC) reported that educational institutions in Ontario were lagging when it came to accommodating people with disabilities (Fagan, 2018). The OHRC found that students with disabilities continued to experience barriers accessing and participating in education (OHRC, 2018, p. 9). The barriers included inadequate classroom resources, long waiting lists for assessments, negative attitudes and stereotypes, physical inaccessibility, inappropriate requests for medical information, ineffective dispute resolution processes, and failure to provide accommodations (OHRC, 2018, p. 9).

The limitations learners with disability face are not unique to Ontario. In 2017, the Canadian Human Rights Commission (CHRC) found that a significant number of Canadians with disabilities faced systemic social and institutional barriers to education. These impediments affect educational attainment, employment, career paths, and overall well-being of Canadians with disabilities (CHRC, 2017). Often, addressing ableism in the education system, be it through calling for change in societal attitudes or through advocating for accommodations and environmental accessibility, is seen as an additional cost. Educational institutions are being pushed by global economic forces to prioritize privatization, marketization, and efficiency. Government support and funding for public schools has continued to shrink. Despite the increasing cutbacks, it is important to continually advocate for equitable education, and teachers can play a vital role in this advocacy. Teacher education programs are fundamental to preparing future teachers for this advocacy.

In this chapter, we draw on our experiences, within the British Columbian (BC) context, and on existing literature to reflect on ways in which disability can be engaged as a social justice and human rights issue in education. We hope to contribute to existing discussions on transforming current and future teacher education initiatives and impact the educational experiences of learners with disability in the school system.

SUBJECT POSITIONING

Levonne identifies as a Filipino, able-bodied, cisgender woman, is a former educator in K–12 schools, and is currently working in student health and well-being at a postsecondary institution in British Columbia, Canada. She is a mother of a child who was diagnosed on the autism spectrum. Having been a teacher in a public school early in her career, Levonne considered sending her son to public school until she experienced ableism in education. Her son had been supported with funding in his early life for over two years. When he was ready to transition to the K–12 system, Levonne connected with administrators of two schools in her neighbourhood to discuss his needs, especially securing the support of an educational assistant (EA). Both administrators, despite having never met her son, acknowledged that they would not be able to guarantee him EA support. The administrators also noted that they were unable to confirm the type of support that would be provided because they could not confirm that the funding allocated to his Special Needs designation would go to the school he attended. Instead, the funding is allocated to the district, which then distributes it to schools, confirming that learners with disability receive more support from their early intervention service providers than from the public schools (Siddiqua & Janus, 2017). This shows how disability funding for education in BC public education comes with many strings. These strings seem to tighten as a student moves from preschool to the K–12 system, leaving a lot to be desired in terms of successful transitions after preschool disability supports and services. Both administrators told Levonne that they would do their best to support her child, but *all the needs of the children in the school* would need to be considered. The administrators' identical responses demonstrate the predominant understandings of inclusive education, one of "fairness," where equal distribution of resources among all students is understood as good practice and perhaps the path to realizing "equitable education," but it was not. Clearly, rigid funding eligibility and vague funding distribution procedures and justifications affect available support for learners with disability in K–12 public schools (Shanouda & Spagnuolo, 2021).

Eventually, Levonne sent her son to an independent school which received direct funding. Despite having a full-time EA, her son still faces challenges in accessing education. Some experiences are subliminal and represent the signs of the ableism that persist. In her role as a continued advocate for her son, Levonne completed a graduate degree focusing on transition planning for students with disabilities. Through this program, she took a course grounded in disability studies. Teacher practitioners enrolled in the course learned to critically reflect on instances of ableism in education and in their practices. They identified instances of ableism in their schools. Some noted that they had not thought about the impact of these experiences on the lives of students with disabilities. Some teacher practitioners shared how some schools had separate wings for students in the Life Skills program. Others talked about "normalized" practices of not taking students with disabilities on field trips due to not having enough EA support. The practising teachers acknowledged that they would have benefited from a similar course in their program so they could support students better. These experiences underscored the need for critical examinations of disability and special education in teacher education and school leadership training.

Bathseba is an educator whose teaching and research interests are in disability studies, anti-racism education, and decolonizing knowledge. She has worked with learners from K–12 to postsecondary settings. She also had opportunities to work with teacher candidates and practising teachers.

A significant moment for her was when she taught a foundations course to teacher candidates and examined disability from a critical disability studies and justice lens. She introduced the case of Rick Moore, a father who won a legal case on behalf of his son, Jeffrey Moore. As described by the Council of Canadians with Disabilities, Jeffrey Moore was diagnosed with a learning disability and needed intensive reading remediation. He received a range of services during his first couple of years of school, but provincial funding cuts to the school district ended a program fundamental to Jeffrey's education. School officials advised Jeffrey that the remediation he required could only be obtained by attending private school. Subsequently, Rick Moore sent his son to a private school. Rick then filed a complaint with the BC Human Rights Tribunal against the school district and the province of British Columbia. Mr. Moore argued that Jeffrey had been discriminated against and denied a "service customarily available to the public." The BC Human Rights Tribunal ruled in favour of Moore, noting that "students like Jeffrey needed a range of educational services, and because of cuts made by the School District, students were unable to access supports (Council of Canadians with Disabilities, n.d.). The tribunal concluded that there was "individual discrimination against Jeffrey and systemic discrimination against students with severe learning disabilities, for which the Province and the School District were responsible" (Council of Canadians with Disabilities, 2012).

When Bathseba finished sharing the case, one teacher candidate (TC) noted that Jeffrey was not the only marginalized student affected by the funding cuts. What the TC failed to acknowledge though was that "different marginalized groups experience different types of oppression. And it's important to understand how the various systems of oppression affect people and groups uniquely" (Mally 2021, para 3). This was not the Oppression Olympics, wherein groups compete to be recognized as the most oppressed (Hankivsky & Dhamoon, 2013). Such comparisons and competitions take away time and attention from the different forces of domination that constitute and sustain oppression (Hankivsky & Dhamoon, 2013). Oppression comparison is a precarious path to follow, as it contributes to erasure and denial of ongoing systemic ableism against people with disabilities. It is important to understand the larger systems of oppression that have historically shaped the experiences of people with disabilities. Pushing schools to support and attend to the needs of students with disabilities during times of funding cuts may be erroneously read as "privileging" students with disabilities over others. The assumption is that all students should be treated equally rather than equitably! The argument that there are other students who are affected negates the reality that ableism is normalized in the education system. Jeffrey's experiences show that although disability is a human rights issue and the BC education legislation mandates provision of learning services for students with disabilities, school districts have yet to live up to the legislation fully. Related to these issues is the fact that neoliberal policies have led to cuts to the BC education system. These policies are used to justify ableist decisions and practices, and they have serious implications for the educational experiences of students with disabilities. There is a need to critically look at the systemic processes, framed in the name of equality, that end up reinforcing inequitable access to education.

This reminds us of Iannacci's (2018) call to consider how disability is taken up in education and dominated by harmful policies, practices, and research, and fueled by unquestioned beliefs and stereotypes. Iannacci (2018) emphasizes destabilizing these taken-for-granted practices, as they are manifest in education, and engaging in critical conversations about how students with disabilities are perceived, understood, and supported in education. Teachers can be important catalysts for changes in the system. The challenge is preparing them to rethink the ableist society they have been socialized into the ableist education they have received.

We ask the following questions: What form of consciousness is needed in teacher education that will equip future teachers with knowledge and skills to problematize the notion of equality and equity in education access and participation for students with disabilities? What preparation would allow future teachers to understand disability beyond the medical model so they could challenge the deficit approaches to disability? How can education institutions prepare teachers to understand systemic ableism and their complicity in it? We realize there are no quick fixes. However, educators can commit to rethinking disability and the implications for teaching and learning.

DYSCONSCIOUS ABLEISM AS A FRAMEWORK

We draw on the notion of dysconscious ableism, informed by Joyce King's (1991) idea of dysconscious racism, to examine the persistent systemic ableism prevalent in society and the education system. King (1991) examined how teacher candidates perceived explanations for persistent racial injustice. King (1991) defined dysconscious racism as "an uncritical habit of mind (including perceptions, attitudes, assumptions, and beliefs) that justifies inequity and exploitation by accepting the existing order of things as given" (p. 135). Elsewhere, King (2015) explained that dysconscious racism is the result of miseducation by an educational system that resists a transformative view of racial inequality. According to Anderson, Narum, and Wolf (2019), the use of *dysconscious* is not to be equated to *unconscious* but rather implies real yet habitually uncontested, indicating that acceptance is almost certainly unrecognized (p. 5). Anderson and colleagues (2019) argue that dysconsciousness is a result of

> the miseducation of students ... that bypasses any precarious ethical judgment about societal inequality and possibly produces teachers who are indiscriminating or altogether unaccustomed to questioning white norms and privilege.... Additional evidence of this miseducation is the fact that textbooks are only recently mentioning the reality of slavery, and most still fall short of discussing the system and prevailing beliefs that made slavery acceptable or the economic benefits gained from slavery. (p. 5)

Although the quote speaks to racism and enslavement in the US context, the same is true of Canada. For centuries, textbooks used in the Canadian education system have erased the history of the enslavement of Black and Indigenous people, the residential school system and its damaging effects on the lives of Indigenous communities, and the racism experienced by racialized groups, among other atrocities. In the case of disability, few texts document the oppression of people with disability in Canada. The eugenics movement continues to target individuals with disability; meanwhile, critics of discrimination in education, healthcare, the judicial system, policing, employment, and the military are silenced. Many teachers fail to examine these textbooks as partial truths (Anderson et al., 2019), leaving learners miseducated.

Anderson and colleagues (2019) proposed that "the concept of dysconsciousness is important, and holds too great a potential in education and research, to remain almost fully in teacher education research and theorizing" (p. 10). They recommended that those in social science fields discuss and thoroughly examine the cause-and-effect elements of dysconscious racism through new theoretical lenses (Anderson et al., p. 11). Broderick and Lalvani (2017) adapted the idea to examine ableism and described dysconscious ableism as an impaired or distorted way of thinking about dis/ability, particularly when compared to criticalist conceptualizations of dis/ability (p. 2). Dysconscious ableism is a form of ableism that accepts and reproduces "the notion of the normative (and normate individual) and the enforcement of a constitutional divide" between abled and disabled identities (Broderick & Lalvani, 2017, p. 2). There is a tendency for Canadians to deny their ableist and racist history (Gulliver, 2018; Lund, 2006). Some could argue that we no longer erect asylums or that we repealed the Sexual Sterilization Act in 1972 or that laws exist that allow for the inclusion of learners with disability in the education system (El-Lahib, 2015). The reality is that the manifestation of ableism and its affiliated normalization schemes keep changing.

Based on these examples, we argue that miseducation and uncritical and limited interpretation of disability reinforce and reproduce ableism (Anderson et al., 2019). There seems to be an assumption that society is constructed upon and functions on meritocracy and that all students need to be treated equally. Yet these are examples of the manifestations of ableism and erasure/denial of the lived realities of learners with disability. When educators believe in a meritocracy and upholding equality, what are the implications for making budgetary and classroom decisions to meet the needs of students with a disability? We echo the work of scholars (Broderick & Lalvani, 2017; Gillberg & Pettersson, 2019; Leonardo & Broderick, 2011; Siuty, 2019) who continue to call for critical race and disability studies in teacher preparation. We consider possibilities to these potential shifts in British Columbia.

RETHINKING INCLUSIVE EDUCATION IN BRITISH COLUMBIA

Inclusive education, as a concept and a practice, has been subject to different definitions, interpretations, and implementations. Forlin, Chambers, Loreman,

Deppeler, and Sharma (2013) explain that "inclusive education is a contentious term that lacks a tight conceptual focus, which may contribute to some misconception and confused practice" (p. 6). Defining inclusive education is problematic; definitions can be impacted by shifts in educational practice, context, culture, and circumstances that can render these features irrelevant and outdated (Forlin et al., 2013, p. 8). Slee (2018) observed that "inclusive education is secured by principles and actions of fairness, justice, and equity. It is a political aspiration and an educational methodology" (p. 9). Inclusion BC notes that inclusive education means that "students attend and are welcomed by their neighbourhood schools in age-appropriate, regular classes and are supported to learn, contribute, and participate in all aspects of the life of the school." Additionally, "inclusive education is about how we design our schools, classrooms, programs, and activities so all students learn and participate together" (Inclusion BC, n.d.). We are mindful of the effects of other identity markers in education and the perils of using inclusion as a code for "special education" (Forlin et al., 2013, p. 9) and therefore prefer to think about inclusive education broadly. However, in this discussion, we pay attention to the experiences of learners with disabilities.

Within BC, there have been changes in the education system, moving from segregation (by ability or disability and race) to a model that aims to be socially just, emphasizing education for all. Despite legislation and individual district policies, students with disabilities continue to be excluded, segregated, and denied access to education. This exclusion is evident in the BCEdAccess *Exclusion Tracker Report 2018/2019*, in which 490 parents/guardians of students with disabilities reported 3,910 instances of exclusion (BCEdAccess, 2019). Examples of exclusion included students not permitted to attend school for the first one to four weeks or until resources were in place; students excluded from field trips and/or extracurricular activities; and students excluded from courses because the content was not adapted. These examples were reported in every district across BC and in public and independent schools (BCEdAccess, 2019).

In their 2017 survey, the BC Confederation of Parent Advisory Councils surveyed over 800 parents, documenting the amount of educational time lost by students with disability, which spanned from half an hour to more than three hours daily. In addition, 132 parents stated that their children were asked to remain home for more than half the school day daily. Lack of resources and insufficient teacher training to support children with disabilities were cited as the reasons why students were instructed to stay home (BC Confederation of Parent Advisory Councils, 2017).

The findings from BCEdAccess (2019) and the BC Confederation of Parent Advisory Councils (2017) contravene Slee's (2018) analysis of inclusive education being based on principles of fairness, justice, and equity and the need to teach inclusively. The findings are contrary to the provisions in Canada's

Sustainable Development Goals commitment to provide inclusive and equitable quality education for all; the United Nations Convention on the Rights of People with Disabilities (CRPD), which Canada ratified in 2010; the BC Ministry of Education Policy (2016) on special education; the BC School Act; and the BC Human Rights Code. Article 24 of the CRPD seeks to ensure that children with disabilities have access to an inclusive, good quality, and free education; reasonable accommodations to meet individuals' learning needs; provision of required supports within the education system; and effective individualized support measures in environments that maximize academic and social development (United Nations, 2006). The BC Ministry of Education (2016) policy on special education states that "all students should have equitable access to learning, opportunities for achievement, and the pursuit of excellence in all aspects of their educational programs" (p. 1). The BC School Act provides for the right to fully funded public education for all, including those with disabilities, while persons with disabilities are protected from discrimination under the BC Human Rights Code.

Ableism in education also overtly excludes students through curriculum and pedagogy. Although Levonne's son had a full-time EA, he was still denied access to a quality education. During second grade, he was struggling with reading. This was affecting his self-esteem, and he developed a disdain for reading. After contacting his teachers, Levonne learned that they had been implementing a traditional phonics program, which was grounded in evidence, to support his learning to read. Since the program was not working, Levonne researched evidence-based practices to teach reading to students with learning and intellectual disabilities. She discovered that intense and repetitive multi-sensory direct instruction in phonological awareness resulted in positive outcomes. After consulting a behavioural specialist and speech language pathologist (SLP), Levonne asked the school to have this implemented. Although the request was heeded, it was not delivered in the systematic way intended. Levonne implemented phonological awareness instruction at home with her son's tutor, under the guidance of the SLP, and her son is now reading fluently. In this example, instruction is given with limited differentiation and adaptation to meet the needs of struggling learners.

Levonne's son struggles with fine motor skills and working memory, which makes printing arduous. She has been advocating for her son to use a keyboard and speech to text to communicate his learning. During one of the IEP meetings, Levonne requested that the goal of writing a paragraph be completed using speech to text first and then edited via the keyboard. The teacher was initially reluctant and did not see value in this method but later agreed to the request, and it was helpful for Levonne's son.

On the surface, it would appear that Levonne's son is doing well; he is attending school, has access to a full-time EA, and is enjoying an inclusive education experience. However, access to an inclusive pedagogy and curriculum, which should be core to inclusive education, is often missing. Unfortunately, the elements of inclusive education are unclear, and there is no consensus among those in education. This leaves novice and veteran educators unsure of what to do in practice (Iannacci, 2018). Many fall back to what they are comfortable doing. Jurisdictions, individual administrators, and teachers are left to interpret and enact inclusive education. Often inclusive education is used to refer to placement in a mainstream classroom, rather than a child's full participation in all aspects of the educational setting (Lalvani, 2013). While placement within a mainstream setting is important, it does not always translate into inclusive education (Ferguson, 2008; Liasidou, 2014).

Legally, the BC School Act provides for the right to fully funded public education for all. Persons with disabilities are protected from discrimination under the BC Human Rights Code. Yet the educational needs of children with disabilities are far from being met equitably. Negative societal beliefs and perceptions of disability in education persist. Changing the attitudes of policy makers, educators, and other education stakeholders is key to realizing the educational needs and rights of learners.

Levonne's experiences show that different educational approaches to inclusive education reflect understandings of disability and what constitutes an equitable education for students with disabilities. Matters pertaining to the education of students with disability ought to be discussed from a critical social justice perspective (Slee, 2001). In teacher preparation, ableism is not addressed in depth when critical pedagogies are examined for racism, sexism, classism, and other -isms. Ableism is woven into K–12 at the individual and institutional levels and often goes unchallenged. Critical disability studies can offer an ethical and human rights approach to inclusive education.

CONCLUSION

We live in a society where education through inclusive education policies is mandated as a right. Yet the realities for students with disabilities are grim. In schools, students with disabilities experience higher rates of bullying, harassment, and isolation, which often leads to mental health problems and leaving school early (Canadian Human Rights Commission, 2017). Overt and covert ableism is responsible for poor post–high school outcomes for learners with disability (OHRC, 2018).

If the aim of education in BC is to develop students' potential and to acquire the knowledge, skills, and abilities needed to contribute to a healthy society and a prosperous and sustainable economy (BC Ministry of Education, 2016), we are failing to support students to achieve this goal. Preparing future teachers who can critically prepare instructional plans that recognize the effects of ableism and create opportunities for learners to thrive in school is imperative (see Hehir, 2007). A critical disability studies perspective can enrich equity and intersectional analyses in social justice education. It will allow for a more nuanced understanding of disability in schools and postsecondary institutions that have been subject to special education's medical model of disability (Connor et al., 2008). This would provide an opportunity for teachers to interrogate "the ableist assumptions they may implicitly carry and which they will encounter in school system" (Gilham & Tomkins, 2016, p. 11).

Courses in pedagogy, curriculum, and leadership can allow for an analysis of ways in which students with disabilities are denied access to learning, guiding practising teachers and teacher candidates in making the connection of physical barriers to inclusion with social and learning barriers to inclusion (Gilham & Tompkins, 2016). During field practica, teacher candidates have an opportunity to include disability history and culture in their lessons. A curriculum that addresses issues of human rights, as in social studies, can include the history of the disability movement and the oppression by people with disabilities throughout history. Science lessons could examine the advancement of technology and ways technology has improved (or not) access and quality of life for people with disabilities. Principles of universal design for learning can be explored in math and physics. Teacher candidates have the opportunity to be teacher inquirers identifying places where ableist assumptions in education persist and then dismantle these.

DISCUSSION QUESTIONS

1. Reflect on examples of what you would consider ableist education that you have experienced or observed in K–12 and postsecondary settings.

2. How does the idea of equality and fairness reinforce ableism in the education system?

3. What systemic changes might you propose, both within the education system and in the wider society, to address ableism?

REFERENCES

Anderson, B., Narum, A., & Wolf, J. L. (2019). Expanding the understanding of the categories of dysconscious racism. *The Educational Forum, 83*(1), 4–12.

Baglieri, S., & Lalvani, P. (2019). *Undoing ableism: Teaching about disability in K–12 classrooms*. Routledge.

BCEdAccess. (2019). *Exclusion tracker report 2018/2019*. https://bcedaccess.com/2019/09/04/exclusion-tracker-2018-2019-final-report/

BC Confederation of Parent Advisory Councils. (2017, November 3). *Summary report: Survey for parents of students who are denied a full day at school*. https://bccpac.bc.ca/upload/2017/11/2017-11-03-Full-Day-Summaryresults.pdf

British Columbia Ministry of Education. (2016). *Special education services: A manual of policies, procedures and guidelines*. https://www2.gov.bc.ca/assets/gov/education/administration/kindergarten-to-grade-12/inclusive/special_ed_policy_manual.pdf

Broderick, A., & Lalvani, P. (2017). Dysconscious ableism: Toward a liberatory praxis in teacher education. *International Journal of Inclusive Education, 21*(9), 894–905.

Canadian Human Rights Commission. (2017). *Left out: Challenges faced by persons with disabilities in Canada's schools*. https://www.chrc-ccdp.gc.ca/en/resources/publications/left-out-challenges-faced-persons-disabilities-canadas-schools

Connor, D. J., Gabel, S. L., Gallagher, D. J., & Morton, M. (2008). Disability studies and inclusive education—implications for theory, research, and practice. *International Journal of Inclusive Education, 12*(5–6), 441–457.

Council of Canadians with Disabilities. (n.d.). *CRPD—10 facts Canadians should know*. https://www.ccdonline.ca/en/international/un/canada/10-facts

Council of Canadians with Disabilities. (2012). *The Moore case: Summary of key points*.

Dunn, D. S. (2019). Outsider privileges can lead to insider disadvantages: Some psychosocial aspects of ableism. *Journal of Social Issues, 75*(3), 665–682.

El-Lahib, Y. (2015). The inadmissible "other": Discourses of ableism and colonialism in Canadian immigration. *Journal of Progressive Human Services, 26*(3), 209–228.

Fagan, L. (August 30, 2018). *Ableism rife in Ontario schools, rights commission says*. CBC News. https://www.cbc.ca/news/canada/ottawa/students-disabilities-discrimination-ontario-1.4803793

Ferguson, D. L. (2008). International trends in inclusive education: The continuing challenge to teach each one and everyone. *European Journal of Special Needs Education, 23*(2), 109–120. https://doi.org/10.1080/08856250801946236

Forlin, C. I., Chambers, D. J., Loreman, T., Deppeler, J., & Sharma, U. (2013). *Inclusive education for students with disability: A review of best evidence in relation to theory and practice*. Australian Research Alliance for Children & Youth. https://www.aracy.org.au/publications-resources/command/download_file/id/246/filename/Inclusive_education_for_students_with_disability_-_A_review_of_the_best_evidence_in_relation_to_theory_and_practice.pdf

Gilham, C. M., & Tompkins, J. (2016). Inclusion reconceptualized: Pre-service teacher education and disability studies in education. *Canadian Journal of Education / Revue canadienne de l'éducation, 39*(4), 1–25.

Gillberg, C., & Pettersson, A. (2019). Between duty and right: Disabled schoolchildren and teachers' ableist manifestations in Sweden. *Disability & Society, 34*(9–10), 1668–1673.

Government of British Columbia. (1996). *British Columbia School Act.* https://www.bclaws.ca/civix/document/id/complete/statreg/96412_02

Government of British Columbia. (1996). *British Columbia Human Rights Code.* https://www.bclaws.ca/civix/document/id/complete/statreg/00_96210_01

Gulliver, T. (2018). Canada the redeemer and denials of racism. *Critical Discourse Studies, 15*(1), 68–86.

Hankivsky, O., & Dhamoon, R. K. (2013). Which genocide matters the most? An intersectionality analysis of the Canadian Museum of Human Rights. *Canadian Journal of Political Science / Revue canadienne de science politique, 46*(4), 899–920.

Hehir, T. (2007). Confronting ableism. *Educational Leadership, 64*(5), 8–14.

Iannacci, L. (2018). *Reconceptualizing disability in education.* Lexington Books.

Inclusion BC. (n.d.). *What is inclusive education?* https://inclusionbc.org/our-resources/what-is-inclusive-education

King, J. E. (1991). Dysconscious racism: Ideology, identity, and the miseducation of teachers. *The Journal of Negro Education, 60*(2), 133–146.

King, J. E. (2015). *Dysconscious racism, Afrocentric praxis, and education for human freedom: Through the years I keep on toiling.* Routledge.

Lalvani, P. (2013). Privilege, compromise, or social justice: Teachers' conceptualizations of inclusive education. *Disability & Society, 28*(1), 14–27.

Leonardo, Z., & Broderick, A. (2011). Smartness as property: A critical exploration of intersections between whiteness and disability studies. *Teachers College Record: The Voice of Scholarship in Education, 113*(10), 2206–2232.

Liasidou, A. (2014). Critical disability studies and socially just change in higher education. *British Journal of Special Education, 41*(2), 120–135.

Lund, D. E. (2006). Rocking the racism boat: School-based activists speak out on denial and avoidance. *Race Ethnicity and Education, 9*(2), 203–221.

Mally, J. (2021). *The dangers of oppression Olympics.* https://www.thegoodtrade.com/features/oppression-olympics

Ontario Human Rights Commission. (2018). *Accessible education for students with disabilities.* Government of Ontario. https://www.ohrc.on.ca/sites/default/files/Policy%20on%20accessible%20education%20for%20students%20with%20disabilities_FINAL_EN.pdf#overlay-context=en/users/aspeller

Shanouda, F., & Spagnuolo, N. (2021). Neoliberal methods of disqualification: A critical examination of disability-related education funding in Canada. *Journal of Education Policy, 36*(4), 530–556.

Siddiqua, A., & Janus, M. (2017). Experiences of parents of children with special needs at school entry: A mixed method approach. *Child: Care, Health and Development, 43*(4), 566–576.

Siuty, M. B. (2019). Teacher preparation as interruption or disruption? Understanding identity (re)constitution for critical inclusion. *Teaching and Teacher Education: An International Journal of Research and Studies, 81*(1), 38–49.

Slee, R. (2001). "Inclusion in practice": Does practice make perfect? *Educational Review, 53*(2), 113–123.

Slee, R. (2018). *Defining the scope of inclusive education.* https://unesdoc.unesco.org/ark:/48223/pf0000265773

United Nations. (2006). *United Nations Convention on the Rights of Persons with Disabilities.* https://www.un.org/disabilities/documents/convention/convention_accessible_pdf.pdf

CHAPTER 12

For Goodness' Sake! Teaching Global Citizenship in Canada with a Critical Ethic of Care

Rae Ann S. Van Beers

INTRODUCTION

With increased attention paid to encouraging global citizenship characteristics in Canadian students, educators now have the opportunity to partner with various NGOs with the expectation that the activities such organizations promote will help to develop desirable qualities in the youth they teach. Even though educators want to teach youth to be "good" local and global citizens, the conceptions of goodness that underlie these activities are not always commensurate with notions of good global citizenship that appear in educational and development studies literature. Such discrepancies can result in the promotion of activities that actually transmit a form of charitable foreign aid mentality to students, all under the guise of global citizenship. This critical analysis of the Right to Play organization serves as an example of how something as simple as children's play can serve neoliberal ends by exporting Western notions of play as integral for both individual and community development, further perpetuating the notion that vulnerable youth are deficient and that their difference must be "fixed" to make them more like the typical Canadian student. This idea becomes even more confused when one realizes that this organization, whose roots were based in development opportunities for children and youth in foreign countries, now uses that same model in Indigenous communities within Canada. These realities call upon us as educators to raise critical questions about how to make being good less problematic in the effort to move toward equity-oriented global citizenship for all regardless of their geographical location or national background. This chapter raises and analyzes such issues, with concluding perspectives on the possibilities of global citizenship teachings that are informed by and mediated via new lenses of what Nel Noddings (1984) characterized as an ethic of care in education.

"GOOD" GLOBAL CITIZENSHIP

Ideas about citizenship feature prominently in educational policy and curriculum documents. In Alberta, for example, the social studies curriculum expresses the desire that young people will "become active, informed, and responsible citizens" (Alberta Education, 2005, p. 1). Grade 6 students are expected to "demonstrate commitment to the well-being of their community by drawing attention to situations where action is needed," while grade 9 students should "develop leadership skills by assuming specific roles and responsibilities in organizations, projects, and events with their community" (Alberta Teachers' Association, 2014, p. 7). This call for students who display "good" citizenship can be found throughout the program of studies, but little direction of how students will learn to become such citizens is provided.

Even with these specific learning outcomes, there seems to be an "uneven approach" to citizenship education (Preece, 2008, p. 383) in schools in Alberta, and likely throughout Canada. In practice, this has often resulted in an overemphasis on acts of service such as fundraising and volunteering for various local and global causes over more activist-driven activities (Westheimer, 2015). It seems the desirable citizen, then, is one who participates in politics through acceptable means like voting, volunteering, donating to charity, and obeying laws, all while self-regulating, making few claims on the state, and contributing positively to the economy (Kennelly, 2009). Such citizenship roles provide relatively few opportunities for individuals to collaborate with others outside their circles, let alone in meaningful global connections, and certainly do not leave room for them to question or work to change the structures in place. The good global citizen has taken on a philanthrocapitalist persona (McGoey, 2015). Someone who has the means to financially contribute to social causes or who can donate their time, energy, or other personal resources is seen as embodying good citizenship, which aligns cleanly with neoliberal ideals of individualism and consumption (Apple, 2016). Such realities and attached actions result in a particular type of citizen who looks good while supposedly doing good and, of course, being credited with that goodness in a public way. NGOs have started cashing in on philanthrocapitalism. Perhaps the most famous—now infamous—Canadian non-profit organization with sturdy school ties is Me to We, which was repeatedly referred to by the organizers as a social enterprise rather than a charity. Previously, it partnered with the Unilever brand to sell school supplies to Canadian students who could then "track their impact" to discover where the donation attached to that product went and "how it changed a life" (Kielburger & Kielburger, 2016).

Interestingly, this NGO seems to have become a victim of its own success, having been connected to some ethically questionable collaborations with the federal government in 2020, and it has since suspended its operations in Canada (but not abroad). Still, many individuals obviously saw validity in this model, as the organization experienced a double-digit increase in sales for its social enterprise because of the collaboration with Unilever. Overall, the general understanding is that "fiscal global citizenship" is, and will continue to be, on the rise (Tallon & McGregor, 2014, p. 1415). While the characteristics of generosity, concern for others, and the need to act in the face of injustice are noble qualities for citizens to embody, there are concerns about viewing global citizenship through a strictly consumerist lens. Unfortunately, this type of citizenship does not always get deconstructed by educators.

The vague sense of citizenship presented in curricular documents has left room for NGOs to provide resources for teachers to fill the gaps in their education programming. Me to We, for example, has stated that their

> goal is to create systemic change by working with educators to inspire a generation of active global citizens. We have seen time and again how young people are looking for something more than what material culture is offering them—and [it is] educators who have the passion and experience to provide it. (Free the Children, n.d., p. 4)

To support this goal, Me to We provided yearly school kits to educators who agreed to partner with them. In return, teachers implemented the lessons in their classrooms or extracurricular clubs and then assisted students in planning and hosting one local and one global project aimed at reducing social inequities. The global projects regularly resulted in students raising money for the Me to We program of their choice. In taking on such work, many educators seemed to assume that students were learning how to be good citizens in their local communities and beyond. But as Benham Rennick and Desjardins (2013) ask, "Whose idea of good should we consider?" (p. 6). It seems that oftentimes Canadian educators allow NGOs to make that call for them, perpetuating shallow constructions of citizenship that shape the thinking and actions of their students.

RIGHT TO PLAY

Right to Play is another organization that has been providing this type of assistance to Canadian teachers for approximately 20 years. Started by Johann Olav Koss, a four-time Olympic speed skating gold medallist from Norway, the organization touts itself as

> an athlete-driven, humanitarian, non-governmental organization committed to improving the lives of the most disadvantaged children and their communities through sport for development. Sport for development evolved out of the

growing evidence that strengthening the right of children to play enhances their healthy psychosocial and physical development, and builds stronger communities. (Clappison, 2004, p. 36)

The organization bases its work on the United Nations Convention on the Rights of the Child (UNCRC), specifically Article 3.1, which in essence outlines the right to play for all children. It states that governments must recognize, promote, and provide age-appropriate opportunities for children to engage in play, recreational, and leisure activities (United Nations, 1989). It is based on the Sport for Development (SfD) model, which utilizes sport to improve the lives of vulnerable children and youth by supporting education, healthy child development, disease prevention, conflict resolution, and community development. Interestingly, Right to Play's global headquarters are located in Toronto, Ontario.

Canadian Students and Right to Play

While the bulk of its work takes place in approximately 15 different countries throughout the world, Right to Play's presence in Canadian classrooms has mainly focused on providing global citizenship and leadership opportunities for what could be deemed "mainstream" students. They claim to "empower youth to be leaders in their community and advocate for the Sport for Development and Peace movement" (Right to Play, n.d.). In the past, Right to Play Canada has offered a playbook along with its signature red soccer ball to educators who agree to partner with them. The playbook consisted of packaged lesson plans for teachers to use, complete with suggestions on how to raise funds for the organization within their schools. The only available literature on how such educational resources play out within Canadian classrooms is a 2014 case study on the use of the playbook by a middle-school physical education teacher. Despite a sense of praise throughout the article for various physical learning activities, such as one that attempted to simulate "a real crisis in Asia, Africa, or the Middle East" (Race, 2014, p. 10), the author notes that the teacher did not observe any noticeable changes in her students' daily behaviour or understanding of global issues after the lessons ended.

The playbook has officially been replaced with the Play Your Part Challenge, which features an online games manual, geared toward students in grades 3 through 8, that teachers can use free of charge, thanks to financial support from Global Affairs Canada. In exchange for this use, educators are asked to consider donating to the organization, with a suggested donation of a toonie per student. Along with the games/lesson plans, teachers can access a toolkit that briefly describes the work that Right to Play engages in throughout the world. In it, play is held up as a means of saving lives by keeping children safe, healthy, and educated. These claims are not verified with any play-based theory or literature but can be found throughout Right to Play's documents. The organization's 2019 annual report stated that it impacted 2.5 million children and youth (Right to Play, 2020). While most of these children live in countries that are considered to be in need of development (a problematically generalized assumption), at least some of these individuals are the ones in Canadian classrooms who engage in the lessons with their teachers. Educators who choose to support the organization use the toolkit to teach leadership skills to their students by encouraging them to design and facilitate a school-wide games event where the second step is to "fundraise, fundraise, fundraise." Such non-critical global citizenship at the school level provides support to McGoey's (2015) notion of philanthrocapitalism, which, by shaping the current understandings of Canadian children, potentially lowers future constructions and practices of critical local and global citizenships.

Sport for Development (SfD)

In direct contrast to the dearth of studies on the impacts of educational interventions on the privileged students who partake in them, there is ample literature on the impacts of SfD organizations in countries they seek to develop. As Spaaij, Oxford, and Jeanes (2016) note in regard to the implementation of SfD lesson plans and activities, "educators cannot simply run through a series of predetermined steps with students and expect this will lead to transformative action" (p. 573). The same could be said for those engaging in NGO-developed lessons in Canadian classrooms. We cannot simply (and simplistically) provide students with a learning experience and expect their lives to be instantly transformed because of it. Such expectations view youth as uniformly deficient and in need of fixing (Nols et al., 2017). While these particular scholars were describing the youth on the receiving end of the care provided by SfD organizations, the youth on the giving end of this care will also not all be equally changed through the same standardized lesson plan, as any educator could attest.

The critique of SfD extends beyond the classroom, however. Concerns that sport is being used globally in the name of development to simply transfer neoliberal colonial ideas have been raised by many researchers (see Arellano & Downey, 2019; Darnell, 2007; Darnell & Hayhurst, 2011; Gardam et al., 2017; Nols et al., 2017; Schulenkorf et al., 2016). Millington et al. (2019) state that historically sport was used by colonizing countries as a means of control over their subjects and that through SfD, "sport is similarly recast as a tool of aid, shaping the actions of youth for the purposes of promoting health, the value of hard work, and fair play" (p. 2135). Right to Play has been noted to be one of the largest SfD organizations in the world (Right to Play, n.d.) and is implicated in these types of concerns and their outcomes. Reinforcing the academic worries about global citizenship education, SfD is thought to solidify global inequities and hierarchies by positioning some individuals as givers capable of global citizenship and others as being in dire need of development. It appears that the neoliberal, colonial, and paternalistic patterns of history simply repeat around the globe, this time with the assistance of Canadian youth who, in their well-intentioned contexts, raise money to support and durably sustain these patterns.

With these pragmatic criticisms having been lobbed in its direction in recent years, Right to Play seems to have become more receptive to community needs and concerns with its programming, resulting in the organization being seen as adaptable and flexible (Arellano et al., 2018). Over time, it has moved from essentially importing sport leaders who present programming to youth to actively hiring mentors from the communities it partners with. Yet changes like this have been slower in Right to Play's programming in Indigenous communities within Canada (Arellano et al., 2018).

Right to Play in Indigenous Communities in Canada

Right to Play provides its development programming in Canada. While some students in Canada are situated as helpers being asked to raise money and awareness for the organization, others are now recipients of the help. Right to Play has extended its work within Canada to 85 Indigenous communities in Ontario, British Columbia, Alberta, Manitoba, and Labrador (Right to Play, n.d.). Through its website, it states that these Promoting Life-skills in Aboriginal Youth (PLAY) programs are funded through partnerships with various organizations, not necessarily through the fundraising efforts of other Canadian students. The Labrador PLAY program was initiated in March of 2019 through a $536,000 grant from Indigenous Services Canada, while the Alberta and Ontario programs are supported by Suncor Energy, an energy company based in Calgary, Alberta. Although not present on Right to Play's list of Canadian programs on its website, a partnership between Right to Play and the Goldcorp company in the Northwest Territories has also been documented in SfD literature (Millington et al., 2019). It appears that the companies in the extractive industries have taken up SfD as a means of "giving back" to the Indigenous communities that they take resources from.

Companies like these partner with various organizations, including Right to Play, as a means of proving themselves to be "good neighbours" to the communities they work in and near, all "while distracting from the deleterious impacts of extractivism" (Millington et al., 2019, p. 2132). Several scholars point out that governmental agencies have outsourced funding for Indigenous youth programming, allowing it to be taken up by companies that have benefited, financially and in other ways, from settler colonial systems (Arellano & Downey, 2019; Gardam et al., 2017; Millington et al., 2019). It is believed that, through this arrangement, companies are attempting to be viewed as good corporate citizens by spending money to improve the "neoliberal employability life-skills" of youth who have been negatively impacted by their actions, with sport being their tool of choice (Arellano & Downey, 2019, p. 467). In Canada, the global headquarters of Right to Play, there seems to be an interesting and alarming disconnect between programming for mainstream students, who get to be characterized as the helpers, and youth growing up in Indigenous communities, who are relegated to the status of needing help. The origins for this discrepancy are never acknowledged in the lessons provided. The federal government's unwillingness to properly fund health, education, and social programs in Indigenous communities throughout Canada, combined with companies' desire to appear to give back to the communities they take from, has resulted in gross inequities within Canada itself. It has also paved the way for private sector funding of social development programs for Indigenous youth (Gardam et al., 2017). In the meantime, most other students in Canada attend adequately funded schools where they learn, often via these uncritical and less-than-inclusive programs, how to become global citizens.

WHAT IS PLAY?

While Right to Play's efforts are focused mainly on the right of children and youth to play sports and games, the organization does utilize other forms of play within its work. According to its website, the development programs it sponsors use games, sport, and creative and free play during weekly activities. As such, it is helpful to consider what is meant by the idea of play more broadly. Isenberg and Quisenberry (2002) note that play theorists overwhelmingly view play as central to children's lives and their healthy development, physically, cognitively, socially, and emotionally. They refer to play as "a serious behaviour that has a powerful influence on learning" (p. 33). Kenneally (2015) notes that play is considered the primary activity of children's lives but worries that recognition of its many benefits will result in it morphing into something to suit adult expectations for the learning and development of children in their care. He warns that "children are positioned as unfinished beings that require guidance and assistance to accumulate the skills and knowledge needed to become functioning members of society … to become the right type of functioning subjects" (p. 258). He echoes Wood's (2012) concern that as adult recognition of the importance of play for children grows, so too does the belief that types of play can be categorized as right or wrong, useful or not, socially acceptable or unapproved.

Right to Play has certainly tapped into the importance of play in that it forms the basis for its global development efforts. On its website, it states that children utilizing their weekly programs are provided with opportunities for creative and free play, along with games and sport. In spite of this support for freedom to play, Kenneally's concerns in regard to purposive play could be applied here as well. There is an underlying current to the way the organization operates that implies that play is of a specific nature and must come from elsewhere. Those in countries in need of "development" must be taught how to play properly. They must be given the tools to *do* play effectively so that they can develop in the way that has been deemed appropriate by others. This is especially apparent in relation to the founding story of Right to Play as an organization, as stated on the website and in the student information pack of the Play Your Part Challenge.

Prior to his Olympic victories, Johann Olav Koss had traveled to Eritrea, where he noticed a particularly popular child within a group. When asked about his popularity, the boy responded, "I have long sleeves." He then showed Koss that once he removed his shirt, he could roll it up and tie the sleeves so that it could act as a ball for them to play soccer with. Koss later made good on his vow to return with a proper soccer ball after the Olympics, and Right to Play was born. In an attempt to be inspiring, this story works like so many other development stories in that it frames children's circumstances as worthy of pity and in need of a (preferably) white person to save them from their sad conditions. The kinds of play that children engage in naturally, with the tools they themselves develop from the resources and creativity they already possess, do not seem to qualify in this imported model of play. By devaluing such context-based creativity, modern sport becomes the appropriate form of physical activity for all (Arellano & Downey, 2019). Interestingly, Indigenous communities within Canada are thrust into this deficient category as well, and the rest of us have the luxury of using the UNCRC to back up our "good" global citizenship actions.

Obviously, the overall story, along with its assumptions and practices, has negative implications for those located as being "helped." Current inequitable structures and hierarchies are perpetuated when specific notions of play and sport become the standard for all countries to adhere to. The deficit lens continues to position the helped as inferior. They are seen to be devoid of agency in their own lives and communities. We know this is not the reality, for, as Nols and colleagues (2017) showed, just because youth live in vulnerable communities we cannot, and should not, assume that they also lack self-esteem, self-efficacy, or related abilities. There are also complicated and problematic implications for those who are viewed—and view themselves—as the helpers. Despite the lure of believing oneself to be a benevolent, selfless, good benefactor who is willing to donate one's time and money to help others, that image does not work to alter the systems that have created the inequities that privileged certain individuals in the first place. It could easily be argued that the privileged do not actually wish to change such circumstances and potentially lose some or all of their privilege and attached "helper/superior" status. Some educators might disagree with that sentiment, especially those who have taught students who were passionate about social justice issues and demonstrated a strong desire to make a positive difference in the world. Sadly, the global citizenship education offered to them through some NGOs may actually result in a failure to promote equity or justice, despite their best intentions. Students may become what Kennelly (2009) referred to as good citizens who follow the rules given to them and stay free of the bad activist label attributed to youth who actively work to challenge unjust systems.

HOW DO WE EDUCATE GOOD GLOBAL CITIZENS?

What might happen if we applied an ethic of care to global citizenship education? Although Noddings (1984) directed her attention to the teacher–student relationship, it does not seem unreasonable to consider other relationships through this lens, including that of students toward other students. If Canadian students are, in fact, raising funds and awareness for their peers in other places, they should be seen as being called into relationship with those peers. In her work, Noddings explains that a dialogical and reciprocal relationship between what she terms the one-caring and the cared-for is necessary for an ethic of care to work. She highlights the problem of indirect caring, which happens when the one-caring is not in relationship with the object of their care. If the cared-for does not, or cannot, respond to the care in some way, the caring loop is not completed. This would seem to be the case when Canadian students simply raise money and awareness for non-profit groups working in other places. Rather than engaging with authentic instances of care where those who are cared-for are able to recognize and respond to the care given, the helpers become caretakers instead of ones-caring. They follow particular caring "rules" that have been set out by NGOs through prepackaged lessons and projects, suggesting that the ones-caring are motivated less by the desire to challenge inequities and more by being publicly credited with the care they provide (Noddings, 1984, p. 24). Noddings notes that those being helped need to be cared for in ways that respect and respond to their specific, individual contexts. Preplanned lessons and projects likely fail in that regard, as they view particular groups as experiencing uniform problems that can be solved in relatively uniform ways. The reciprocal relationships required for true caring relationships to occur can only be fostered through contextualizing the experiences of individuals who wish to receive the care being provided. While the two-way dialogues between caring parties that are needed for this to happen may be difficult for schools to arrange, they are vital to teaching more privileged students to see those living in circumstances different from their own as capable and valued agents of change in their own lives, as well as in the lives of others. This is especially important considering that the helper/helped divide that current global citizenship education practices can delineate occur not just globally but within the nation-state known as Canada.

An awareness that the global citizenship education tools provided to educators by organizations like Right to Play are potentially problematic is important. As shown through the example of play presented above, the activities promoted by some of these organizations actually transmit a form of neoliberal, charitable foreign-aid mentality to students, framed as good citizenship. Without questioning our ideas of what it means to be good, some educators may continue to support these types of organizations, with similar results. However, through careful consideration of the activities shared by these groups, teachers can help their students to critically digest both the overt and covert lessons being presented to them. An increasing number of educators are becoming more aware of this and are starting to provide thoughtful opportunities for students to enhance their critical global citizenship skills and knowledge and perhaps become the "good" global citizens whom we hope for and who will change systems for the better. After all, "human play should be understood as one of the special places for the conjuring of possibility" (Hendricks, 2009, as cited in Wood, 2012, p. 5) and true global citizenship education should open up possibilities for students everywhere.

DISCUSSION QUESTIONS

1. What did citizenship education look like when you were a student? Do you feel that those lessons helped you to become a better citizen? If so, what made them effective? If not, how could they have been improved?

2. What are attributes of global citizenship that you believe are important for students to learn and embody?

3. Does raising money and awareness for certain causes have a place in citizenship education?

4. What role does play have in K–12 classrooms? Can play be used to teach citizenship? If so, how?

REFERENCES

Alberta Education. (2005). *Program of studies: Social studies, kindergarten to grade 12.* Alberta Education.

Alberta Teachers' Association. (2014). *Not so random "acts of kindness": Engaging students in thoughtful social justice actions participant guide.* Alberta Teachers' Association.

Apple, M. W. (2016). Challenging the epistemological fog: The roles of the scholar/activist in education. *European Educational Research Journal, 15*(5), 505–515. https://doi.org/10.1177/1474904116647732

Arellano, A., & Downey, A. (2019). Sport-for-development and the failure of Aboriginal subjecthood: Re-imagining lacrosse as resurgence in Indigenous communities. *Settler Colonial Studies, 9*(4), 457–478. https://doi.org/10.1080/2201473X.2018.1537078

Arellano, A., Halsall, T., Forneris, T., & Gaudet, C. (2018). Results of a utilization-focused evaluation of a Right to Play program for Indigenous youth. *Evaluation and Program Planning, 66*, 156–164. https://doi.org/10.1016/j.evalprogplan.2017.08.001

Benham Rennick, J., & Desjardins, M. (2013). Towards a pedagogy of good global citizenship. In J. Benham Rennick & M. Desjardins (Eds.), *The world is my classroom: International learning and Canadian higher education* (pp. 3–15). University of Toronto Press.

Clappison, S. (2004). Going international: Right to Play. *Physical and Health Education, 70*(2), 36–38.

Darnell, S. C. (2007). Playing with race: *Right to Play* and the production of whiteness in "development through sport." *Sport in Society: Cultures, Commerce, Media, Politics, 10*(4), 560–579. https://doi.org/10.1080/17430430701388756

Darnell, S. C., & Hayhurst, L. M. C. (2011). Sport for decolonization: Exploring a new praxis of sport for development. *Progress in Development Studies, 11*(3), 183–196. https://doi.org/10.1177/146499341001100301

Free the Children. (n.d.). *Educator's guide: Free the Children.*

Gardam, K., Giles, A. R., & Hayhurst, L. M. C. (2017). Understanding the privitisation of funding for sport for development in the Northwest Territories: A Foucauldian analysis. *International Journal of Sport Policy and Politics, 9*(3), 541–555. https://doi.org/10.1080/19406940.2017.1310742

Isenberg, J. P., & Quisenberry, N. (2002). Play: Essential for all children. *Childhood Education, 79*(1), 33–39. https://doi.org/10.1080/00094056.2002.10522763

Kenneally, N. (2015). "Be careful!" Using our words as a discursive exploration of early childhood educators regulating children's play. *Global Studies of Childhood, 5*(3), 255–265. https://doi.org/10.1177/2043610615597139

Kennelly, J. (2009). Good citizen/bad activist: The cultural role of the state in youth activism. *Review of Education, Pedagogy, and Cultural Studies, 31*(2–3), 127–149. https://doi.org/10.1080/10714410902827135

Kielburger, C., & Kielburger, M. (2016, January 25). *Together we can change the world.* Presentation at University of Alberta, Edmonton, AB.

McGoey, L. (2015). *No such thing as a free gift: The Gates Foundation and the price of philanthropy.* Verso Books.

Millington, R., Giles, A. R., Hayhurst, L. M. C., van Luijk, N., & McSweeney, M. (2019). "Calling out" corporate redwashing: The extractives industry, corporate social responsibility and sport for development in Indigenous communities in Canada. *Sport in Society*, *22*(12), 2122–2140. https://doi.org/10.1080/17430437.2019.1567494

Noddings, N. (1984). *Caring: A feminine approach to ethics and moral education*. University of California Press.

Nols, Z., Haudenhuyse, R., & Theeboom, M. (2017). Urban sport-for-development initiatives and young people in socially vulnerable situations: Investigating the "deficit model." *Social Inclusion*, *5*(2), 210–222. https://dx.doi.org/10.17645/si.v5i2.881

Preece, J. (2008). A social justice approach to education for active citizenship: An international perspective. In M. A. Peters, A. Britton, & H. Blee (Eds.), *Global citizenship education: Philosophy, theory and pedagogy* (pp. 381–393). Sense Publishers.

Race, D. L. (2014). Teaching social responsibility: Feasibility of the Right to Play Playbook. *Revue phénEPS / PHEnex Journal*, *6*(1), 1–21.

Right to Play. (n.d.). Right to Play: Schools. *Right to Play Canada website*. http://www.righttoplay.ca/Act/join/Pages/Schools.aspx (Website was available when the information was downloaded on August 20, 2020 but has been since taken down).

Right to Play. (2020). *Right to Play 2019 annual report*. https://righttoplaydiag107.blob.core.windows.net/rtp-media/documents/2019_AnnualReport_SinglePages_LowRes_PDF.pdf

Schulenkorf, N., Sherry, E., & Rowe, K. (2016). Sport for development: An integrated literature review. *Journal of Sport Management*, *30*(1), 22–39. https://doi.org/10.1123/jsm.2014-0263

Spaaij, R., Oxford, S., & Jeanes, R. (2016). Transforming communities through sport? Critical pedagogy and sport for development. *Sport, Education and Society*, *21*(4), 570–587. https://doi.org/10.1080/13573322.2015.1082127

Tallon, R. A. M., & McGregor, A. (2014). Pitying the Third World: Towards more progressive emotional responses to development education in schools. *Third World Quarterly*, *35*(8), 1406–1422. https://doi.org/10.1080/01436597.2014.946259

United Nations. (1989). *Convention on the rights of the child*. United Nations.

Westheimer, J. (2015). *What kind of citizen? Educating our children for the common good*. Teachers College Press.

Wood, E. (2012). The state of play. *International Journal of Play*, *1*(1), 4–5. https://doi.org/10.1080/21594937.2012.655477

CHAPTER 13

Education for Refugee Learners under the Framework of Social Justice and Racial Equity

Neda Asadi

INTRODUCTION

There are over 70 million people globally who have been forcibly displaced from their homes due to overriding geopolitical conflicts (United Nations High Commissioner for Refugees [UNHCR], 2018). This collective, signified as *refugees*, was created as a sociopolitical class (with attendant legal and economic implications) after World War II. Although the United Nations High Commissioner for Refugees has mandated international protection and assistance to refugees under the Geneva 1951 Convention, their safety and resettlement has not been safeguarded. Policies that address refugee populations have been delayed, sporadic in nature, and difficult to enforce, if they are enforced at all. In many instances, the human rights of the displaced population are not upheld during the resettlement process; by extension, children's welfare and best interests, although stated to be of prime importance, in practice are not taken into consideration (Crowe, 2006). The lack of understanding of and the lowered value accorded to refugees is evident through the sparseness of public policies and spaces to allow for equitable success; the limited policies and practices are also extended into educational settings.

The review of the literature on policies and educational trajectories related to the education of refugee youth reveals the lack of targeted policies and lower levels of educational attainment for refugee learners (Asadi, 2016; Gunderson et al., 2012; Roessingh & Field, 2000). Ironically, there exists a wealth of knowledge on the importance of integrating refugee learners into the mainstream educational model and the means through which to enhance the spaces and practices to ensure refugee learners' engagement with schooling (Dei & Rummens, 2010; Lund, 2008; Rossiter & Rossiter, 2009; Rutter, 2006). It has been argued that the underlying framework that educational institutions are built upon maintains the hierarchy of values placed on learners, which perpetuates the educational achievement of those deemed to be valued and creates the "Other" (Abdi & Richardson, 2008; Apple, 2000). As such, it is imperative to reimagine an educational framework that allows for educational policies and practices that would redress the injustices faced by refugee learners. In this chapter, I propose a theoretical framework of racial equity and social justice that allows the unfolding of educational policies and practices in a manner that creates equitable educational opportunities, where learners can access knowledge, develop their sense of self, and understand the destructive power of "Othering."

REFUGEE LEARNERS IN CANADIAN SCHOOLS

Challenges faced by refugees to integrate into their new homes and countries have been studied and documented over the last seven decades. An array of pre- and post-migration challenges effectively impedes refugee integration into mainstream society; some of the major hindrances for children and youth include interrupted education or inability to access any formal education during pre-migration experiences. Additional post-migration challenges faced by refugees include lack of familiarity with the new predominant culture, the language barrier, lack of proper documentation, economic challenges, and racism (Kanu, 2007; Lund, 2008). The combined challenges make navigating the Canadian system difficult and lead to low-paying employment and family income and the inability to access essential services such as healthcare and education, which further drive this vulnerable population to the margins of society.

Refugee youth and their families highly value educational institutions, but the Canadian education system has failed to meet their needs and ensure their engagement with schooling (Kanu, 2007; Ngo, 2009a). A review of policies and practices from the provinces of Alberta and British Columbia indicates the lack of targeted policies and practices needed to meet the needs of refugee learners (Asadi, 2016). Data from the literature on the education of minorities and refugees in Canadian educational institutions indicate that the intentions of inclusion and diversity policies are not realized (Dei, 2008; Ngo, 2009b; Parkin, 2012; Shields, 2004). The broad policies under the umbrella of multiculturalism homogenize all migrant learners and students with varying needs. Such policies exist despite research emphasizing the importance of developing a sense of belonging in children and youth, and theories and practices on a variety of alternative educational practices to enhance language acquisition and academic learning for newcomers (Cummins, 2009; Gunderson et al., 2012; Meyers, 2006). Therefore, there is an evident gap between existing policies and practices and the existing knowledge in identifying and addressing the educational needs of refugee learners. To uncover the root causes that have made refugee learners invisible in our education system and educational practices, which relegates them to the margins of society, existing hegemonic belief systems and practices need to be interrogated and replaced. A framework based on racial equity and social justice will disrupt hegemonic belief systems and provide a platform to address the multi-factorial societal issues that impact the education of refugee youth. The framework is built upon the earlier work of two critical theorists: racial equity, as inspired by the work of Frantz Fanon, *Black Skin, White Masks* (1967), and social justice, from the work of Nancy Fraser (2005b, 2008).

FRAMEWORK: RACE EQUITY AND SOCIAL JUSTICE

Why a Racial Equity and Social Justice Framework?

Schools, as substructures of the larger society, mirror the predominant values, practices, and social orders of their larger environment. Canada, similar to other Western nations, is built upon a neoliberal discourse and thus driven by neoliberal values. Schools and learning institutions are created as vehicles to advance the cause of capitalism, and for capitalism to thrive, there is a need for the perpetuation of inequity and the superiority of a small, selectively elite group over others. Given this overall national context, ongoing inequities are created as a result of differences in background, history, and socioeconomic situation as well as gender, race, and ability/disability assumptions. Additionally, building the foundations of schools solely upon one cultural perspective, that is, Eurocentric values and practices, creates a superiority of one culture over all others and erases the enfranchisement of diverse cultures, knowledges, and subjective beings. Building an educational framework that encompasses racial and other equities goes beyond tolerance based on skin colours, ethnicities, and religious beliefs, and endeavours to decolonize the education system. The decolonization of education embodies valuing all learners and their full inclusion, accepts all knowledges, and promotes educational resources and practices that learners can relate to in both cognitive and embodied ways. As Isaacs (1968) argued,

> Habits of mind created by this long history of mastery and subjection are part of the culture itself in all its many manifestations. Conscious and unremitting effort will be needed to free the culture of the many gross and subtle ways in which it has shaped whites and non-whites to these patterns. This effort begins in the political, legal, and economic systems, but then must move into society's

educational systems and religious establishments, its great bodies of sacred and profane literature, folklores, and languages and vernacular. (p. 78)

The decolonization of education therefore encompasses not only policies that adhere to equity of education but also promote the educational environment and curriculum that relate to students' epistemological and ontological standings. For education to meet the needs of all learners, there is a need to shift the policy and practice of education to valuing all learners, highlighting their strengths and meeting their needs.

While the cornerstone of decolonization of education involves racial equity and awareness of biases and stereotypes, race consciousness alone will not create an equitable society or learning environment (Varma, 2012). Learning and education are multi-factorial and largely dependent on students' families, their socioeconomics, and the larger society's economic, cultural, and political influences. Therefore, for education to allow the learner's growth and educational achievement, there is a need to be conscious of societal factors impacting education. Education as a means to fulfilling one's potential and ability to serve in a meaningful way is only attainable in a just society with political, economic, cultural, and racial equities. Lack of social justice will deny exploration of the Self and continue the perpetuation of marginalized others. As Shultz (2012) states, lack of parity of participation in all spheres of society perpetuates the existing societal hierarchy:

> Processes of participation can perpetuate humiliation when they continue to misrecognize and silence people, their knowledges, and experiences. Forced inclusion, like exclusion, are dehumanizing and de-citizenizing when they perpetuate the ideal citizen as one who is obedient and agreeable, supporting the myths of harmony, compliance, and universal Enlightenment. (p. 38)

Given that educational success is highly dependent on the provision of specific support as needed for each learner or group of learners, this framework provides a platform to unfold the educational practices in a way that paves the way to the educational success of all learners regardless of their social, economic, racial, or other specific attributes.

Racial Equity

Fanon's (1967) work *Black Skin, White Masks* involved the experiences of the colonized during European colonization; his work to this day can inform societal inequities based on the racialization of peoples. Fanon's work creates an awareness on the impact of colonization, which has caused the devaluation of the sense of self and erasure of the knowledges and histories of the Other. For Fanon, race was not defined based on genetic disposition but as a political and historical construction mediated through culture, "for not only must the black man be black, he must be black in relation to the white man" (p. 90). He discussed the creation of the Black man through culture when he described "the white man who had woven me out of the thousand details, anecdotes, and stories" (p. 91). In his analysis, Fanon described the misuse of race through power relations and creation of the Other that is objectified and, therefore "recreated," as inferior.

Furthermore, Fanon acknowledges the relation between the racialization process and class; he contends that the creation of the inferior race, the colonized, is directly linked to being of lower economic status (Hussain, 2006). That is, "production relations under modern capitalism have historically remained race relations in such a way that race itself comes to constitute class, and that, thus, one cannot sufficiently account for class formations without considering race as a determining factor (p. 129)." Fanon (as cited in Hussain, 2006) stated, "In the colonies the economic subculture is also a superstructure. The cause is the consequence; you are rich because you are white, you are white because you are rich" (p. 134). Fanon underlines the intersectionality of becoming oppressed and its impact on identity development, cultural devaluation, and economic impediment. Therefore, objectifying the Other creates a class of citizens who are constructed as less capable of social participation or who are disengaged from citizenry.

Similarly, racism in schools has been attributed to social marginalization, the devaluation of students' knowledges and experiences, low expectations for student achievements, streamlining students to non-academic routes, and improper placement (Guo, 2015; Henry & Tator, 2006; Kanu, 2007; Zinga & Gordon, 2016). There is a negative relationship between ethnicity and success in learning institutions. The crafting of the narrative of the Other in educational institutions and the resulting negative educational outcome go even further for refugee learners, as they are characterized as victims, traumatized, and affected by disrupted schooling (Kumsa, 2006). The phenomenon that Fanon referred to as the creation of his narrative by the colonizers through "the stories and anecdotes" is similarly being played out in the school systems, where stories of students based on their ethnic lines, race, and class are predefined. The consequences of these practices, embedded in stereotypes by the host country, are limited educational outcomes for students from minority backgrounds and the perpetuation of the marginalization of communities based on race and ethnicity.

Racial stereotypes play a significant role in educational and identity development of youth within the learning centres. Cui (2015), in her study of Chinese students in rural and urban Alberta, discovered that racialized minority youth felt marginalized and "still regarded themselves as outsiders even if they were educationally successful and economically included" (p. 1155). In their study,

Zinga and Gordon (2016) established that while minority students acknowledged the existence of racism, they downplayed the issue and attempted to fit in with the mainstream school population. Strategies included "minoritized individuals often repress their race to fit in with white majority contexts due to the difficulty that individuals face in discussing race and racial issues" (p. 3). Fanon described Black individuals' internalization of white values as epidermalization, a process of devaluing one's own behaviour, language, and culture and internalizing the values of the white to be accepted as an equal, thereby accepting and internalizing inferiority based on race and ethnicity. Recognizing the impacts of racial inequity and the significant role it plays in identity development and educational attainment of youth, racial equity needs to be one of the pillars informing any framework within which education unfolds. Racial equity takes away the power and privilege that is given to one group over another. Racial equity creates an environment within which learners as valued members can thrive based on their own stories and experiences and grow into their authentic selves.

Fanon's work, even after so many years, is particularly suitable in achieving racial equity. In *Black Skin, White Masks*, he expresses hope for the possibility of overcoming the barriers set by race as defined and practised in historical and contemporary power relations:

> I believe that the fact of the juxtaposition of the white and black races has created a massive psychoexistential complex. I hope by analyzing it to destroy it.... I seriously hope to persuade my brother, whether black or white, to tear off with all his strength the shameful livery put together by centuries of incomprehension. (p. 5)

Fanon, in his analysis of race and racialization, unravels the possibility of moving beyond the construction of the Other, if people of all ethnicities are willing to understand Self and the Other and to go through recognition and "authentic communication" (p. 180) between them. In doing so, it becomes possible to challenge racism and disrupt the existing prescribed narratives and labels directed toward students from ethnic backgrounds. It is through racial equity, therefore, that students and their ways of being, as well as knowledge and knowledge creation, must be valued and their specific needs met in a way that supports their growth and educational goals.

Social Justice

Social justice theories were developed in response to existing societal inequities as a means to redress lived injustices. Throughout history, various philosophers, politicians, and scholars have proposed varying means of achieving social justice;

each theory comes with its own focus on one or the more factors that can cause injustice. In this chapter, social justice is, as drawn from Fraser's (2007) definition, accessibility to social needs and arrangements for all members in order for all to participate on par on matters concerning their society. In order to achieve participation parity, Fraser has developed a three-dimensional model of recognition, representation, and redistribution, referring to it as *post-Westphalian democratic justice* (Fraser, 2007, p. 19).

Redistribution was in response to members of society being denied full participation in economic spheres. Parity of participation can be denied when the status of members—based on their race, country of origin, or value system—is devalued, and individuals are misrecognized. Hence the need for recognition to achieve social justice for all is crucial, particularly in the face of socially created attributes and identification factors. In inquiring whether justice requires the recognition of groups or what is distinct about individuals, Fraser argues that both universalist recognition and distinctiveness of individuals can be utilized to redress the injustice, as the case requires.

Representation is the third dimension in Fraser's understanding of social justice; it underscores the importance of political inclusion, that is, who can be represented. Fraser explains that while economics and culture are political, as they are impacted by power relations, the representation dimension constitutes a more specific definition of politics: "I mean political in a more specific, constitutive sense, which concerns the constitution of the state's jurisdiction and the decision rules by which it structures contestation" (p. 20). In identifying who should be included, Fraser writes, "all those who are subject to a given governance structure have moral standing as subjects of justice in relation to it" (Fraser, 2005b, p. 65). According to Fraser (2005a), all three dimensions are equally important and must be interlinked in order for parity of participation to be possible: "no redistribution or recognition without representation" (p. 23).

Research conducted in Alberta has demonstrated that peoples of colour and Indigenous people live in a disadvantaged position in every sphere of our society: housing, justice, employment, and education (Lightman & Good Gingrich, 2018). Lack of social justice negatively impacts the development of children and youth. Children in many low-income families exhibit a reduced motivation to learn, delayed cognitive development, lower achievement, less participation in extracurricular activities, lower career aspirations, interrupted school attendance, lower university attendance, an increased risk of illiteracy, and higher dropout rates (Ferguson et al., 2007). Redistribution, recognition, and representation are vital in the formation of a healthy society where the ills of society have been addressed and all citizens have access to basic needs.

Racial Equity and Social Justice Framework

By merging the concepts discussed by Fanon and Fraser, the framework of racial equity and social justice makes explicit and highlights the multitude of factors that contribute to the marginalization of individuals or groups of people. By highlighting the interconnection of all the factors discussed above, this model can help policy makers and educators to be cognizant of how different aspects of education, alongside learners' existing realities, impact learning and the educational journey of students with refugee backgrounds.

As depicted in figure 13.1, the framework is comprised of four segments, the first of which consists of the economic, cultural, and political factors that influence equity of education. This segment of the framework creates an awareness of the existing inequities and acknowledges histories, policies, and practices that have created economic inequities, cultural devaluation, and political disenfranchisement. In the context of education for refugee learners, this awareness allows educators to be cognizant of the impact of the inequalities and the constructed myths about refugees placed on these learners and to then take the necessary proactive steps to bring forth equitable policies and related educational practices.

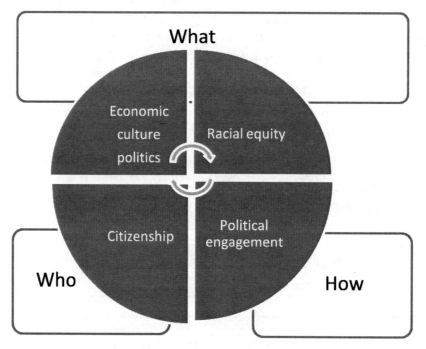

Figure 13.1: Racial Equity and Social Justice Framework

Source: Created by Neda Asadi.

For example, in drafting policies or educational activities, it is important to consider whether goals are attainable for all students or will create presumed helpless victims who are marginalized more. Therefore, educators and administrators should (1) be conscious of students' perspectives on the existing power-relations in their interactions with these youth and (2) develop programs that address problematic power and social justice relations through the teaching of learning outcomes that engage students by relating learning to their life experiences. This form of education alleviates the imbalance in educational provisions and outcomes and promotes learning that develops the sense of self for all.

The second segment in figure 13.1 is concerned with the question of citizenship and inclusion. As Fraser (2005b) stated, inclusion is not just based on membership and

> is amongst the most consequential of political decisions. Constituting both members and non-members in a single stroke, this decision effectively excludes the latter from the universe of those entitled to consideration within the community in matters of distribution, recognition and ordinary-political justice. (p. 19)

Given some refugees' stateless position and their lack of citizenship globally, which led to their precarious situation in Canada, the second segment is an important element in ensuring that refugees have access to their rights and, by extension, that children have access to the resources needed for successful inclusion in the education system. Here, it is important to locate refugee populations within the larger society and understand how their positions as members or nonmembers, as prescribed by society, has influenced their accessibility to resources. It is through this level of understanding that educators can identify the specific needs of their refugee learner populations and ensure those needs are met.

Refugee students' interrupted or lack of formal education and their experiences of being forcibly displaced are examples that educators and school administrators need to consider creating equitable inclusive education. School placement for all students is based on their age upon arrival; these newcomer refugee students are also placed in classes based on their age as opposed to their experiences of schooling. Furthermore, given refugee students' limited fluency in English or French (in Quebec), which requires them to catch up fast, they are generally unable to partake in other core subjects, such as math and science. As placement is based solely on age, refugee newcomers are expected to participate on par with other newcomer students who have different migration experiences; on the other hand, they are limited in the subject matters in which they can enrol. Problematically, it is also assumed that if they do not have sufficient knowledge of the English language, they must also lack or be limited in their knowledge of other school subjects. To counter this, placement policies and practices must embody valuing the whole learner through designing programs that meet their needs while building on their strengths. To do this, proper assessments that values all students' knowledges and educational practices and that help students experience success are essential in creating sustained engagement with schooling for refugee learners.

The third segment of the figure informs the process of social justice: who should become involved in voicing the injustices. Fraser argued that the responsibility for seeking equitable society needs to include all members of society and not only those who are being negatively impacted by the existing policies and practices. She asserted that those "who already enjoy parity of voice will need to engage in critical reflection and dialogue" (as cited in Hölscher, 2014, p. 25), with the goal of ensuring social justice for all. In order for the existing systems, which create a hierarchy of the population based on economic, political, racial, religious, and cultural values, to be challenged, individuals need to examine their own values and practices and take part in the process of creating change. While it is essential for refugee learners to demonstrate a sense of agency and pave their educational success through perseverance, resilience, and by becoming familiar with their new surroundings, these efforts would be a struggle in the face of non-acceptance and non-recognition. As such, it is essential for educators, administrators, community support networks, and families to understand the struggle and participate in creating learning spaces where learners feel seen, valued, and provided with opportunities to grow into their authentic selves.

The fourth segment focuses on ensuring racial equity for all students within Canadian educational institutions. The literature related to race in the education system in Canada has acknowledged the power of "whiteness" (Carr, 2008, p. 5) and the need for an equitable educational system. Although it is tempting to believe that racial inequities are features of the past and that humans have progressed to an understanding of one another based on their essence rather than socially constructed attributes, daily events and documented studies outlined earlier reveal otherwise. Undertaking education under the pillar of racial equity shines a light on how Eurocentric views and practices have marginalized students whose histories are not recognized and whose knowledges are not included. Therefore, policies and practices need to consider and value diverse knowledges and histories. A curriculum that is representative of diverse knowledges and practices and that includes learners and their families in its creation of knowledge can be an example of creating equitable learning spaces and exemplifies the decolonized classroom.

Under the lens of a racial equity and social justice framework, institutionalized and societal barriers such as racism impeding the educational success of refugee learners are under scrutiny. It is through such increasing scrutiny that all stakeholders—administrators, teachers, students, parents, and community members—are called upon to examine individually and collectively their deeply held assumptions on race and the effects of racism in our educational institutions. The racial equity and social justice framework discussed in this chapter must shift the blame from students' identities to societal barriers. The framework of equity and social justice fills the gap created by liberal multiculturalists who, on one hand, have argued that there is only one human race without considering the existing differences and, on the other hand, have marginalized students who are the most dissimilar to the mainstream culture. Kincheloe and Steinberg (1997, as cited in Shields, 2004) reminded us that "being colour-blind is a hegemonic practice that only White people have the luxury of believing" (p. 120). The focus on critical racial equity and social justice frameworks opens the dialogue on the differences within our educational institutions and acknowledges the presence of diversity. Further, it allows diversity to become part of the educational experience in meaningful ways, such as through inclusion in the curriculum, appropriate evaluation systems, student support, and students' socialization experiences within schools.

CONCLUSION

The creation of a forcibly displaced population is a result of a complex interplay between geopolitical, economic, and racial circumstances, but above all, it is an unimaginable breach of justice for those who have been uprooted from their lands and their lives. Therefore, any action taken to remediate this grave injustice must be considered under a framework that highlights interrelated sociopolitical factors. In the context of racial equity and a social justice framework, various societal and educational factors are dissected, analyzed, and scrutinized to develop an awareness of how educational factors such as curriculum, disciplinary guidelines, role modelling, teacher education, and existing biases, along with other societal factors, impact students' learning. By drawing attention to the entrenched biases that have created the marginalized population of refugee and other pedagogically and knowledge-wise excluded students, educators and their school systems can take the needed measures to reimagine their classrooms as spaces that provide inclusive and equity-oriented learning for all their students.

DISCUSSION QUESTIONS

1. What are the main pillars of the social justice and racial equity framework discussed in this chapter, and what injustices do they address?

2. Reflecting on your own beliefs and practices, identify some areas of your own blind spots with respect to cognitive justice. What are some approaches that can help better incorporate cognitive justice into your practices?

3. In your experiences of educational practices, whether as an educator or an administrator, how would educational practices and outcomes differ if they unfolded within the framework of social justice and racial equity?

4. How does the social justice and racial equity framework mitigate current policies, such as inclusive educational policies or general multiculturalism, that are guiding your practices in educating minority learners?

5. What are some of the difficulties that educators and administrators might face in providing education within the framework of social justice and racial equity?

REFERENCES

Abdi, A. A., & Richardson, G. (Eds.). (2008). *Decolonizing democratic education: Transdisciplinary dialogues*. Sense Publishers.

Apple, M. (2000). *Official knowledge: Democratic education in a conservative age*. Routledge.

Asadi, N. (2016). *From recognition to knowledge creation: Education of refugee youth learners in Alberta and British Columbia* [Doctoral dissertation]. University of Alberta.

Carr, P. R. (2008). The "Equity Waltz" in Canada: Whiteness and the informal realities of racism in education. *Journal of Contemporary Issues in Education*, *3*(2), 4–23.

Crowe, S. (2006). *Immigrant and refugee children in middle childhood: An overview*. National Children's Alliance.

Cui, D. (2015). Capital, distinction, and racialized habitus: Immigrant youth in the educational field. *Journal of Youth Studies*, *18*(9), 1154–1169.

Cummins, J. (2009). Multilingualism in the English-language classroom: Pedagogical considerations. *TESOL Quarterly*, *43*(2), 317–321.

Dei, G. J. S. (2008). *Racists beware: Uncovering racial politics in the post modern society*. Sense Publishers.

Dei, G. J. S., & Rummens, J. A. (2010). Including the excluded: De-marginalizing immigrant/refugee and racialized students. *Education Canada*, *50*(5).

Fanon, F. (1967). *Black skin, white masks*. Grove Press.

Ferguson, H., Bovaird, S., & Mueller, M. (2007). The impact of poverty on educational outcomes for children. *Paediatrics & Child Health*, *12*(8), 701–706.

Fraser, N. (2005a). Reframing justice in a globalized world. *New Left Review*, *36* (Nov–Dec.), 69-88.

Fraser, N. (2005b). *Scales of justice: Reimagining political space in globalizing world*. Columbia University Press.

Fraser, N. (2008). Rethinking recognition: Overcoming displacement and reification in cultural politics. In K. Olson (Ed.), *Adding insult to injury: Nancy Fraser debates her critics* (pp. 121–141). Verso Books.

Fraser, N., & Bourdieu, P. (2007). *(Mis)recognition, social inequality and social justice*. Routledge.

Gunderson, L., D'Silva, A. R., & Odo, M. D. (2012). Immigrant students navigating Canadian schools: A longitudinal view. *TESL Canada Journal, 29*(6), 143–156.

Guo, Y. (2015). "Unlearning privileges": Interrupting pre-service teachers' deficit thinking of immigrant students with origins in the south. *Cultural and Pedagogical Inquiry, 7*(1), 34–59.

Henry, F., & Tator, C. (2006). *The colour of democracy: Racism in Canadian society*. Nelson.

Hölscher, D. (2014). Considering Nancy Fraser's notion of social justice for social work: Reflections on *misframing* and the lives of refugees in South Africa. *Ethics and Social Welfare, 8*(1), 20–38.

Hussain, A. (2006). Towards political economy of racism and colonialism: A re-reading of Frantz Fanon's *Wretched of the earth*. In J. Young & J. E. Braziel (Eds.), *Race and the foundations of knowledge: Cultural amnesia in academy* (pp. 127–144). University of Illinois Press.

Isaacs, H. R. (1968). Group identity and political change: The role of color and physical characteristics. In J. Hope Franklin (Ed.), *Color and Race* (pp. 75–97). HMH.

Kanu, Y. (2007). Educational pathways to successful social integration for African refugee students in Manitoba. *Our Diverse Cities, 2*, 114–119. https://publications.gc.ca/collections/collection_2010/cic/Ci2-1-6-2009-eng.pdf

Kumsa, K. M. (2006). "No! I am not a refugee!" The poetics of belonging among young Oromos in Toronto. *Journal of Refugee Studies, 19*(2), 231–255.

Lightman, N., & Good Gingrich, L. (2018). Measuring economic exclusion for racialized minorities, immigrants and women in Canada: Results from 2000 and 2010. *Journal of Poverty, 22*(5), 398–420. https://doi.org/10.1080/10875549.2018.1460736

Lund, D. (2008). *Fostering acceptance and integration of immigrant students: Examining effective school-based approaches in prairie schools*. https://sites.ualberta.ca/~pcerii/Virtual%20Library/FinalReports/Lund%20FinalReport%20PCERII.pdf

Meyers, M. (2006). Myths and delusions: English language instruction in Canadian schools. *Education Canada, 46*(2), 31–34.

Ngo, H. V. (2009a). *Evaluation of ESL education in Alberta: Perceptions of ESL students in four major school boards*. https://fdocuments.net/document/evaluation-of-esl-education-in-alberta-evaluation-of-esl-education-in-alberta.html?page=1

Ngo, H. V. (2009b). Patchwork, sidelining, and marginalization: Services for immigrant youth. *Journal of Immigrant & Refugee Studies, 7*(1), 82–100. https://doi.org/10.1080/15562940802687280

Parkin, S. (2012). *Inclusive education in Alberta: Is it possible?* https://dtpr.lib.athabascau.ca/action/download.php?filename=mais/700/Capstone%20Revised%20January%202013%2014th.pdf

Roessingh, K., & Field, E. (2000). Time, timing, timetabling: Critical elements of successful graduation of high school ESL learners. *TESL Canada Journal, 18*(1), 17–31.

Rossiter, J. M., & Rossiter, R. K. (2009). Diamonds in the rough: Bridging gaps in supports for at-risk immigrant and refugee youth. *Journal of International Migration and Integration*, *10*(4), 409–429.

Rutter, J. (2006). *Refugee children in the UK*. Open University Press.

Shields, C. M. (2004). Dialogic leadership for social justice: Overcoming pathologies of silence. *Educational Administration Quarterly*, *40*(1), 109–132.

Shultz, L. (2012). Decolonizing social justice education: From policy knowledge to citizenship action. In A. A. Abdi (Ed.), *Decolonizing philosophies of education* (pp. 29–42). Sense Publishers.

United Nations High Commissioner for Refugees. (2018). *Global trends: Forced displacement in 2018*. https://www.unhcr.org/statistics/unhcrstats/5d08d7ee7/unhcr-global-trends-2018.html?query=canada

Varma, P. K. (2012). The assault on culture through education. In C. Alvares & S. Saleem Faruqi (Eds.), *Decolonising the university: The emerging quest for non-Eurocentric paradigms* (pp. 21–30). Penerbit Universiti Sains Malaysia.

Zinga, M. D., & Gordon, K. M. (2016). "Racism under the radar": Student perceptions of school experiences in a multicultural context. *Race Ethnicity and Education*, *19*(5), 1088–1116.

CHAPTER 14

Interrogating Equity Issues on Inclusive Postsecondary Education for Refugees and New Immigrants in Canada

Michael Kariwo

INTRODUCTION

Canada is a popular destination for refugees and immigrants. Between 2015 and 2017, 20,046 refugees landed in Canada (Immigration, Refugees and Citizenship Canada [IRCC], 2017; United Nations High Commissioner for Refugees [UNHCR], 2019). According to the 2016 census, almost 2.2 million children under the age of 15 were foreign-born (first generation) or had at least one foreign-born parent (second generation), representing 37.5 percent of all Canadian children. This is an increase from 2011, when this proportion was 34.6 percent. This population of children with an immigrant background could continue to grow from 39.3 percent to 49.1 percent of children under the age of 15 by 2036. In 2016, the majority (74.0 percent) of these first- or second-generation children were from countries of ancestry in Asia, Africa, the Caribbean and Bermuda, or Central and South America (IRCC, 2017).

This growth in the immigrant population has implications for education, particularly at the postsecondary level. In this chapter, I focus on the following problems: (a) refugees' lower rates of access to postsecondary education and (b) the challenges faced by refugees and other immigrants in postsecondary education. Here, a distinction is made between refugees and those who migrate for economic reasons. This includes international students who, by definition, can support themselves while studying in Canada. This group faces challenges and barriers, although not to the same extent as refugees. Several studies have found that enrolment in post-migration schooling is associated with improved income and labour force participation among immigrants

(Anisef et al., 2010; Banerjee & Verma, 2009; Bratsberg & Ragan, 2002; Rollin, 2011). However, there has been little empirical analysis focusing on refugees' participation in Canadian postsecondary education (Ferede, 2010).

Higher education has been long viewed as a pathway to upward social and economic mobility. However, the inaccessibility of postsecondary education disadvantages refugee youth in obtaining a future of economic stability and social mobility (UNHCR, 2016). Indeed, 1 percent of refugees worldwide have access to postsecondary education, compared to global enrolment rates of 34 percent (UNHCR, 2016). In view of this disparity, it is clear that access to higher education is problematic for refugee youth.

There are complex issues at local, national, and international levels when dealing with policies associated with the distribution of resources and services for migratory populations such as refugees. This means an engagement in political, economic, and educational policies is essential for transformation. In Canada the discourse on equitable resource distribution is very much alive and pertains to marginalized groups such as Indigenous people and refugees. Any democracy that ignores these issues cannot be seen as adhering to principles of social justice and equity (Government of Canada, 1982).

Que (2020) observed that despite Canada's renowned generosity toward refugees, negative attitudes about refugees seem to be on the rise in Canada. Many working-age adults who immigrate to Canada enrol in postsecondary education after their arrival to upgrade their educational credentials or improve their employment prospects. Overall, 28 percent of immigrants (between the ages of 25 and 54) admitted from 2002 to 2005 enrolled in Canadian postsecondary educational institutions within the first seven years after admission into Canada. Those who were admitted into Canada as refugees were less likely to participate in postsecondary education during their first seven years after admission compared with immigrants in other admission classes—such as economic immigrants or family class immigrants. Specifically, 19 percent of government-assisted refugees and 20 percent of privately sponsored refugees reported studying at the postsecondary level (IRCC, 2017).

THEORETICAL FRAMEWORK

This chapter adopts a theoretical framework that is a combination of transnationalism, neoliberalism, intersectionality, and social capital. Transnationalism states that immigrant life and experience are not contained within one geographic space (Morawska, 2003). This lens foregrounds strong linkages between immigrants and their homelands and how those linkages mediate their present experiences (Bauböck, 2003). Transnationalism is relevant in analyzing the factors that influence immigrant youths in postsecondary education in Canada because it brings in multiple intersecting influences across diverse social locations. Intersectionality is concerned with simultaneous intersections of diverse aspects of social locations, social differences, identity, and how multiple forms of oppression intersect in complex and independent ways (Crenshaw, 1990). With this reading of intersectionality and attached realities, immigrant youths face a crisis of identity. On the one hand, they are trying to be Canadian like their peers from the dominant white community; on the other hand, however, their parents wish them to remain in their traditional culture (e.g., African family norms and culture). In general, and related to the intersecting contexts of these immigrant youths' intersectional lives, operational forms of identity may include race, nationality, gender, class, geography, age, and migration status. In addition, an intersectional perspective recognizes how power and power relations across intersecting social locations are reproduced and how these power relations may affect migrant experiences. Crenshaw (1990) used the concept to highlight the interconnection of social identities and systems of oppression and domination. This theory is relevant when analyzing issues such as class, racial, or gendered barriers to education. As such, it is important to include the history and journeys that refugees take to their new country as part of the analysis and, later, into educational design and dispensation. Taking a historical perspective will reveal pre-migration challenges, such as trauma, which help us understand the barriers faced by this population in pursuing a career and education. The difficulties experienced by racialized, gendered, and poor refugees are connected to geopolitical, racial, and economic processes.

Spivak's (1988, 2005) analysis on social capital highlights the need to pay attention to the voices of the most vulnerable and to create channels of agency to bring their experiences and challenges to the broader public and policy discourses. Social capital plays an important role for refugees and immigrants because they need new networks and supports, particularly when attending postsecondary education. According to Putnam (2000), social capital refers to "social networks and the norms of reciprocity and trustworthiness that arise from them" (p. 19). Putnam concludes that ethnic diversity correlates with low social capital. In ethnically diverse neighbourhoods, residents of all ethnicities tend to "hunker down." The inhabitants have less trust and fewer networks and participate less in voluntary organizations. According to Putnam (2000), however, the negative effect of diversity on social capital should be expected to be temporary. "In the long run societies have overcome such fragmentation by creating new compassing identities that dampen the negative effects of diversity" (pp. 138–139). The literature on social capital has also stimulated research on the social and political integration of immigrants. Putnam (2000) makes a distinction between "bonding" and "bridging" organizations. Bonding social capital is made up of social ties between people who are similar along important dimensions; such capital works to strengthen exclusive identities and homogenous group constellations and may, in its extreme, be harmful to society. Bridging capital, on the other hand, is constituted by ties across social distinctions, between people who, in one social category or more, are different from each another.

LEGAL AND POLICY FRAMEWORK

Que (2020) observed that the 1976 Immigration Act was the first Canadian immigration legislation that recognized refugees as a distinct class of immigrants. The 1951 Geneva Convention Relating to the Status of Refugees and the 1967 Protocol defined the status of refugees. The clauses include any person who

a. by reason of a well-founded fear of persecution for reasons of race, religion, nationality, membership in a particular social group or political opinion,
   i. is outside the country of the person's nationality and is unable, or by reason of that fear, unwilling to avail himself of the protection of that country, or
   ii. not having a country of nationality, is outside the country of the person's former habitual residence and is unable or, by reason of that fear, is unwilling to return to that country (Government of Canada, 1976).

The Canadian Charter of Rights and Freedoms

Another legal instrument relevant to this discussion is the Charter of Rights and Freedoms. Paragraph 15 of the Charter states that "Every individual is equal before and under the law and has the right to the equal protection and equal benefit of the law without discrimination and, in particular, without discrimination based on race, national or ethnic origin, colour, religion, sex, age or mental or physical disability." Canada is therefore legally bound on issues of equity for all its citizens, including refugees.

PARTICIPATION

Sixty percent of domestic university students are now female; however, international and refugee student enrolments remain male-dominated (see table 14.1). These disparities indicate that broader structural and sociocultural issues that impact university participation for members of certain groups and communities remain factors in university participation and completion (Anderson, 2020).

Table 14.1: Participation of Refugees and Immigrants in Postsecondary Education (ages 25-54)

	Family Class (%)	Economic Class (%)	Government Sponsored (%)	Privately Sponsored (%)
Male	18	39	22	21
Female	23	51	17	18
Married	21	39	18	16
Single	28	51	25	27
Widowed/divorced/separated	11	46	13	16

Source: Statistics Canada, 2018

Refugee students and children of refugees have among the lowest participation and graduation rates in Canadian universities, due largely to language and literacy barriers and their status as first-generation postsecondary students (i.e., students whose parents did not attend postsecondary education). A study by Hou and Bonikowska (2016) found that refugee youths' lower university completion rates were correlated with their fathers' lower levels of education and language ability. There are disparities in the system that require broader structural and sociocultural adjustments. In the following section, I discuss barriers that hinder participation of refugees and immigrants; afterward, I suggest possible solutions.

BARRIERS

Unlike refugee students who encounter nuanced and persistent challenges accessing postsecondary education in the country, international students are, by definition, people who come to Canada on student visas with the expressed intent to study in Canadian schools. Grayson (2008) observed that, in general terms, international university students are reported to experience relatively high satisfaction levels and graduation rates.

Level of Parents' Education

Children of refugees in Canada have among the lowest university completion rates and subsequent job earnings compared to both domestic populations and other immigrant classes in the country (Hou & Bonikowska, 2016). One of the major barriers for refugees and their children's success is the fact that parents did not attend postsecondary education. Fewer than 15 percent of refugee fathers have university degrees from their home countries upon landing. Segmented assimilation theory (Portes & Rumbaut, 2001) discusses the importance of immigrant parents' human capital on their children's development. The theory provides various pathways to assimilation in a foreign country.

Refugee parents also face a lack of recognition of their academic and professional credentials, forcing them into precarious employment positions and having to work multiple jobs, resulting in limited time to concentrate on their children's academic work (Guo, 2009). Therefore, the level of parental education is one of the strongest preconditions affecting university participation and completion for refugee families in Canada. Parents with high levels of academic success themselves are more likely to influence the academic aspirations of their children. Refugee families are among the lowest wage earners in Canada, and this economic reality contributes to their low participation in university education in the country.

Language Barrier

Language poses a great barrier for refugees and some groups of immigrants from countries where English or French is not the official language. Instruction at the university level in Canada is in either English or French, depending generally on the province where the institution is located and, in some cases, on the nature of the university or college. Seventy-five percent of newly landed refugees speak neither English nor French. Being a first-generation university student from a low-income family can be especially prohibitive. These issues are evidenced in the university completion rates of refugees at Canadian universities (only 27 percent) compared to other immigrant classes, such as skilled workers (50 percent) and the Business Class (59 percent) (Hou & Bonikowska, 2016).

Language and literacy issues for many international students and refugees hinder full participation in universities where there are requirements to engage in presentations and seminars and produce scholarly papers and assignments. Clearly, therefore, competency and fluency in English and/or French can facilitate academic and social success at the postsecondary level.

Tuition Fees

As shown in table 14.2, financing university education is another barrier for refugee learners that needs to be analyzed.

Universities in Canada set their own fees depending on several factors, such as program, immigration status, and whether the applicant is a Canadian citizen or international student. The average fees for international undergraduate students in 2019–2020 was $29,714 per year. Humanities courses are generally less

Table 14.2: Postsecondary Undergraduate Tuition and Accommodation Fees, 2020–2021

Institution	Tuition (CAD) for Canadian Students, Faculty of Arts	Accommodation on Campus	Tuition (CAD) for International Students	Accommodation on Campus
University of British Columbia	5,507	10,700–13,850	39,574	10,700–13,850
University of Alberta	5,692	7,118	23,156	7,118
University of Toronto, Ontario	6,100	11,973–20,571	52,890	11,973–20,571
Brock University, Ontario	6,089	8,340	26,558	8,340
Memorial University, Newfoundland and Labrador	2,550–3,330	2,202	11,460	2,202

Sources: University websites (2020)

expensive compared to business, medicine, and engineering. Living on campus incurs an additional cost. The highest average undergraduate tuition fees were in dentistry ($21,717), medicine ($14,162), law ($12,388), and optometry ($11,236). In 2019–2020, the average tuition fees for international students studying business, management, or public administration was $28,680 (Statistics Canada, 2019).

Racism and Discrimination

In a study by Bajwa and colleagues (2018), an intersectional perspective was critical in identifying barriers to refugees that were rooted in patriarchal gender relations in Canada and their home countries, which create a racialized and gendered refugee subject, who is either seen as passive and needy or dangerous and needing to be securitized. They found that racism and patriarchy tend to create gendered and racialized representations of refugee women, which lead to isolation and "Othering" in the host society, devaluing them and their labour (Bajwa et al., 2018).

In a study conducted in Newfoundland and Labrador by Bittner and Baker (2013), postsecondary students in their second year or beyond reported their attitudes toward and experiences with racism. Among respondents, 90.48 percent indicated that they had witnessed a racist comment or behaviour; this was slightly higher than the rate found for first-year students, which was 82.35 percent. In addition, respondents indicated a mindfulness of racial discrimination in their country and institution, with 53.85 percent disagreeing and 41.43 percent strongly disagreeing that there is no racial prejudice in Canada, while 54.23 percent disagreed and 19.65 percent strongly disagreed that there is no racial prejudice at their college/university. These results illustrate the awareness that students in Newfoundland and Labrador have of racial discrimination in the country.

Student Mental Health Issues

Compared to other classes of immigrants, refugees tend to experience and report more mental health issues, even in postsecondary institutions. Often, they have post-traumatic stress disorder (PTSD) from the violence experienced during war in their home countries. "Refugees may experience vulnerable mental health and cognitive concerns that affect their learning, including insomnia, flashbacks, and problems with memory concentration and processing information (Bajwa et al., 2017).

STRATEGIES TO SUPPORT REFUGEE AND IMMIGRANT YOUTHS

Faculty and Peer Support

Some universities in Canada have developed mentorship programs for immigrant students. Examples include the University of Toronto, Dalhousie University, and the University of Alberta. The University of Alberta (2020) states that the objectives of the Black students mentorship program at the institution include (1) understanding and creating awareness of issues affecting the full participation of Black youth in society and the economy; (2) increasing leadership skills of Black youth; (3) increasing postsecondary entry and completion rates for Black youth; (4) fostering community belonging for Black youth; (5) creating a positive cultural identity for Black youth; and (6) increasing the ability of Black youth to tackle issues of *racism and discrimination*.

Dalhousie University's (2020) mentorship program aims at creating meaningful connections between industry, professionals, and students. The guidelines state that students and mentors will be matched based on their educational backgrounds and career goals; once matched, students are responsible for initiating and maintaining contact with their mentor; and the student–mentor relationship will be confidential and professional. In addition, students should ensure a minimum of two points of contact with their mentor; students are responsible for preparing questions and topics for discussion. The role of a mentor is not to find a job for the student, and mentors and students have the right to conclude their mentorship match at any time.

The University of Toronto (2020) mentorship program is much more comprehensive and covers a diverse range of students and their needs and includes support from upper-year students, mentoring, leadership, and coaching skills. It provides opportunities to network and make important connections, and there are themed cafés organized and led by peer mentors.

The Access & Inclusion Peer Programs at the University of Toronto is a mentorship program for students from historically underrepresented and marginalized communities. It offers academic, career, wellness, and social supports that foster a sense of belonging and community. Overall, this mentorship program emphasizes exposure to different points of view and perspectives of student life and success.

Family Support

The social support system has four main components, namely emotional, affirmational, material, and informational. Social support serves several functions for refugees and immigrants in postsecondary education. Several studies (Simich et al., 2005; Wong & Yohani, 2016) have suggested that using all available personal and social resources to obtain social support is critical to reducing stress and maintaining health. Social support helps individuals cope with stress in an immediate way during crisis situations and reinforces the self-confidence needed to manage ongoing challenges critical to the adaptation process. Many newcomers to Canada rely on friends and family for support to overcome settlement difficulties (Simich et al., 2005). Many refugees arrive from camps and will have left family and friends back home after fleeing wars and related political and civil unrest. By and large, they start off without any familial support. Those who arrive with their families find it hard to get jobs, and many refugee parents cannot give financial support to their children because they do not earn a lot of money from the menial jobs they usually hold. Compared to other classes of immigrants, refugees also lack informational support and therefore are less prepared to plan their postsecondary journey, and they often receive conflicting information (Bajwa et al., 2017). In addition, refugees face language barriers, as many do not speak English or French, and this limits their access to and contextual interaction with relevant and necessary information about opportunities in their new land and within their general surroundings.

WORLD UNIVERSITY SERVICE OF CANADA PROGRAM

The World University Service of Canada (WUSC) program assists students from refugee camps who show academic potential. The program works in partnership with Canadian universities. WUSC-sponsored postsecondary refugee students are required to find jobs when their first year of undergraduate education is completed. Such a transition is difficult, as it requires refugee students to be independent when many of their first-year resources are taken away. Refugees have problems finding appropriate employment due to lack of networks. Also, the most difficult period for refugees to find work is within their first year of arrival. Here is how one WUSC Local Committee member at the University of Toronto (St. George Campus) describes the situation:

> I was very inspired by the direct, positive impact I could have in refugee students' lives by being an active member of our WUSC Local Committee. I realized I could be a friend, a welcoming peer, and a mentor all in one to help make the students' experiences in Canada the best they can be. The best part about being involved with my Local Committee is the opportunity I get to glimpse the network of brilliant students that have come to study in Canada. I have had the chance to meet so many SRP students, and I have to say, I am humbled by the joy, positivity, and perseverance they all share. (WUSC, 2022)

RECOMMENDATIONS FOR POSTSECONDARY INSTITUTIONS

In order to increase access to postsecondary learning for refugees, institutions of higher education in Canada should consider alternative assessments for students who have experienced forced migration and all the traumas that accompanied it. Applicants are often measured on high school grades, which do not take into account refugee students' special needs. Admissions policies might draw from current practices for Indigenous students, which include bridging programs. Given the complex lives of refugee and immigrant students, academic support services need to be flexible, accessible, and personalized. This is critical because refugee students especially lack access to navigational skills within their familial and social networks to deal with the limited and selectively competitive postsecondary environment.

Because refugee students in postsecondary education face many challenges after migration, they need to develop resilience. These young students face understandable difficulty achieving that by themselves, so Wong and Yohani (2016) recommended establishing community supports to foster support, which can lead to educational success. There is, therefore, a need to develop programs that empower refugee and immigrant students, including but not limited to mentorship programs. In their study, Bajwa and colleagues (2018) demonstrated that "Knowledge Is Power" and developed a program that created awareness within participants and were subsequently able to match power, oppression, and powerlessness to their own experiences. This understanding allowed them to experience a transformation in the relationship between their assessment of a situation, their personal experiences, and the action they need to take. Ms. HJ, who was experiencing racism and discrimination, stated, "I wish I knew this earlier, that even as a refugee I had rights. Nobody can make me not eat with others because I am a woman and I am Black" (p. 118).

CONCLUSION

Refugees have lower participation rates in postsecondary institutions and face many barriers during their journey into and through higher education. As a result, they have lower economic outcomes compared to other Canadians. Refugee students experience challenges in navigating the postsecondary system, and the development of mentorship programs is one way of solving this and similar problems. Research points to the important role of a supportive educational model that promotes self-esteem and a sense of belonging as critical to combatting the structural, financial, and intersectional factors that restrict access to higher education and the pursuit of educational/career goals for refugee students. Que (2020) summarized the barriers faced by refugees in accessing postsecondary education. She observed that refugee youths' access to postsecondary education was impeded by a number of barriers, including financial difficulties resulting from the repayment of transportation loans and a lack of targeted scholarships for refugee students pursuing postsecondary education. In addition, there was a lack of information about postsecondary admission requirements, scholarships, and on-campus employment opportunities, negative peer influence from refugee students who were less motivated, limited communication with local peers, and fear of the unknown as well as of the academic challenges they would face in postsecondary education.

In the Black youth mentorship program at the University of Alberta, students emphasized the need for guidance in selecting a field of study and subsequently a career path. They tended to have little knowledge about the requirements that they needed to meet in order to reach a specific destination. In their study, Bajwa and colleagues (2017) highlight these informational barriers and suggest ways to overcome them. Usually, parents, guidance counsellors, and teachers are the sources of information helping students set postsecondary goals and identifying the necessary steps to achieve these goals. However, refugee parents do not have adequate information to do this.

Moreover, the situation of refugees is complicated by untreated pre- and trans-migration psychological stresses as well as post-migration academic, economic, and psychosocial challenges, which all negatively affect the ability of refugee students to adapt to and acculturate into their host country's academic contexts and progress. These challenges are compounded by perceived or real attitudes of prejudice, marginalization, and racism from fellow students, professors, and administrators.

DISCUSSION QUESTIONS

1. What is a relevant theoretical framework to use in a discussion on refugee and immigrant postsecondary education in Canada?

2. Given the current state of postsecondary education, which policy issues should be addressed to make the environment more conducive to refugees and immigrants?

3. Which legal instruments need to be reviewed, and how, in order to achieve equity and social justice within Canadian postsecondary institutions?

4. How can postsecondary institutions in Canada respond to the growing numbers of refugees and immigrants wanting access to education?

REFERENCES

Anderson, T. (2020). International and refugee university students in Canada: Trends, barriers, and the future. *Comparative and International Education/Éducation Comparée et Internationale, 48*(2), 1–17. https://doi.org/10.5206/cie-eci.v48i2.10787

Anisef, P., Sweet, R., Adamuti-Trache, M., & Walters. D. (2010). *Recent immigrants: A comparison of participants and non-participants in Canadian post-secondary education.* Government of Canada. https://www.canada.ca/en/immigration-refugees-citizenship/corporate/reports-statistics/research/recent-immigrants-comparison-participants-non-participants-canadian-post-secondary-education.html

Bajwa, J. K., Abai, M., Couto, S., Kidd, S., Akbari-Dibavar, A., & Mckenzie, K. (2018). Examining the intersection of race, gender, class, and age on post-secondary education and career trajectories of refugees. *Refuge: Canada's Journal on Refugees / Refuge: Revue canadienne sur les réfugiés, 34*(2), 113–123.

Bajwa, J. K., Couto, S., Kidd, S., Markoulakis, R., Abai, M., & Mckenzie, K. (2017). Refugees, higher education and information barriers. *Refuge: Canada's Journal on Refugees / Refuge: Revue canadienne sur les réfugiés, 33*(2), 56–65.

Banerjee, R., & Verma, A. (2009). *Determinants and effects of post-migration education among new immigrants in Canada*. Working Paper no. 11. Canadian Labour Market and Skills Researcher Network.

Bauböck, R. (2003). Towards a political theory of migrant transnationalism. *The International Migration Review, 37*(3), 700–723.

Bittner, A., & Baker, J. (2013). *Building an inclusive society: Post-secondary youth perspectives on immigration, multiculturalism and racism in Newfoundland and Labrador*. Discussion Paper. The Harris James Centre, Memorial University.

Bratsberg, B., & Ragan, J. F. (2002). The impact of host-country schooling on earnings: A study of male immigrants in the United States. *The Journal of Human Resources, 37*(1), 63–105.

Crenshaw, K. (1990). Mapping the margins: Intersectionality, identity politics, and violence against women of color. *Stanford Law Review, 43*(6), 1241–1299.

Dalhousie University. (2020). *Mentorship program*. https://www.dal.ca/campus_life/career-and-leadership/employerservices/engagement/mentorshipprogram.html. (Website no longer available).

Ferede, M. K. (2010). Structural factors associated with higher education access for first-generation refugees in Canada: An agenda for research. *Refuge: Canada's Journal on Refugees / Refuge: Revue canadienne sur les réfugiés, 27*(2), 79–88.

Government of Canada. (1976). Canada: Immigration Act, 1976–1977, c. 52. https://www.refworld.org/docid/3ae6b5c60.html

Government of Canada. (1982). *Charter of Rights and Freedoms*. https://laws-lois.justice.gc.ca/eng/const/page-12.html

Grayson, J. P. (2008). The experiences and outcomes of domestic and international students at four Canadian universities. *Higher Education Research & Development, 27*(3), 215–230.

Guo, S. (2009). Difference, deficiency, and devaluation: Tracing the roots of foreign credentials for immigrant professionals in Canada. *Canadian Journal for the Study of Adult Education, 22*(1), 37–52.

Hou, F., & Bonikowska, A. (2016). *Educational and labour market outcomes of childhood immigrants by admission class*. Social Analysis and Modelling Division, Statistics Canada.

Immigration, Refugees and Citizenship Canada. (2017). *Facts and figures 2016: Immigration overview—Permanent residents*. https://www.cic.gc.ca/opendata-donneesouvertes/data/Facts_and_Figures_2016_PR_EN.pdf

Morawska, E. (2003). Disciplinary agendas and analytic strategies of research on immigrant transnationalism: Challenges of interdisciplinary knowledge. *The International Migration Review, 37*(3), 611–640.

Portes, A., & Rumbaut, R. G. (2001). *Legacies: The story of the immigrant second generation*. University of California Press.

Putnam, R. D. (2000). *Bowling alone: The collapse and revival of American community*. Simon & Schuster.

Que, H. (2020). *Surviving to thriving: Post-secondary education for refugee youth in smaller centres in Canada* [Doctoral dissertation]. Memorial University.

Rollin, A. (2011). The income of immigrants who pursue postsecondary education in Canada. *Perspectives on Labour and Income*. Catalogue no. 75-001-X. Statistics Canada.

Simich, L., Beiser, M., Stewart, M., & Mwakarimba, E. (2005). Providing social support for immigrants and refugees in Canada: Challenges and directions. *Journal of Immigrant and Minority Health*, 7(4), 259–268. https://doi.org/10.1007/s10903-005-5123-1

Spivak, G. C. (1988). Can the subaltern speak? In C. Nelson & L. Grossberg (Eds.), *Marxism and the interpretation of culture* (pp. 271–333). University of Illinois Press.

Spivak, G. C. (2005). Scattered speculations on the subaltern and the popular. *Postcolonial Studies*, 8(4), 475–486.

Statistics Canada. (2018). *Refugees and Canadian post-secondary education: Characteristics and economic outcomes in comparison*. https://www150.statcan.gc.ca/n1/en/pub/89-657-x/89-657-x2018001-eng.pdf?st=_LOCPNdt

Statistics Canada. (2019). *Tuition fees for degree programs, 2019/2020*. https://www150.statcan.gc.ca/n1/daily-quotidien/190904/dq190904b-eng.htm

United Nations High Commissioner for Refugees. (2016). *Global trends: Forced displacement in 2015*. https://reliefweb.int/report/world/unhcr-global-trends-forced-displacement-2015

United Nations High Commissioner for Refugees. (2019). *Canada refugee resettlement fact sheet 2017*. https://www.unhcr.ca/wp-content/uploads/2017/03/Canada-Resettlement-Fact-Sheet-March-2017.v2.pdf

University of Alberta. (2020). *Black youth mentorship and leadership program*. https://www.ualberta.ca/nursing/media-library/research/health-immigration/black-youth-mentorship-program-final-report.pdf

University of Toronto. (2020). *Mentorship & peer programs*. https://studentlife.utoronto.ca/department/mentorship-peer-programs/

Wong, A. H. C., & Yohani, S. (2016). An exploratory study of resilience in postsecondary refugee students living in Canada. *Canadian Journal of Counselling and Psychotherapy*, 50(3), S175–S192.

WUSC. (2022). *Student refugee program*. https://srp.wusc.ca/about/

EPILOGUE

Edward Shizha

Global societies and nations have become multi-racial, multicultural, and very diverse. In turn, educational institutions, which are microcosms of society, mirror this diversity, and the main challenge that they encounter is how to provide all-around equity and inclusion for their populations. Equity, diversity, and inclusion are important principles that every educational institution should anchor its policies and programs on in order to distribute opportunities and privileges among its members. These are social justice issues in education. An educational approach that interrogates the homogenization of thoughts, practices, and treatment of students and educators is desirable in highlighting the uneven awkwardness of the changing contexts of real classes, schools, colleges, and universities (Griffiths, 2014). These are the themes that this book has adequately addressed. The term *social justice* and its place in education are contested, and there are different and competing philosophical and sociological arguments on what social justice involves. However, many Canadian education scholars, including those in this book, agree that it relates to equality of opportunities and treatment, representation, and inclusivity. It means implementing change and reform in schools and redefining what it means to have educational equality. In the Canadian context, as scholars in this book have highlighted, it means deracializing educational institutions (treating Indigenous people and racialized groups as equals despite colonizing racial differences)—including a variety of personal experiences, values, and worldviews that arise from race, ethnicity, religious and spiritual beliefs, class, age, colour, disability, immigrant status, and national origin—to empower students and enrich their learning potentials and experiences. Social justice in education is a roadmap that incorporates the diversity that exists in educational institutions and a human rights principle that integrates and treats diverse students' and educators' experiences as strengths rather than impediments to participation in educational programs. Educational institutions should not be warehouses of hegemonic colonial, traditional, and conservative values, attitudes, and mentalities that valorize the superiority of colonial, patriarchal, and normalized hierarchies of power.

Social justice in education can be achieved through the processes of decolonizing and Indigenizing the education system and applying inclusive education that incorporates all disadvantaged groups. The Canadian education system, and its institutional culture, mirrors a colonial legacy of white middle-class values and power structures that marginalize other cultural worldviews. The absence of diverse cultures disadvantages the sociocultural groups that are excluded. Student success and collegiality among faculty and administrative staff can be promoted when hegemonic values and oppressive power structures are transformed and become inclusive. This is what this book is about, and the various authors have successfully identified and interrogated the systemic racism faced by minoritized students, who include Black/African, immigrant/refugee, and Muslim students, as well as students who might be excluded from the education system because they live with disabilities or they are not able to pay tuition fees for higher education. Canadian educational institutions are multi-racial and multicultural, with their populations comprising students and academic and administrative staff with different backgrounds and experiences. As the earlier work of Courchene (1996) showed, the ethnocultural diversification of our society resulting from our immigration policy along with its concomitant racist sentiments, the political tensions between Quebec and the other provinces in Canada, the claims by Canada's Indigenous people for justice in the areas of land claims and self-government, and the absence of any effective policy to promote Canadian "culture" by the federal government have forced Canadians to search anew for the essence of their culture and identity. Whatever this culture is, the role of educational institutions is to lead in research that is inclusive and does not promote one culture above the others. The otherization of some cultures would perpetuate the colonial legacy and injustices that some Canadians continue to experience. As revealed in this book, African students, Muslim students, students living with disabilities, immigrant/refugee students, and other minority students who are perceived as inadequate and possessing cultural or cognitive deficits are excluded from participating adequately in the Canadian educational institutions.

Canada is a country with (a) two hegemonic cultures, French and English, with different languages and histories; (b) Indigenous people with a variety of colonially "undervalued" languages, histories, and cultures, most of which have been excluded from the mainstream Canadian society; and (c) a long tradition of immigrants from a wide variety of countries, languages, and cultures (Griffiths, 2014). In addition to these cultural differences, there are social groups that are defined by sexual orientation and by ableism (which normalizes certain bodies and abilities). This mixed pot of cultures calls for an education system that is sensitive to these cultural differences (such as implementation of a critical multicultural education approach, a pro-Black/African approach to schooling, a decolonial education perspective to education, an Islamic duoethnographic approach to support Muslim students, and Indigenization and an anti-oppressive education approach). It is an education system that does not promote the Bourdieusian analysis on the oppressive white middle-class cultural capital and symbolic capital that reinforces the exclusion of marginalized groups' knowledges. The fact that Canadian educational institutions are a mixed bowl of players calls for a critical pedagogy that applies a decolonial anti-hegemonic approach to curriculum planning and implementation. A decolonial education curriculum is an expression of the changing geopolitics of knowledge where the modern epistemological framework for knowing and understanding the world is no longer interpreted as universal and unbound by geohistorical and biographical contexts (Mignolo, 2011). The challenge for educators is to learn how to manage knowledge and disseminate it, and to teach beyond the distorted cultural and/or historical hegemonic and imaginary impoverished subjectivities that are colonially and hierarchically ranked according to Eurocentric concepts, standards, and assumptions. The avoidance of such subjectivities can be achieved by transforming the educational space that welcomes knowledge multiplicities and educators from diverse backgrounds.

Decolonizing education for social justice goes beyond the "add-on" of other knowledges and educators through the buzz phrase of "equity, diversity, and inclusion," which seems to be a reactive policy and an afterthought resulting from human rights violation crises and overt symbolic and physical violence against racial groups such as Black and Indigenous people. Is the current stampede to hire Black and Indigenous professors in Canadian universities a Damascene moment? Have these institutions, whose administrative hierarchy is predominantly white, able-bodied, and heterosexual men and women, suddenly realized that there is an underrepresentation of Black and Indigenous people on their faculty complement? Are they also going to have a Damascene moment to realize that their institutions are skewed toward heteronormative sexual orientation and normalized "able" bodies? A crucial question that remains unanswered is whether this Damascene moment that has resulted in the stampede to hire Black and Indigenous professors implies that there is a resultant change in racial attitudes toward non-white academics and minoritized groups in general? Before this hiring spree, the Employment Equity Act existed in Canada, requiring institutions or employers "to identify and eliminate employment barriers against persons in designated groups that result from the employer's employment systems, policies, and practices that are not authorized by law" (Minister of Justice, 2021a, p. 5). Universities should strive to meet representation levels, based on estimated workforce availability, for the four employment equity designated groups: women, Indigenous people, persons with disabilities, and members of visible minorities.

This Employment Equity Act came into force in 1986 with the objective to build a foundation for equal access to employment opportunities or benefits and to correct the conditions of disadvantage in employment. If this act has been in existence for this long, why has it not been applied effectively to provide opportunities for disadvantaged groups? As noted in this book, the answer is in racism, stereotypes, prejudice, and overall attitudes against "otherized" communities and in the dominant hegemonic cultural capital in institutional hierarchies of power.

The equality rights in the Canadian Charter of Rights and Freedoms of 1982 guarantee "the right to the equal protection and equal benefit of the law without discrimination and, in particular, without discrimination based on race, national or ethnic origin, colour, religion, sex, age, or mental or physical disability" (Minister of Justice, 2021b, p. 50). Together with the Employment Equity Act, these rights are meant to ameliorate conditions of disadvantaged individuals or groups so that they are treated fairly in all sectors of life, including in having access to education and access to power structures in educational institutions. However, despite the legal instruments, as noted in this book, educational institutions have remained embedded in racial white supremacy that promotes dominant cultural capital and white bodies defined through ableism, heterosexuality, and birthright citizenship that excludes immigrants, especially those from the Global South. As noted by scholars in this book, for social justice to be achieved, educational institutions—structurally and epistemologically—should be ruptured, restructured, reimagined, and deracialized to meet the needs of students and teachers/professors. The rupturing, restructuring, and deracialization should be directed at ultimately promoting accessibility to academic and institutional privileges for all previously disadvantaged and excluded groups. Barriers to equity, diversity, and inclusion are mainly attitudinal and are based on stereotypes. These are barriers to access to physical spaces, ethnic and Indigenous epistemological foundations of teaching and learning, access to financial capital to enter and complete postsecondary education, and to power structures. As argued by contributors to this book, these barriers should be critically interrogated, continuously confronted, resisted, and dismantled to bring about educational transformation premised on equality, equity, diversity, inclusion, and social justice in Canadian education system.

Decolonization, Indigenization, global citizenship education, and inclusive education that considers differences in abilities and sexual orientations should be the cornerstone of educational transformation and education for social justice. Equal and equitable access to epistemological opportunities and institutional positions and power structures viewed through multiple perspectives should be the hallmark of social justice in education. Canadian society is multicultural, and educational institutions are a hybrid of diversity; thus, social justice in education should also be reflected through the promotion of diverse perspectives that include the ethnic cultural capital of immigrant students and teachers/professors rather than the Bourdieusian cultural capital of the dominant white society that is hegemonic, oppressive, racist and that problematizes and otherizes those who are not represented by the culture. Multiple perspectives incorporate diverse teaching and learning styles that promote educational success for students and build opportunities for them to become global citizens who are open-minded and can think critically to solve problems, make decisions, and communicate ideas effectively using a cross-cultural lens. Embedded in multiple perspectives and learning styles are representations that do not distort knowledge and social reality. As highlighted in this book, these perspectives are a tool for deconstructing racism, ethnocentrism, ableism, stereotypes, biases, and cultural distortions. The perspectives also entail redistribution of knowledge and privileges that are representative of the disadvantaged students and teachers, and privileges that are not impacted by power dynamics that promote defensive and paternalistic white supremacy culture. According to Fraser (2009), the ability of each individual to participate equally in social and political life is the primary aim of social justice. Education is both political and social and has economic consequences; therefore, multiple perspectives in education will promote participation. Participation comes through educational epistemes that are applied using social justice pedagogy, educational/social reconstructionism, and anti-oppressive education (Cho, 2017).

THE WAY FORWARD

Evidently, for a deeper understanding of the complexities and realities of the social justice landscape in Canadian educational institutions, there is a need to conduct an environmental scan to determine the extent to which the social injustices discussed in this book are particularly salient. It is also not enough to theorize or re-theorize anti-colonial theory or anti-racism (Dei & Demi, 2021) and philosophize on social justice in education (Abdi, 2011) without practicalizing these philosophies and theories. Practical answers should be sought on how social justice programs can best be implemented in education without masking and window-dressing existing and continued overt and covert injustices. Programs such as the hiring of Black and Indigenous professors in universities should not be an end in themselves but a means to continuous conversations that endeavour to bring about genuine equality, equity, diversity, and inclusion in education. Social justice in education should focus on continuous practical social transformations, building and promoting a society that is based on anti-racism and equality of opportunity for all disadvantaged groups.

REFERENCES

Abdi, A. A. (Ed.) (2011). *Decolonizing philosophies of education*. Sense Publishers.

Cho, H. (2017). Navigating the meanings of social justice, teaching for social justice, and multicultural education. *International Journal of Multicultural Education, 19*(2), 1–19.

Courchene, R. (1996). Teaching Canadian culture: Teacher preparation. *TESL Canada Journal, 13*(2), 1–16.

Dei, G. J. S., & Demi, S. M. (2021). Reframing the anti-colonial for new futures: An introduction. In G. J. S. Dei & S. M. Demi (Eds.), *Theorizing the "anti-colonial"* (pp. 1–14). Dio Press.

Fraser, N. (2009). *Scales of justice: Reimagining political space in a globalizing world.* Columbia University Press.

Griffiths, M. (2014). Social justice in education: Joy in education and education for joy. In I. Bogotch & C. M. Shields (Eds.), *International handbook of educational leadership and social (in)justice* (pp. 233–251). Springer.

Mignolo, W. D. (2011). Geopolitics of sensing and knowing: On (de)coloniality, border thinking and epistemic disobedience. *Postcolonial Studies, 14*(3), 273–283.

Minister of Justice. (2021a). *Consolidation: Employment Equity Act. S.C. 1995, c. 44.* Government of Canada. https://laws-lois.justice.gc.ca/PDF/E-5.401.pdf

Minister of Justice. (2021b). *A Consolidation of the Constitution Acts 1867 to 1982.* Government of Canada. https://laws-lois.justice.gc.ca/PDF/CONST_TRD.pdf

CONTRIBUTOR BIOGRAPHIES

Ali A. Abdi is a Professor of Social Development Education at the University of British Columbia (Vancouver campus). His areas of research include citizenship and human rights education, social and cultural foundations of education, anti-colonizing education, and epistemic decolonization. His previous works include the edited volume *Decolonizing Philosophies of Education*.

Levonne Abshire is the Co-Director of Health Promotion and Education in the Office of the Vice President of Students at the University of British Columbia. She provides leadership and oversight for the development and implementation of health education programs and services to support student health and well-being. Current special interests include her work in organizational development and capacity building for staff and faculty in the area of mental health, health equity, and teaching practices that support student well-being.

Neda Asadi is an educator at NorQuest College in Edmonton, Alberta. She is also a community-based researcher bridging research between community and academic settings. She obtained her PhD from the University of Alberta, department of Educational Policy Studies. She is the co-editor of *Interrogating Models of Diversity within a Multicultural Environment* (2019). Her work and research are centred around anti-racism and decolonization of educational policies and practices as well as settlement laws and practices impacting marginalized populations.

Dan Cui is an Assistant Professor in the Department of Child and Youth Studies at Brock University. Her research interests include sociology of education, sociology of children and youth, immigration, integration and transnationalism, social justice and equity studies, comparative and international education, and qualitative research methods. Drawing on Bourdieu, she elaborated on the concept of "racialized habitus" in her research with Chinese Canadian youth.

George J. Sefa Dei is a Ghanaian-born educator and a foremost scholar on race and anti-racism studies. He is a Professor of Social Justice Education and Director of the Centre for Integrative Anti-Racism Studies at OISE, University of Toronto. He is also "Professor Extraordinaire," University of South Africa. In 2017, he was elected Fellow of the Royal Society of Canada, the most prestigious award for an academic scholar. Professor Dei was also installed as a traditional chief in Ghana.

Sameena Eidoo is an award-winning educator and an Assistant Professor in the Department of Curriculum, Teaching, and Learning at OISE, University of Toronto. Sameena is the author of *Shaping Muslim Futures: Youth Visions and Activist Praxis*, a "guidebook" that amplifies the counternarratives of activist Muslim youth living into their desired futures and creates space for readers to clarify their own.

Antoinette Gagné is an Associate Professor and the Associate Chair for Student Experience in the Department of Curriculum, Teaching, and Learning at OISE, University of Toronto. Her research has focused on teacher education for diversity and inclusion. She has explored the experiences of young English language learners and their families as well as internationally educated teachers in Canadian schools and universities. Antoinette is also the convenor of the Network of Critical Action Researchers in Education (NCARE).

Ratna Ghosh is a Distinguished James McGill Professor and William C. Macdonald Professor of Education at McGill University, where she was the Dean of Education. She publishes on education and social justice issues and more recently on the radicalization of youth. She was elected Fellow of the Royal Society of Canada, Fellow of the World Academy of Sciences, and Full Member of the European Academy of Arts, Letters, and Sciences. She is also a Member of the Order of Canada.

Yan Guo is a Professor of Language and Literacy in the Werklund School of Education at the University of Calgary. Her research interests include critical pedagogy of language learning, immigrant parent engagement, diversity in teacher education, transnational identities, translanguaging of immigrant and refugee children, and language policy. Her publications include *Home-School Relations: International Perspectives* and *Spotlight on China: Changes in Education under China's Market Economy*.

Claudette Howell Rutherford is an MEd candidate in Social Justice Education at OISE, University of Toronto. Claudette is a wife and the proud mother of three beautiful children. She is an educator of over 19 years and a devout community organizer and advocate. She is an op-ed contributor for the Centre for Integrative Anti-Racism Studies. She also serves on the OACAS Strategic Educational Outcomes Committee and as a Roster Member at the Ontario College of Teachers.

Michael Kariwo is an Instructor at the University of Alberta; a Research Fellow at the Centre for Global Citizenship Education and Research, in the Faculty of Education; and a Research Associate in the Faculty of Nursing. His published books include *Interrogating Models of Diversity within a Multicultural Environment*; *Resources and Performance of Academics at Universities*; *Education and Development in Zimbabwe: A Social, Political and Economic Analysis*; and *A Comparative Analysis of Higher Education Systems: The Issues, Challenges and Dilemmas*.

Anna-Leah King is Anishnaabe kwe from Wikwemikong Unceded Reserve, Manitoulin Island, Ontario. She currently works in the Faculty of Education, University of Regina, as Associate Professor, Chair of Indigenization for the faculty, and Chair of the Indigenous Advisory Council for the university. Her teaching role includes anti-oppressive education, art, Indigenous literatures, language acquisition, and Indigenous spirituality in education. Her research is in the area of Indigenous literature, Indigenous oral story, and Indigenous language revitalization.

Bathseba Opini is an Associate Professor in the Department of Educational Studies, Faculty of Education, at the University of British Columbia. Her research interests are in critical race studies and anti-racism education, disability studies, decolonizing education, teacher education, and international education. She is the author of a chapter in *Course Syllabi in Faculties of Education Bodies of Knowledge and their Discontents* (edited by A. E. Mazawi and M. Stack, Bloomsbury Academic Publishers, 2020).

Edward Shizha is a Professor in Youth and Children's Studies at Wilfrid Laurier University in Canada. His scholarly work focuses on social justice; anti-racism; education; and Indigenous knowledge systems, migration, and transnationalism. He has 12 books to his credit, which include *Living Beyond Borders: Essays on Global Immigrants and Refugees* (Peter Lang, 2018) and *African Indigenous Knowledge and the Sciences: Journeys into the Past and Present* (Sense Publishers, 2016), among others. He is the book series editor for Africa in the Global Space, which is published by Peter Lang.

Marlon Simmons is an Associate Professor and Associate Dean of Graduate Programs at the Werklund School of Education, University of Calgary. His scholarly work is grounded within the diaspora, decolonial thought, qualitative research, and sociology of education. Related to Marlon's teaching and research interests are network learning, governance of the self, and the role of socio-material relations with enhancing educational delivery.

Alison Taylor is a Professor in Political Economy of Education working in the Educational Studies Department at the University of British Columbia. Her current research, the Hard Working Student study, focuses on undergraduate students and their term-time work. Her previous research focused on community-engaged learning in Canadian universities and vocational education in K–12 schooling.

Robyn Taylor-Neu is a PhD candidate in sociocultural anthropology at the University of California, Berkeley. Her dissertation research explores questions of non/human relationality through an ethnography of animation and object theatre artists in Berlin (Germany) and Granada (Spain).

Rae Ann S. Van Beers has completed her PhD at the University of Calgary having studied in the Curriculum and Learning specialization. Her doctoral research focused on secondary students' conceptions of social justice through the work they do with their school-based social justice groups. Framing her research through the lens of children's rights is a touchstone for all her work, be it research or teaching.

Dania Wattar is a sessional lecturer, research associate, and Online Teaching Coach in the Department of Curriculum, Teaching, and Learning at OISE, University of Toronto. Dania has experience teaching at different universities and at the pre-tertiary level. Dania's research explores inclusion and equity, curriculum, professional development, and policy. She is currently working on projects related to supporting language learners and utilizing multilingual technology to fill the learning gap created by the COVID-19 school closures.